Leabharlann Chontae Luimni

Lansdowne Through the Years

Edward Newman graduated from University College Cork with a degree in English and Irish, and has been reporting on rugby for thirteen years. He contributes to various national publications including the *Irish Examiner*, *The Irish Times*, the *Irish Daily Mail* and *Village* magazine. He is a secondary school teacher (and rugby coach) at Christian Brothers College in Cork city.

Lansdowne Through the Years

EDWARD NEWMAN

HACHETTE
BOOKS
IRELAND

First published in paperback in 2010 by Hachette Books Ireland

A division of Hachette Livre UK Ltd

1

A CIP catalogue record for this title is available from the British Library.

ISBN 978-1-4447-1137-0

Typeset in Adobe Garamond by Claire Rourke
Cover design by Anú Design, Tara
Printed and bound in the UK by CPI Mackays, Chatham, ME5 8TD

Hachette Books Ireland's policy is to use papers that are natural, renewable
and recyclable products and made from wood grown in sustainable forests.
The logging and manufacturing processes are expected to conform to the
environmental regulations of the country of origin.

Hachette Books Ireland
8 Castlecourt Centre
Castleknock
Dublin 15
Ireland

A division of Hachette Livre, 338 Euston Road, London NW1 3BH, England

Contents

Foreword by Edmund Van Esbeck ix

Introduction xv

1   Ollie Campbell 1

2   Gareth Edwards 13

3   Ciaran Fitzgerald 24

4   Mick Galwey 37

5   Gavin Hastings 49

6   Denis Hickie 59

6   Martin Johnson 74

7   Tom Kiernan 91

8   Jack Kyle 99

9   Donal Lenihan 112

10   Michael Lynagh 123

11   Willie John McBride 135

12   Colin Meads 144

13   Syd Millar 151

14   Munster Supreme 162

15   Noel Murphy 186

16   Bertie O'Hanlon & Jimmy McCarthy 197

17   Nick Popplewell 208

18   Fergus Slattery 219

19   Peter Stringer 229

20   Ulster's Triumph 243

21   Tony Ward 257

22   Keith Wood 268

Acknowledgements 283

Permission Acknowledgements 286

Bibliography 288

In memory of my dear mother,
Maria O'Donovan-Newman,
who never stopped believing in me

'And so may a slow
wind work these words
of love around you,
an invisible cloak
to mind your life.'

John O'Donohue, 'Beannacht'

Foreword

Edmund Van Esbeck

The Lansdowne Road ground always held a very special place, not alone in the annals of Irish rugby, but also sport in Ireland on an even broader scale. Since the middle of what historians refer to as the Victorian era, the tumult and the shouting that are an integral part of a big sporting occasion echoed around the ground in Dublin 4.

We owe an immense debt to the man who started it all, Henry Wallace Doveton Dunlop. A noted athlete in his day, he had a vision of creating a sporting complex in the Dublin area. With that in mind, he purchased a twenty-one-year lease on the ground from the Pembroke Estate at an annual rent of £70. He was the founder of The Irish Champion Athletic Club and the committee of the club raised £1,000 for the purpose of enclosing and levelling the ground, laying down a running track and erecting a pavilion. Dunlop's dream had been realised. In addition to his main interest and prowess in athletics, he was also the founder of the Lansdowne Rugby Club in 1872, thus there is a very tangible rugby connection from the outset of the ground as a sporting theatre.

It was in Lansdowne Road that the first athletics international in history took place when Ireland met England in 1875. By that time, Ireland had entered the international rugby arena but, in fact, Lansdowne Road was rejected by the rugby authorities as being unsuitable as the venue for the first international played in Dublin. The game was played instead at the Leinster Cricket Ground in Rathmines.

When Ireland played England for the second time in Dublin, on 11 March 1878, Lansdowne Road was the venue and, since that match until the ground closed for renovation at the end of 2006, every senior international played in Dublin took place at the ground.

Dunlop eventually sold the lease to Harry Sheppard, who was honorary treasurer of the IRFU, but Sheppard died a young man in 1906 and his mother then sold the lease to the IRFU for a nominal sum. The lease was extended and, thus armed, the IRFU set about major development, which has been ongoing through the years. However, by the start of the twenty-first century, it was decided the ground was no longer able to meet the needs of the modern game and so the grand old aristocrat of rugby stadia was demolished to be replaced by a grand new structure. It is, in the circumstances, opportune to reflect on that very brief history of the ground and how it came into the possession of the IRFU.

One man who has made a major contribution to the ongoing development of the ground is Ronnie Dawson, assuredly one of the great figures in the history of the game in this country. A former captain and coach of both Ireland and the Lions, and a former president of the IRFU, he was also one of Ireland's representatives on the International Rugby Board. An architect by profession, he used his professional expertise on a voluntary basis to help maintain the ground and oversee improvements. He is owed an immense debt of gratitude for a magnificent contribution.

Lansdowne Road has, of course, been the venue for soccer internationals and international athletics, but this publication deals with some of the happenings, the days of great joy and indeed occasions of acute disappointment, for those rugby players who were centre stage at a ground unique in the annals of rugby football, the oldest international rugby stadium in the world.

Generations of Irish rugby followers will have their special memories and, on a personal level, I will never forget the excitement of my first visit to Lansdowne Road over sixty years ago. I was, at the time, a schoolboy living in Cork, and was brought by my late brother Frank to see Ireland play Australia in December 1947. Ireland lost comprehensively that afternoon, but there was some compensation in the fact that I had made the pilgrimage as I saw my hero, Jack Kyle, play for Ireland for the first time.

We were not to know it on that December afternoon but the Irish rugby team was about to enter a 'golden era' with Kyle at the heart of the triumphs of a Grand Slam, two Triple Crowns and three championships between 1948 and 1951. It was my good fortune to have been at those matches.

Through the years that followed, those of us who write about rugby for a living were able to view the drama from a position of great advantage – the press box, situated ideally in line with the halfway line, initially from the old East Stand and then, from 1974, from the West Stand.

Lansdowne Road was the mecca for a multitude, its situation is ideal and as one old rugby international once said to me, 'You know, it was not just the rugby and the atmosphere, but it was also a social meeting place for so many of us.'

Many have played a part in the history of the ground. In *Lansdowne Through the Years*, Edward Newman concerns himself in the main with those who wore the green and enjoyed glory and, at times, disappointment.

Through the years, there were great occasions to savour and to relive as long as memory holds. Victories over the big powers of the southern hemisphere, Australia and South Africa and a famous draw against the All Blacks. But it is what is now known as the Six Nations Championship (and which was initially the International Championship) that has always had a special place in the game in these islands. The Triple Crown and the Championship wins at Lansdowne Road in 1982 and 1985 are especially precious memories, as is the 2004 Triple Crown success achieved at the ground.

Each person will hold their own memories. In the pages that follow, some of the great players who displayed their talents on the old green sward give us the benefit of their memories. In giving those men the opportunity to share their experiences with us, Edward Newman has served us well.

The changes have been immense since the days when Dunlop saw his dream come true when the affluent arrived in their horse-drawn carriages, the rest by train and tram. Now, we look back with great affection on the days that are gone and look forward with great expectation to a time when, in its new life, the stadium will retain the unique atmosphere that has pervaded the great old ground.

History gives value to the present hour and its meaning.

Edmund Van Esbeck

Introduction

Three years after the wrecking ball reduced the old Lansdowne Road to dust, a curvy, glassy sphere has risen from the ashes, replacing a structure that served Irish rugby so well down through the years.

Irish rugby (and soccer) has a new home of which to be proud; a stadium for the twenty-first century.

The only comparison between the old Lansdowne Road and the new €410 million, 50,000-seater Aviva is the site. The pitch remains the same – even the old soil had been preserved through the construction phase, and will be used for the new surface that comes complete with under-soil heating. Also during construction, the old Wanderers pavilion was used as a pivot to move the field by about 15 degrees, though the iconic old house in the Lansdowne Road/West Stand corner could not be retained: its location was, we are told, vital to the construction of the pedestrian overpass.

The war memorials, however, remain, but so much more has changed – and for the better. An overpass means the supporters will no longer be detained by a passing Dart, while, inside, the view from any of the stands is simply terrific. Premium and corporate entertainment, which used be housed in tents on the old Lansdowne FC field behind the East Stand, is inbuilt into this impressive swirling-shaped arena. But for most people, however, small details will impress: extra leg room between the seats, for example, and a view to rival any in the world. That's something to keep the sentimentalists happy; there's a sense supporters will be close to the pitch and the re-creation of the old Lansdowne vibe should come back naturally.

For the players, gone is the simple hook on the wall and the small showers, replaced by comfort-line dressing rooms, hot and cold hydrotherapy baths and Astroturf areas for warming up. There was a time when visiting sides used to jump in and out of large wheelie bins that acted as ice baths. The players will also have easy access to the impressive new media room, a far cry from the long walk they once faced to a tent behind the old West Stand.

Ideally, the IRFU wanted a capacity for 60,000 and, yet, even that number seems conservative given the upsurge in popularity Irish rugby has enjoyed since Croke Park opened its gates to rugby and soccer in 2007. Croker, with its 82,300 capacity, was often sold out for rugby tests between 2007 and 2010; the great shame is that over 30,000 people will now be locked out of the new Aviva.

So, rugby makes its journey back from its temporary home on Jones's Road, where it enjoyed some memorable days, to Lansdowne Road (remember that's the address of the new Aviva so the name, at least, remains with us).

When the old Lansdowne Road stadium closed its doors on 31 December 2006 for reconstruction, it had been at the epicentre of Irish rugby for 130 years; a venue for epic matches, great tries and memorable individual feats. It opened with an old inter-pro between Leinster and Ulster and closed – in a touch of nice symmetry – with the same sides battling it out in a Magners Celtic League game, Jamie Heaslip scoring the last ever try.

Whatever the nay-sayers may say about its antediluvian facilities, there was no more vibrant a sight in world sport than when Lansdowne Road was packed to capacity, and nothing more uplifting than the raucous sound created inside as an Ireland player hurtled towards the tryline at either the Lansdowne Road or Havelock Square ends.

Lift the lid on the past and there's Willie Duggan handing his cigarette butt to the referee as the former Number 8 took the final step of fourteen from the tunnel under the West Stand; the emotion locked between the shaky boards of this old structure when John Pullin's England walked onto the hallowed turf in 1973 and the crowd rose to their feet for a five-minute standing ovation. Pullin's men travelled amidst threats from paramilitary groups as the Troubles raged across Ireland and Great Britain. 'We may not be very good but at least we turn up,' said Pullin in his post-match speech at the dinner reception at the Shelbourne Hotel, to which men wept as they stood again to applaud the England captain and his team. I think Con Houlihan wrote later that what happened on 10 February 1973 was the first Anglo-Irish agreement.

When the crowd is in full voice, when its roar is at its most throaty, and especially when Ireland is winning, there was no greater venue in world rugby as players in this book testify.

Players from both Ireland and abroad echo this sentiment – and mean it. Keith Wood, one of Irish rugby's most iconic figures, called the famous Lansdowne Roar 'the beat'.

So many words have been used to describe what Lansdowne Road was and what it represented. It was at one time unique and magical and, in many ways, timeless. For the home team, it was their citadel and, for visiting teams, it became known as the lion's den. There might be similarities with other old, atmospheric grounds – such as the ivy-covered Wrigley Field, home to the Chicago Cubs baseball team, or Carisbrook in Dunedin, New Zealand – but Lansdowne stood as a queen amongst them.

Will there ever be its like again? Certainly the time had come to move on and, in that regard, Lansdowne became outmoded. But the atmosphere generated through three different centuries will hopefully not be lost inside the new Aviva.

The dawn of the multipurpose corporate stadium made old Lansdowne (ironically built as a multipurpose complex) redundant. One can only wonder whether the brainchild behind Lansdowne Road, Henry Wallace Doveton Dunlop, ever envisaged that his stadium venture would evolve into a structure that would house some of the world's most epic rugby matches.

Early in its history, Lansdowne began hosting teams from the southern hemisphere and none came bigger than the visit of the first All Blacks in 1905 – 'the Originals' – captained by Dave Gallaher, a Letterkenny native. On their tour of Great Britain and Ireland, the Originals played thirty-two matches and won thirty-one, but such was their popularity that when they arrived on these shores, the IRFU decided to make the international an all-ticket affair; thus Lansdowne became the first stadium in the world to host an all-ticket international.

A powerful All Black side overwhelmed the Irish 15–0, but they also happened to keep twenty-four of their opponents on the tour scoreless. In total, the All Blacks scored 830 points and conceded just thirty-nine. When the Centenary All Blacks toured in the autumn of 2005, they visited the birthplace of Gallaher in County Donegal, just a few days before over-whelming Ireland, 45–7; a performance you could say in homage to the Originals.

Lansdowne Road is also closely linked to world history. The British cavalry from nearby Beggar's Bush barracks originally used this sixteen-acre site to graze and water their horses. And they indulged in a bit of rugby there, too. The morning after the outbreak of the First World War in August 1914, rugby players – mainly from Wanderers and Lansdowne clubs – enlisted there for service. A monument to mark this occasion stood behind the old ivy-coated South Terrace and a plaque to the Wanderers and Lansdowne players who were part of the first 'pals regiments' hung beside the former Wanderers pavilion. Both these memorials have been retained within the new structure.

In September 1914, it was decided that all club games and representative matches be suspended for the duration of the Great War, though schools and inter-provincial matches did continue. Full internationals were not played again until the 1919–1920 season.

Though relations between Ireland and England had dipped to an all-time low during the War of Independence and, despite the parlous state of Dublin, the England rugby team fulfilled its fixture in 1920, travelling to Lansdowne and winning the Five Nations game, 11–14. (It had moved from a Four to a Five Nations Championship in 1909 and France won their first game on their first visit to Lansdowne in March of that year.)

At this point, the IRFU was secure in its tenancy, and had set about a major rebuilding and planning programme for the stadium. The ground had been swung on its axis from an east–west to a north–south alignment and a covered stand had been erected on the west side of the ground and an uncovered stand to the left of it. This cost £6,000 and had been finished in time for the visit of Scotland in February 1908, a game Ireland had won to mark the occasion. In 1928, the east side of the ground was fitted with a stand.

In 1955, it was felt the West Stand had run its course, and it was decided to build a modern two-tier structure, one which arched over the railway line that served the busy suburban route to Sandymount, Blackrock and southeast Dublin. In 1974, the lower tier of the West Stand underwent major renovation and, in 1983, it was decided that the old East Stand should be demolished to be replaced by a modern structure. One man who devoted a huge amount time to the development of Lansdowne Road is former Ireland and Lions captain, Ronnie Dawson. An architect by profession, Dawson served on the IRB for twenty years as well as a term as the President of the IRFU.

Internationals were suspended again after the outbreak of the Second World War but, in 1947, the coming together of a golden generation of Ireland players resulted in Ireland's first Grand Slam in 1948. Ireland played only one game in that Grand Slam year in Lansdowne Road – a 6–0 win over Scotland – before claiming the title with a 6–3 win over Wales in Ravenhill, Belfast.

In the late 1940s and 1950s, great athletics meets were hosted at Lansdowne Road. The late Dutch sprinter, Fanny Blankers-

Koen, who won four gold medals at the 1948 London Olympics, ran in Lansdowne, while, in the late 1950s, Ronnie Delany, who won a gold medal in the 1,500 metres at the 1956 Melbourne Olympics, displayed his athletic prowess on the Lansdowne grass track.

While at the epicentre of Irish international rugby, Lansdowne Road has provided the pulse for Irish soccer's glory days, especially during the Jack Charlton era from 1986 to 1995. During the Englishman's tenure, the Republic of Ireland qualified for a European Championship (1988) and two World Cups (1990 and 1994) – with many of the most epic qualification games played out at the Dublin 4 venue. There's no doubt that Lansdowne Road has been the focal point for the fostering of Irish international soccer teams and the theatre for some of soccer's greats. Indeed, during the Charlton years, Irish soccer reached its apogee, and, you could argue, Lansdowne was at the heart of soccer's glory years too.

It became a field of dreams for schoolboys from Leinster where Junior and Senior schools cups were decided at the venue. And while playing host to its tenants, Lansdowne FC and Wanderers FC through the decades, Lansdowne also opened its doors to the club game in this country with many All-Ireland League finals played there. Leinster Senior Cup games have also been hosted there, and, in the 2005–2006 season, the inaugural AIB All-Ireland Cup final was won by Cork Constitution in Lansdowne Road.

Lansdowne has also been a venue for concerts – a stand-out one being the visit of U2 in August 1998. They brought their infamous and somewhat brash Pop-mart tour to the oldest stadium in the world but, somehow, it didn't look out of place. The acoustics, for some strange reason, were always good there, and on a rainy night in May 1989, old blue eyes himself, Frank Sinatra, swooned a captivated audience inside Lansdowne. Seated tickets for that show cost just £35. The Aviva, meanwhile, is geared towards hosting concerts as well, and the designers and architects have taken acoustics into account – though, in respect to the IRFU/FAI's neighbours, just three concerts will be held there each year.

The players in this book describe the old Lansdowne ground as a theatre of dreams – sometimes broken dreams. They describe how a passionate Lansdowne crowd could, at different times, make them run ten seconds faster or feel ten inches taller. Many of Lansdowne's great days have been recounted by the players – Ireland's golden years between 1948 and 1951; how Ireland nearly beat, and should have beaten, the All Blacks in 1963 and 1973; Ollie Campbell's twenty-one points helping 'Dad's Army' to the 1982 Triple Crown (the first to be won at Lansdowne Road); Michael Kiernan's drop goal that gave Mick Doyle's boys the 1985 Triple Crown; Donal Lenihan's inner torment at losing to a last-minute try to Australia in the 1991 World Cup quarter-final; Irish rugby's dark ages; the transition to professionalism and its associated problems; Ronan O'Gara single-handedly beating Australia (2002) and South Africa (2004); Brian O'Driscoll's hat-trick against Scotland in 2002 as well as our current golden generation's successes.

The fans, too, helped make Lansdowne, as the Welsh great Ieuan Evans says, they are, 'vibrant and raucous'. Bill McLaren says that Irish fans were philosophical about their rugby football – that, win or lose, a good time was had by all. McLaren felt the Irish 'kind of skidded along'. It is felt by others that the supporters, especially those in touchline seats or the East Stand terrace, must have had a mischievous quality about them too. Former England hooker Brian Moore remembers one particular day when he got a dose of Lansdowne 'hospitality', Moore remembers, 'I was playing with England at Lansdowne Road, and at the bottom of a ruck five yards from our line, I felt an Irish hand grab my ankle. All I could think was, "He is going to try and sprain my ankle now." But he pulled his hand away and, with it, my boot! He promptly turned around and threw it into the crowd. Sure enough, when I, as you can imagine, politely asked for my boot back, they refused. The referee ordered play to continue. It was a five-yard scrum and I'd only one boot! Eventually, the boot was thrown back at me and we carried on.'

I'm sure Brian Moore will look back wistfully at that moment and smile and say – 'that's Lansdowne and that's the Irish'. Keith Wood used say that Lansdowne seemed to live for the big occasion; that when it came to life, it struggled one last time to hold its place.

Lansdowne will forever hold its place in many people's hearts. That's a guarantee. But here's to the next 125 years of memories inside the new Aviva.

Edward Newman
June 2010

Ollie Campbell

Fly-Half

1976–1984

Before he scraped the Lansdowne Road mud from his boots and placed it in a plastic bag for keeps after Belvedere College won the Leinster Schools Senior Cup in 1971, and before he talked his way into Lansdowne Road to witness the emotion and magic of the historic Five Nations game between England and Ireland in 1973, Ollie Campbell sat in the West Upper alongside his father, James Oliver, bewitched by the All Blacks who fashioned a 6–5 victory over Ireland in December 1963.

It might be expedient to say that Campbell was deeply influenced by the genius of the All Blacks full-back, Donald Clarke, but the truth is that he did become a keen student of Clarke's kicking game. He would always look back on that winter's afternoon in 1963 as a pivotal moment in his life. It was the day Clarke left an indelible mark on Campbell's psyche and, more importantly, on his kicking game, which he would put to good use in kicking Ireland to Triple Crown glory in 1982.

'From the moment my father took me to see them, I would have had a fascination with the whole All Blacks mystique – what they stand for and what they mean,' says Campbell. 'There is just something about the All Blacks. Even the name – it's not just New Zealand, it's the All Blacks. As a team they've rarely disappointed.'

Twenty years after he first set eyes on those famous black shirts, he toured with the Lions in New Zealand 'playing in all these grounds that I'd only ever read about or seen briefly on TV'. Their aura of invincibility had gone around the world like the wind – and Campbell was caught in the slipstream. For ever. 'The 1963 side was captained by Wilson Whineray who, to this day, would be considered one of the great captains of New Zealand rugby – he's certainly an MBE if not a Sir Wilson Whineray for his services to New Zealand. He has been very successful in everything he has done. You also had Colin Meads, Stan Meads and Donald Clarke, of course, at full-back. Donald was probably the first really great kicker – he kicked the old-fashioned way with the toe and, for many years, he was actually the biggest man who ever played for New Zealand. Even though he was a full-back, he was a colossus. Those were the sort of names that caught my eye.

'Johnny Fortune got a try for Ireland in that 1963 test, but, if I remember right, it was a fairly late, long penalty by Don Clarke that actually squeezed victory for the All Blacks. The Irish side that day included Willie John McBride, Ray

McLoughlin, Noel Murphy and Tommy Kiernan – the last two would also have a massive influence on my career. So in many, many ways that first day was really a defining day for me in my life, in my career and how things evolved after that.'

The visit of the All Blacks in 1963 lodges lovingly in Campbell's memory but when the modern batch arrived on these shores for a test in November 2005, the bond Ireland has with the All Blacks grew even stronger. On the week of the test, players like Keven Mealamu and Jerry Collins took a breather from their hectic schedule (which included a visit to Letterkenny, County Donegal, to the birthplace of Dave Gallaher, captain of the 1905 Originals – the first All Blacks) to drop out to Campbell's beloved Old Belvedere on Angelsea Road to meet some of the kids.

It was Gareth Edwards who said that 'rugby is really a simple game and it's only the coaches who make it compli-cated' and, as is de rigeur in the professional era, Campbell didn't have three different kicking advisors at provincial, national and Lions level to blunt his edge. He was old school and self-taught, untainted by opinion and input from others. For someone who never kicked a ball at school, who hadn't done so much as a twenty-two drop-out or a halfway kick and who had never even punted or place-kicked at school, his record at test level was a result of sheer hard work. He was nineteen before he assumed kicking duties – on an Old Belvedere thirds side – the captain presuming that if he was at fly-half, he was also a kicker.

In fact, back at school Ollie was fifth-choice place-kicker on the Belvedere College side that won the 1972 Leinster Schools Senior Cup. Those, he says, were special days for the north Dublin school completing, as it were, back-to-back titles.

Campbell's first appearance at Lansdowne was in the 1971 final, as a fifth-year student and as a fringe player, who was only fleetingly involved in senior rugby that season, playing in just five friendly games. He remembers Tony Duane getting injured in the last few minutes of the semi-final, and on cup final day, Campbell was told just two hours before kick-off that he'd be playing. It didn't allow him much time to notify family, but the short notice carried long-term benefits: there was no time to even think of nerves. 'Only afterwards do you realise what a huge occasion it was. It all happened a bit quickly. But that was my first time playing in Lansdowne Road and, as I've mentioned many times before, I kept the mud from my boot in a plastic bag for a long, long time afterwards.'

His coach at the time was a Jesuit, Jim Moran, who would have played things very calmly, very coolly, telling young Ollie that he should play the match, rather than the occasion. 'That would have been very much his mentality at that time: "It's just another game of rugby," he'd keep telling me. I was very proud of that medal. There wouldn't be anything near the media hype that is there now. Today you even have a satellite station, Setanta, covering the Leinster Senior and Junior Schools Cups. The exposure would have been more modest in my time.'

The following season, he had the medal in his pocket and the temperament to match the emotional longevity of a cup final campaign as well. Belvedere faced Terenure in the final, their long-time adversaries. 'They had beaten us solidly at under-9s, under-10s, all the way up, twice a year, every year,' says Campbell. 'OK, we beat them at under-16, but they had half their team playing for a senior team that day. It didn't look good when, in Senior Cup year, we lost to Terenure before Christmas, 25–3. In the final, we were losing 10–3 after twenty

4

minutes and facing another drubbing. Suddenly, we turned it around. Whatever happened, we won 20–10. Michael Hickey, a brother of David Hickey (of the Dubs teams of the 1970s), was a superb place-kicker. He could kick them from anywhere and, in fact, that day against Terenure, he kicked four penalties from all sorts of angles and distances and that helped us win the cup. He was the man of the match. They're great memories and there's nothing that I experienced or achieved in my subsequent career that surpassed the experience of representing the school and winning a couple of cup medals.'

Ollie returned to Lansdowne Road in 2005 to watch his alma mater lift the Leinster Schools Senior Cup for the first since his team of all talents walked the steps of the West Stand in 1972 to collect the famous silverware. 'Over half the 1972 team live outside of Ireland now,' recounts Campbell. 'It was a sign of our era, I suppose, but we got as many as we could for a function in Old Belvedere before the match (in 2005) and then we walked down from Anglesea Road. We all agreed afterwards that the sweetest sound we had ever heard was the sound of the final whistle going in Lansdowne Road that day. We said we can get on with our lives now! But, suddenly then, we were consigned to history!'

Campbell scored his first try at the ground in 1973 in a provincial schools victory for Leinster, but later came a memory that still burns brightly within him.

The occasion? England's visit to Dublin during the Troubles. 'There was such emotion, gratitude and admiration all rolled into one for the English team that day. That was certainly a very poignant moment.' In 1973, John Pullin's England side travelled to Dublin despite paramilitary threats. (In 1972, Wales and Scotland had refused to play at Lansdowne because of the threats players had received). Campbell shouldn't even have been there that day. He had no ticket. 'My dad was allowed to drive down Lansdowne Road, drop myself and Albert Horton, an elderly man, outside and I was only to talk my way in, bring Mr Horton up to his seat and then leave the ground. But I didn't leave. I ended up sitting on the steps of the West Upper and, as long as I'll live, I will never forget the applause when the English team ran out. It really does to this day send a shiver up my spine, and I also remember how Ireland captain Tom Kiernan, sensing what was happening, held back his team from running out so that the applause rang out even more.'

Campbell made his entrance on the international stage in January 1976 against Australia – he arrived like a whirlwind, but left the field with a whimper. The loud thud within his head was the sound of his kicking game imploding, but, in a game of inches, the misses just came down to sheer fractions.

The circumstances around the announcement of his first cap came at the Shelbourne Hotel twenty-four hours before the game. It was all rather casual, he says. He was eating a steak when Roly Meates gave a tap on his shoulder and said, 'Ollie, Barry's out [Barry McGann], you're in for tomorrow. Congratulations.'

The week before, he had played for Old Belvedere against Galwegians on a pitch that would have resembled the Battle of the Somme, a match that should never have gone ahead. 'Probably the worst match that I played in my life and that was my preparation for playing at Lansdowne Road the following week!'

Inside the dressing room, everything was calm and Campbell felt humbled to be seated amongst some legends of Irish rugby.

The pre-match speeches from Meates and captain Mike Gibson were less of the chest-thumping variety and more intrinsic motivation, to use modern parlance. The tendency, it seemed, around that time would have been to signal your intent through loud passionate blasts from the heart. 'Roly was very quietly spoken, a cerebral guy in his approach to rugby as was Mike Gibson, which was fantastic. On that particular day, it was very low-key which, to be honest, suited me much better than the rabble-rousing stuff that would often have gone on around that time.'

The game? Best forgotten if you were Ollie or Irish. 'And it wasn't even a full house,' he says now. 'They beat us 20–10. I had a 100 per cent record with my kicking – I missed four out of four! But they were all by just a fraction. I was dropped and I didn't play for Ireland again until the infamous Australian tour of 1979. It was the only team I was ever dropped from, from when I started under-9s until I retired. I was one of five new caps that day – Ian McIlrath, Johnny Cantrell, Feidhlim McLoughlin (who got his one and only cap aged thirty-four) and John Robbie, a great friend of mine. Johnny was twenty and I was twenty-one. I have a photograph at home and the two of us look like twelve-year-old kids! I'd be thinking sometimes, "What were we doing there?"'

This time there was no mud collected and preserved to go alongside that from his Belvedere days, just a thought that glory was fleeting and obscurity was for ever. Ollie wasn't too inclined to read newspapers when he was playing, but, the following Monday, the temptation to reach for the experts' views was too great to resist. 'I was in the College of Commerce in Rathmines at the time. I remember going to college on the Monday after the match and it took all day to even open *The Irish Times*. I told myself that there wasn't much good that could be said. I remember reading the report from the bottom to the top – literally starting at the bottom and working my way up through it. I said it to the writer, Ned Van Esbeck, over Christmas 2005 – I'd never said it before and I thought it was about time that I did – that he didn't even mention my name, which was fantastic because he really couldn't have said many positive things. I was young, it was my first cap, I was only twenty-one. It wasn't the fact that I missed a few kicks that we lost – we were outplayed. I really appreciated what Ned did and I've never forgotten that. After reading it I said, "What a relief to not even to be mentioned." If I'd been aware of any criticism out there, well, I would have been affected by it. It all happened a bit quickly. I was too young and wasn't ready and I'd be the first to admit it.'

He also wasn't ready when a mysterious brown envelope came through the letter box six months later. 'Today you're formally presented with your cap at a function the evening after the match. In June of that year, I got my cap in a brown envelope in the post with not so much as a compliment slip. That would have been quite standard as well. So things have moved on a lot.

'And to show how long ago it was, after winning your new cap, you were allowed keep your jersey and your socks. But, if it wasn't your first cap and if you wanted to keep your jersey, it cost £10 and your socks cost £3.'

When he arrived home from Australia after kicking Ireland to two test wins in 1979, Campbell was a home-town hero. But he had taken the place of Tony Ward on tour. The battle for the Number 10 shirt intensified and the attention their relative merits drew as out-halves was the talk of the nation – and divided the country. Before the 1980 Five Nations, due mainly to their heroics Down Under, Ireland were tipped to win the Triple Crown but, after losing away to England at Twickenham, Scotland came to Lansdowne Road. The pressure was back on Ireland. And back on Ollie. 'We were tipped to win the Triple Crown that year because of what we'd done to Australia. Against England, we got a bit of a pasting – 24–9 – so any hopes of a Triple Crown were blown to pieces.'

Ireland beat the Scots 22–15 thanks to Campbell's three penalties and a drop goal and a conversion from Terry Kennedy's try. 'That would have been my first win for Ireland at Lansdowne Road. We beat Wales at home that year as well. Wales were probably still the team to beat and that was at the end of their long decade of dominance. I'd say beating Wales carried more kudos to beating Scotland – that was certainly one not to forget.'

The Campbell–Ward debate raged on yet again before the following year's Five Nations. Campbell started at 10 for the French game but, after a loss and in an effort to accommodate two of the brightest talents of the same era, Ward returned to out-half and Campbell moved to the centre. But it proved a difficult championship for the Irish and they went on to lose all their games, though only by narrow margins. 'As Moss Keane says, "It was Ireland's best ever whitewash!" I think we were in the lead in every game at half-time and we lost every game by a single score. Tommy Kiernan had taken over as coach at that stage and he was quite fantastic during that period. He kept saying we were doing the right thing, that it was only a question of time and that the wins would come.'

Going into the 1982 campaign, Ireland were aiming to bring a seven-game losing streak to an end and Campbell returned to out-half for that year's Five Nations. 'We beat Wales but nobody was talking about a Triple Crown – the only thing was the sheer relief of breaking a long, losing sequence. We went to England two weeks later and won 16–15, with Ginger McLoughlin's famous try. A fortnight later, we had Scotland at home and, suddenly, the chance of a Triple Crown, which we hadn't done for thirty-three years – and we'd never won a Triple Crown at Lansdowne Road – seemed possible. So, all that again happened quite quickly and out of the blue. The only change in the pack that went on the tour to Australia in 1979 was Donal Lenihan coming into the second row. The pack was seasoned, and they knew what they were about. In the backline, I was the only one remaining from 1979, so suddenly I was one of the veterans.'

He tried to put the atmosphere out of his head, and one of his abiding memories is playing into a gale-force wind for the whole of the second half. 'We only turned around 15–6 at half-time. It wasn't a big enough lead. Most of the game seemed to have been played down the East Stand side. I don't think anyone on the East Stand sat down for the whole match – and, naturally, they were all standing up on the lower terrace, singing 'Cockles and Mussels'. I've often said it, but they sort of willed us to victory. They just would not have accepted anything but a victory and I think they were as responsible as anyone on the pitch for us winning that match.'

He remembers, too, the sound of silence after John Rutherford's try levelled matters. He says it was like having the television at full blast and suddenly pressing the mute button. 'I remember a lineout on the halfway line on the East Stand side, Roy Laidlaw making a brilliant break, feeding John Rutherford who went racing under the posts. You could hear a pin drop. This wasn't in the script because that made it 6–6. However, we turned over 15–6 ahead, then Jim Rennick and Andy Irvine missed a couple at the start of the second half which would have made it a very uncomfortable ride for us, but we came through and it was just euphoria afterwards. Looking back on it now, a 21–12 win seems comfortable and, by and large, we were in control for most of the game but when Jonno went over for that try …

'I was brought up on the Grand Slam and Triple Crown winning teams of 1948 and 1949, the Jackie Kyles, the Karl Mullens, the George Nortons, the Bill McKays, the Des O'Briens – it's almost like I was there. My dad would talk particularly about Jackie Kyle, and all of my life they were my heroes, they were up on a pedestal – imagine winning a Triple Crown, a Grand Slam – and then you're on the next team to actually win a Triple Crown. That certainly wasn't lost on me: being the first Irish side to win a Triple Crown in Lansdowne Road for only the fifth time in Ireland's history.'

Many say it was Campbell's Triple Crown. He kicked six penalties and a drop goal that afternoon against Scotland, but his meticulous attention to detail had brought the man who would eat, sleep and drink rugby to undergo intensive surgery to his place-kicking before Triple Crown day.

'I remember against England I hit a ball from about forty yards just to the left of the post. I hit it absolutely beautifully just hoping the wind would draw it in. And it never moved an inch. I was furious with that. So when we got back on the Sunday, I went straight to Anglesea Road with my five balls in the boot of the car. I was probably out for a couple of hours, practising exactly from that spot. So, for whatever reason – and I had never done it before and never did it since – but 90 per cent of the kicks I took that day in the Scotland match were from that one spot on a field where I missed against England. Three minutes into the Scottish match – penalty for Ireland. Where is it from? From exactly the same spot as the one I missed in Twickenham! My feeling was that I could hit it with my eyes closed after I had hit two or three hundred from exactly that spot. Put it down, over the bar and we were away. So I suppose that day did make sense of all the practice.'

Campbell's late father, who played as a Louth county minor as well as propping with Suttonians, hardly ever missed an international at Lansdowne Road – and his enthusiasm rubbed off on young Seamus Oliver. Campbell talks of how his father 'got a great kick' out of his career, and of how it was his father who set those Lansdowne dreams alight when he tossed a new leather rugby ball to him in their back garden onr day when Ollie was six years old and said, 'If you catch this, you can keep it.' Campbell did.

One of Campbell's earliest memories of Lansdowne was, as a young lad, running onto the pitch after matches. While his dad was having a couple of drinks in the Lansdowne or Wanderers pavilion, Ollie would be out on the field using a pair of rolled-up gloves as a ball and, if there were other kids around, they'd have a game. They'd knock around and it just seemed to go on for hours in the dark. Only the lights from the two pavilions kept their game alive. Ollie would pretend to be Mike Gibson – drop kicking and grubber-kicking and running as any kid would do. Then his dad would come out and they'd go home. But Ollie would be back.

Gareth Edwards

Scrum-Half, Wales

1967–1978

Gareth Edwards arrived for his first senior Wales game at Lansdowne Road in March 1968. Though only twenty, the Welsh great had heard much about the unique Lansdowne atmosphere, and had got glimpses of the old lady on cinema in Wales.

That spring afternoon, he walked into the Lansdowne Pavilion, one that nestled cosily between the West Stand and the Havelock End terrace. 'It was like a little house in the corner,' mused Edwards. He recalls a dressing room resembling someone's front room – quaint and welcoming, in an Irish sort of way. 'It was a surreal setting,' he says now, 'so welcoming and cosy, but it seemed there wasn't enough room to swing a cat in there. Although, that said, it was a contrast to the reception you got from the Irish team when you hit the ground!'

After nearly ninety minutes of rugby, he was seen galloping back to the sanctuary of the dressing room; the atmosphere had become fairly heated outside. Though Ireland had won 9–6, his debut at Lansdowne would be remembered for all the wrong reasons.

The debris that had accumulated around the perimeter of the field was a result of an Edwards 'drop goal' and the contentious refereeing decision in awarding the score. The build-up to the score wasn't a play Edwards or his team had premeditated; instead he had intended passing the ball along the line but changed his mind at the last moment. He does remember connecting sweetly with the ball but now is sorry he ever did. 'I hit it very well, it travelled straight and true, but the ref was watching the Irish back-row line for possible offside. He looked up a little late to watch the ball swing. I thought for a moment that it might very well have gone over because the ball just swirled in the wind and turned around the post. I think the ref thought it was going to go one direction, and he was cricking his neck to sort of see it go over. The next thing I knew he had given it. I think there were 40,000 in Lansdowne that day who didn't agree with him!'

The result of Edwards' drop goal precipitated some angry scenes on the terraces. He was told on the bus to the match that the Lansdowne crowd was a very knowledgeable one, but, after his kick, he hadn't too much time to ponder the merits of the Lansdowne crowd. The ball was retained by the Irish supporters, and then bottles, tin cans, even fruit were hurled onto the field – though nothing it must be said was thrown at any player. Soon, sections of the crowd began to spill onto the field as well.

'There was a lot of controversy surrounding that drop goal. I remember there were loads of coins, even loads of Guinness landing all around us. In fact, there were enough coins to have taken care of us for a good night out in Dublin! It was mayhem really. The game looked like it would end up a draw.

'I don't think any of us were hit but some of us were laughing at the sight of all these objects being hurled down from the terrace.'

Approaching full-time, the Welsh players harboured a suspicion that the referee might add enough injury-time in an effort to assuage 'the angry mob'. And, ten minutes later, Mick Doyle touched down on a patch of grass in the corner near the then Lansdowne Pavilion – a patch that, years later, would become known as 'Currow Corner'. Soon after, the ref called time.

'I remember there was a lot of injury-time that gave Ireland an opportunity to score a winning try right down near the dressing room. I think it was a bit more than a coincidence than just the fact they had scored in the corner. From Ireland's point of view, justice was served when Doyler scored in the corner.'

Two years later Wales suffered a 14–0 defeat to Ireland at Lansdowne Road. While the Edwards drop goal from Wales' previous visit to Dublin was still vivid in the Irish memory, the Ireland players had preserved the hurt after the beating they received at Cardiff Arms Park the previous season when the principality went on to win the Triple Crown. Others, meanwhile, were still not over the punch Noel Murphy received when Welsh forward Brian Price ghosted from a ruck and hit the Ireland flanker in what was his last international match.

The retribution was cold and calculated. Wales were squeezed and suffocated. The result didn't exactly precipitate rioting in the streets in Wales, says Edwards, but there were plenty of inquests in the Valleys afterwards. The star-studded Welsh side, men of so-called genius, never got close to Ireland in 1970. In the aftermath, they started looking within themselves in an effort understand where it all went wrong.

The visitors learned one very important lesson that day: you never underestimate the Irish, especially on their home patch. 'They were all over us. We all played badly. Barry [John] and myself at half-back were given a torrid time. Ken Goodall was quite sensational, as were all the Irish forwards. There was no response from us at all. Barry McGann slammed over a beautiful drop goal and I remember Alan Duggan and Ken Goodall scoring fantastic tries. It was a comprehensive defeat.

'14–0 doesn't sound much by today's standard, but we were well beaten on the day. We lost a match that we thought we might conceivably win. As a commentator of the time said, "We were lucky to get nil!" When we went to Ireland we always knew it was going to be tough, but we had experienced players with us at that time. We never really got off the ground and the Irish took a grip of proceedings from the very beginning. We all had a bit of a nightmare really.'

And though the greatest Welsh scrum-half of all time was rubbing away the tears of a comprehensive defeat, he was later saddened by the news that Ken Goodall would be moving to rugby league the following season. 'Ken was the star of that game in 1970. He was a great loss to British and Irish rugby. I played all too briefly with him in the 1968 Lions tour but I have so much respect for him. As a Number 8, he was such a talented player and though we had Mervyn Davies, Ken was right up there with the very best. If he hadn't gone to rugby league, who knows what the future would have held for him.'

The fall from grace of the Triple Crown champions at Lansdowne Road brought with it feverish inquests in Wales. The gossip-mongers and tabloid press had a field day. Some of the stories got quite personal and showed how far people and newspapers would go to finding the solution for a sudden collapse in form. 'I can laugh about it now but the rumours were that the Welsh team were fighting behind the scenes. Another was that on the Friday night before the game, we were out having drinks and fighting them on the lawn outside the hotel. Then they were saying that myself and J.P.R. Williams were fighting after the game because my girlfriend and J.P.R. were now an item! Such was the sting of the defeat that the Welsh fans felt there had to be more than just the fact that Ireland were so much better than us.'

Wales and Scotland did not travel to Lansdowne Road in 1972 because of the Troubles in Northern Ireland, and so Ireland lost out on an opportunity to play the 1971 Grand Slam champions. Wales were a team of all talents, playing a brand of rugby that today would mark them out as innovators and entertainers.

Whether the Lansdowne Road faithful had their appetite sated by the excellence of some of their own like Mike Gibson, Barry McGann, Tom Kiernan, Tom Grace and Fergus Slattery, the Welsh brought a mystique to the table, as the All Blacks did. Superlatives were spun out lavishly by the media in an attempt to paint as effusively as possible the talents of Edwards, John, Gerald Davies, Williams and Phil Bennett, or of their much-vaunted Pontypool front-row of Price, Faulkner and Windsor.

Amidst the hype and hoopla of Welsh rugby, the potential and capabilities of the Irish seemed to have been undermined. Indeed, the Irish team was not far off winning a Grand Slam that year.

'In 1972, we didn't go over and that was a huge disappointment for us but the political scene wasn't conducive to travelling. I know England did go the following year. The players were quite prepared to play but the WRU made the decision and said no. It's easy on reflection to look back but people in the union were very concerned and the threat was very real as we all know. The union said, "This will not be the players' decision, this will be our decision", and they pulled the plug on it.'

When Wales travelled to Lansdowne in 1974, Edwards recalls it was probably a better result than the team could have envisaged. Still, it was a stadium where this Welsh team had yet to break loose and win the respect of the Irish rugby public. But the vagaries of the wind coupled with a litany of incomprehensible decisions by the referee left Wales playing a more conservative brand of rugby, alien to their innate attacking instincts. Free expression had to wait for another day.

The game was less about inventiveness and playing with abandon and more about a sleeves-rolled-up attitude – a very un-Welsh thing especially for this group of superstars.

'By that time, the Welsh team was maturing. We were playing some great rugby coming into that match. Then we came to Dublin. There was a very strong wind, as there tended to be in Lansdowne. We played very well into the wind in the first half and I just thought, "If we turn around – and I think it might have been 6–6 at half-time – there's a chance of winning this." All we have to do is win a few balls and keep

Ireland down there. We got penalised out of the game in the second half whether it was justified or not, but, naturally, I'd have a blinkered view about it. We were hard done by. The referee was penalising Wales in the lineout for pushing and, having played with Willie John McBride over a number of years, I knew exactly who was doing most of the shoving!

'But that's only a whinge,' he says with a smile. 'It was an awful game spoilt predominantly by the wind. But we had the advantage in the second half. We had the wind and I thought surely it would be a matter of time before we got a couple of penalties. We only got a few in the second half and the match ended all square (9–9), which was a huge disappointment to me. I think both sides nullified one another. We had to wait a few years before we had a decent game of rugby against one another at Lansdowne Road.'

When they clashed in Dublin two years later, it was time for the Welsh to put on their most extravagant show. Edwards, so often 'the man' in Welsh victories, capped off one of his most inspiring displays with a try in a 34–9 victory. Still, Edwards would let you believe that scoreline was deceptive, that somehow Wales sneaked a win. 'That was a very, very tough game. It was only in the last fifteen minutes that we pulled away. It had been very tough, very close and it all just came together. We were young but there was a lovely way about the game we played. We had control of the pack and we could also play an expansive game. In that period of time – 1976, 1977, 1978 – we won three Triple Crowns in consecutive years and two Grand Slams. We only lost out narrowly in Paris for the third Grand Slam. Unlike 1970 and 1974, we were able to hold on and match Ireland's aggression – and we were then able to ride the storm so to speak.'

Sadly, we were to see the last of Edwards at Lansdowne Road in 1978. He went on record afterwards saying that the game had become too physical, that the fun had gone out of it for him. 'I put it on record as saying that the game was so physically hard that I thought, WWhat am I doing here? I'm not really enjoying this." It's a peculiar thing to say, you know. The responsibility and the intensity of the occasions were just wearing me down.'

He remembers a couple of stand-out moments in that 1978 game, despite the nasty undercurrent. 'We had a wonderful start and I thought, "This is too easy." I remember turning to Gerald Davies and saying, "Gerald, I don't like this because it's too easy!"' But, as soon as we thought that way, the opposite always seemed to happen. Nothing is how you would expect it at Lansdowne.'

And if it's believed that Lansdowne Road does strange things to players, it certainly had done strange things to great Welsh sides in the 1970s. 'When we thought we were going to do well, we came away with our tail between our legs.

'But nothing is easy at Lansdowne Road and Ireland dominated the next hour of the game until the Welsh side showed its experience and resolve. The forwards knew it; they knew they had to get their hands on the ball because they hadn't seen it for about an hour.

'Our pack eventually got a hold of the ball, drove down the middle of the field and worked it into a position. The improvisation of the Welsh back division meant we were able to conjure up a try in the dying minutes which I suppose epitomised the way we played. It showed our spirit and character. And if we were to put our names on the record books, then Ireland had contributed significantly by pushing us to the very, very limits. That try in the last minute won the match for us. We trundled off into the dressing room and there was hardly any noise because the boys were shattered, nobody was shouting or jumping up and down. We were just far too physically tired to do anything else. I remember the delight on the faces of the selectors who came in, but the boys just sat there, too tired to even take their shirts off. "You don't realise what you have achieved," I think is what they said to the team. Nobody responded. Don't get me wrong – there was obviously great delight and elation but people were just completely shattered.

'I remember that I had to go down the corridor from the dressing room to do some television work after getting dressed and changed. About an hour afterwards, lots of the forwards were just sat there, the Pontypool front-row were sitting there in their shirts – they were absolutely drained.'

After the match, Edwards met up with his tormentor-in-chief that afternoon, Fergus Slattery. 'Slatts', he remembers, was 'all over the place in a flanker sort of way' that afternoon, trying to dictate which way the game should be played. 'We've discussed that game with a laugh many times since. I remember saying to him afterwards, "Christ, you were clattering everyone, Slatts." He said, "No I didn't." Then one of the Irish lads, S.A. McKinney turned around and said, "Yes you did, you clattered me as well!" We all had a laugh about that and had a good drink as well.'

Edwards went on to work for the BBC when his playing days ended in 1978. The charm of Lansdowne, the laid-back attitude of the people and the miracle of the BBC technicians around the commentary positions always amazed him. 'The ageing stadium was always causing panic for the BBC technicians. I'd be sat in the commentary position with Bill McLaren just before kick-off, panicking about the transmission and whether or not we could get through to London. Then minutes before kick off, Bill and myself would find somebody hanging by the windowsill tapping a few wires and meddling around with switches. Then some one would say, "That'll be all right now." Or I could be standing on the field ready to do a live piece to camera on *Grandstand* which was starting at one o'clock I'd be thinking, "My word, we haven't got London. What's going to happen? What's going to happen?" And with a minute to go somebody taps a thing or pulls something and suddenly I'm saying, "All right, we're through." So it always worked by and large. But, many's the time we were left biting our knuckles wondering whether or not it was going to work.'

From a playing point of view, Edwards has mixed memories, but he always found Lansdowne an enchanting arena. 'There was a terrific atmosphere there. It seems everybody just poured into the stadium. It defied logic really the number of people could get in there. It created an electric atmosphere, and was a wonderful arena in which to play rugby. We came off the wrong side of results on too many occasions, though the crowd certainly got behind their team and made it a very intimidating place for anyone to play.

'The new Lansdowne Road is long overdue … but we in Wales have great memories of the old one – where else would you have a major sporting arena with a main line station underneath? It is sad that Lansdowne Road changed because I have very, very fond – and not so fond – memories, but the old ground will live long in the memory. Whenever you played at Lansdowne Road, the game always seemed to be played at a huge pace, at a hundred miles an hour. There was no time to take a deep breath, have any kind of control of the whole thing.'

At least Lansdowne can be thankful to have witnessed not just a great Welsh team but a diamond of a scrum-half like Garreth Edwards.

Ciaran Fitzgerald

Hooker

1979–1986

Your imagination might not need too much prodding to picture Ciaran Fitzgerald pacing the dressing room under the West Stand at Lansdowne Road before either of the Triple Crown deciders against Scotland (1982) or England (1985). An army officer by day, in the dressing room Fitzie was equally adept at drilling his team, bringing presence and charisma and force of will to the entire Ireland squad.

You can't help but conjure an image of the Ireland hooker finger-wagging and giving instructions when he paced the room to gee up each player. Or an index finger pointed to his temple stressing the importance of mental toughness or, to paraphrase Kipling, of keeping your head when all around you might be losing theirs. And then, for good measure, you must factor in an appropriate level of 'colourful' language to capture the importance of it all.

Before Big Jack Charlton, Mick McCarthy and the giddiness of a soccer World Cup in Italy, Ireland had Ciaran Fitzgerald – rugby's Captain Fantastic. He was the original of the species and Lansdowne Road will hardly see his likes again. Just ask Tony Ward.

Lansdowne Road was packed for the Triple Crown decider in 1985. The win – for a few weeks at least – dimmed the horrible reality of economic depression and rising unemployment, symptoms of Ireland's lumbering economy of the 1980s. The nation's self-esteem was at an all-time low but at least Fitzie and his boys raised hope.

To underline Fitzgerald's legendary motivational skills we got a snapshot on television during that 1985 Triple Crown decider. It came in a moment of the match when Ireland was struggling. You didn't need to be the world's most qualified lip reader to interpret his immortal words during an interlude in the second half when he bellowed, 'Where's your f***ing pride?' You almost stood to attention yourself.

It wasn't a premeditated outburst, but it came nevertheless from the heart and perhaps that vignette – as well as the free-flowing style of rugby they were encouraged to play – captured the free-spiritedness of Mick Doyle's team, a coach who inspired his players to express themselves. As Hugo MacNeill, who played full-back on that Triple Crown winning team, said, 'Doyle caught the spirit of an already confident group, he lit the touchpaper … it was youth gone mad, given its head.' They didn't play in a straitjacket; it was rugby from the heart – just like Fitzie's moments of motivational genius.

Tony Ward describes Fitzgerald as the greatest-ever Ireland captain, and how can you dispute that – to lead Irish teams to two Triple Crowns (1982 and 1985), a share of the championship (1983), and a championship (1985) in the space of five years is no mean achievement.

Many considered the Connacht man the perfect choice as captain. From a province that has always been seen as the poor relation when it came to international selection, Fitzgerald brought a new dimension to his role as captain. He empowered those around him to play with a cause. His rise to instant recognition, to an elevated plateau in the story of Irish international sport, is part fairy tale, part romance. As a boy growing up in Loughrea, County Galway, he joined the local boxing club and, if in later years showed fighting qualities as a rugby player, he was a real scrapper inside the ring, winning two All-Ireland championships.

He also was an avid GAA fan and attended each of Galway's three-in-a-row All-Ireland football wins between 1964 and 1966 in Croke Park. On the field, he distinguished himself as a promising hurler at Garbally College. In 1970, he impressed the Galway minor selectors so much they put him on a team alongside Iggy Clarke and Sean Silke in an All-Ireland minor final against Cork where he marked Martin O'Doherty.

It was during his early teenage years that he remembers travelling to Lansdowne for the first time, and the game left an indelible mark on the young sportsman. 'I came up with my father, a friend of his and his son. I remember watching Wales play Ireland. I must have been thirteen at the time. I hadn't played rugby, but I remember watching it from the South Terrace and saying something to my father like, "I could play that, I'd like to play it." That was my first introduction to rugby really.'

After being knocked out of the Connacht colleges' senior hurling competition early in his Leaving Cert. year, Fitzgerald was approached to try his hand at being hooker for the school team. 'They were stuck for a hooker to play against Blackrock. It was my last year in Garbally – they weren't allowed play cup rugby at the time because the local bishop felt that the rugby ethos was a corrupting influence on our Catholic sensibilities. I remember playing that match – I didn't have a clue what the rules were but I remember reading offside and other laws of the game going up in the bus. We played Blackrock and gave away loads of penalties. I played a couple of matches that year and then I went on to UCG and played with them in the Connacht League.' Not long after he was making his mark with the Connacht senior side in the inter-provincial series.

Fitzgerald made his Ireland senior debut against Scotland in Lansdowne Road in 1980. He wasn't too intimidated by Lansdowne then – he even went as far as to say he was inspired by the environment. 'I don't think I ever got that nervous about any match. I always felt going out that I couldn't wait to get out there and the first thing you'd notice – as anyone will tell you – was the roar. Lansdowne Road was so compressed, the crowd was really in on top of you. And I will always remember that. I remember saying to myself, "How could you not play well in an environment like this?" They always said that the good players on a stage like that would be better players whereas the guys who are not as mentally strong would suffer a bit because they'd get distracted, because it was just one big roar.

'And, in my time anyhow, the one thing about Lansdowne Road was the constant roar. I think the proximity of the touchline seats as well added to the atmosphere.'

As a hooker, he had the onerous task of communicating calls to his lineout jumpers and a scrum-half in the Lansdowne din. Amidst the relentlessness of test rugby, he smiles now at the proximity of the fans, of how he found himself stopping for a chat with some supporters or with the person who was handing back the ball. Often he had to coax back a ball – a priceless piece of memorabilia – from a supporter's grasp. 'In the old days, when there weren't ball boys, the ball would be in amongst the crowd. You wouldn't get it back immediately, so you then would have to interact with them, nod or something like that. Only then was it brought back to you again. Even when you're knackered in the second half, it had to be done. I would always remember comments from people encouraging me and that would lift me further because I would be going in to get the ball whereas other lads wouldn't get as close to them.'

Fitzgerald remembers days in Lansdowne when the noise level reached such a pitch he could only communicate lineout moves by hand signal or through his scrum-half who would then relay the information to his jumpers. 'It was difficult in Parc des Princes and Cardiff Arms Park when it was full din, but I think that Lansdowne Road was a far more intimate ground than any of the other ones because of the proximity of the people. I think it was a reason a lot of the visitors used to hate playing in Lansdowne. One reason was because the Irish used go bananas there. The passion in the old days was a huge factor and the Lansdowne crowd was always part of that. And the breezes around Lansdowne Road were unlike any other ground. You'd think you're playing with the wind and suddenly it's coming against you.'

Fitzgerald played in an era when there was little, if any, of the finely choreographed lineout moves of today. Organised mayhem might be one description of life in the lineouts in the old days. 'It was a bit of a lottery. In those days, there was no lifting in the lineout. As the late Mick Doyle used to say, "You were pushing in the lineouts and jumping in the scrums."'

Fitzgerald's first outing at Lansdowne Road in January 1980 passed off smoothly when Ireland triumphed 22–15 against Scotland. He says his mother didn't go to Lansdowne but stayed behind in the Shelbourne Hotel lighting candles and saying decades of the rosary.

He believes the tour to Australia the previous summer – where he earned his first cap – steeled him for what lay ahead in the Five Nations and he felt he had earned some respect from his team-mates, grizzled old warriors like Willie Duggan, Phil Orr and Fergus Slattery. 'The benefit for me going into Lansdowne Road was that I had been with the Ireland team for six and a half weeks out in Australia. I felt when I came back that I was a hardened tourist, a member of the squad and because of that had earned a bit of respect from the other guys as well. I didn't feel like the novice or young garsún going out in the first match. I was confident I could deliver on the first day as well. For me, it was a much easier transition. I wasn't afraid going out that I was going to make a clown of myself in front of all these people who knew me.'

He scored a try in the Welsh match at Lansdowne Road that March, and remembers an almost volcanic eruption of noise after he crossed the line. Ireland won 21–7. His mother's candles were burning brightly in the Shelbourne that afternoon.

Fitzgerald missed the entire 1980–1981 season after dislocating his shoulder in a club match with St Mary's. The 1981 Five Nations saw Ireland lose all their games with a combined total of just thirteen points, but Fitzgerald could not believe how Ireland had suffered a whitewash given the possession they enjoyed in each outing. When he returned the following season, Fitzgerald took over the captaincy from Fergus Slattery. He had an inclination there would be a change and prepared himself mentally in case he was chosen.

He remembers a group of players low on morale and noticed that many were annoyed by the criticism of their play and a pack labelled 'Dad's Army'. 'A lot of fellows were coming to the end of their careers. The Mossies [Keane], the Willies [Duggan], the John O'Ds [O'Driscoll], the Slatts [Fergus Slattery] of this world were clearly fed up. They were pissed off because there was dog's abuse that year and people didn't want to finish up like that.'

The timing of Fitzgerald's coronation as captain could not have been better. Yes, he was younger than many of his peers and his army background might have allowed him to slip on the mask of a sergeant major. But he didn't dictate. Fitzie admonished players without alienating them. He inspired but was never insipid. He once described himself as 'sensitive to people and curious about people', and his people skills coupled with Tom Kiernan's coaching brought about a first Triple Crown in thirty-two years. More importantly, it was the first Triple Crown to be won at Lansdowne Road.

'There's no precedence for captains – everyone is different, there's no captaincy school in the IRFU. From my point of view, I wanted to get Moss Keane, Willie Duggan, Slatts, all these guys moving and once they moved everything else happened and fellows followed them. They weren't difficult to motivate because they were all pissed off, labelled "Dad's Army" or "on the scrapheap", "gone". I used say, "Is this the way we're going to finish or not?" Even though I was relatively youngish – more than they were – they accepted that what I was saying was the way to go. I didn't feel shy about saying it because, at the end of the day, the older guys weren't going to finish like that and the younger guys like Trevor Ringland and Paul Dean could create out wide when the guys did the business up front. Those were the tactics.'

A look at the video of the 1982 Scotland match shows Fitzgerald impressing upon Ginger McLoughlin, the Shannon prop, to give one more big scrum for the cause.

And, for many, 1982 was Ollie Campbell's Triple Crown, his six penalty goals and one drop goal propelled Ireland to a 21–12 win over the Scots. 'That day against Scotland everyone was up for it, so it was a question of keeping it as cool and as calm as you could and then, in the last few minutes before leaving the dressing room, you would hit the few vocals. You'd be pulling some fellows off the ceiling and some fellows you'd be doing the opposite to. Everybody is different and people had their own routines. You'd know when guys were uptight – they'd go to the same spot and things had to be the way they always wanted them. Fellows slot into their own zone because you have to get to a certain pitch mentally before you get out of the dressing room. Because once you get out there, the first ten or fifteen minutes of any match like that, you have to be really impervious to any noise, injuries or pain.

'Were Scotland as formidable as us? I think we had the stronger pack. I think the biggest thing about Scotland that day was that they were very good on the offside line or killing ball on the ground, and we had to be fairly physical in the loose. I'll never forget the sight of Scots going down on the ball and being rucked out of it. Irish fellows were hitting rucks harder than I had ever seen. And, even with that, the Scots still put their bodies on the line. I think most of Ollie's penalties that day came from them killing the ball or coming in from the side. And that's the sort of day it was – they were a difficult team to put away. Scotland had very good teams right through the 1980s and they played a very fast game. But that's what you had to deal with.'

Fitzgerald's favourite Lansdowne memory was the 1985 Triple Crown win. He was injured in 1984, a season when Ireland got the Wooden Spoon, but the arrival of Mick Doyle brought with it sweeping changes and a new attacking philosophy. The country liked Doyler's way and got behind the arrival of a new generation of Ireland players. 'There was only Donal Lenihan and Phil Orr left from 1982 and all the rest were young guns with Paul Dean at out-half, Brendan Mullins, Michael Kiernan – they were all young and talented, new kids on the block, full of enthusiasm, who had a great attitude to the game and didn't see a problem with doing anything. It was probably the most enjoyable year I played rugby because there was no expectation from anybody. We were just a side that had come together. You could see in the training there was a special thing developing there from inside the squad, not from outside. Mick, in fairness, let it all develop and let us do our thing. So the more we played together and trained together, the more we developed as a unit.'

Ireland's rugby that season, particularly away from home in Murrayfield and Cardiff Arms Park, was a thrilling concoction of fifteen-man rugby. Here was a team playing with a real *joie de vivre*, colouring the occasions with spontaneity and splendidly worked tries. 'Looking back at the tries scored that season, they were ahead of their time in terms of skill. We had a vision to look for those sort of scores. If 1982 was all about forward strength, in 1985 we had a young pack and real dynamic back-row in Carr, Spillane and Matthews and loads of speed in the backs. In Cardiff, we lost the battle up front, but the backs played some brilliant rugby that day. It was all teed up for the last day. And I'd say the only pressure that came on the lads was for the last match because people realised that we could actually play good rugby. All of our games that year were won against the odds. The first match in Murrayfield was ding-dong. They had the upper hand near the end and we produced a score in the last five to eight minutes with Trevor Ringland's try in the corner. That was a well-executed try.'

On to Lansdowne Road and those immortal words – 'Where's your f***ing pride'. One wonders where they came from. 'I don't even like repeating it. Very rarely would I repeat it. I just knew my own thought-process at the time. I really felt we were backed into the corner. We were trying to keep the tide out because, physically, they were a much bigger team and the match was played in real wet, heavy conditions. We were getting out-mauled in the second half, smothered nearly. Guys were getting tired and you could see it. I don't know where those words came from. It might have been out of pure desperation. There was nothing else there to think of. And that's about it.' Michael Kiernan's drop goal won Ireland the Triple Crown and Fitzgerald will forever remember the scenes in the immediate aftermath of that win. If Munster have built up a special rapport with their fans in today's European Cup, then this team gripped the imagination of the success-starved Irish in the 1980s. 'After the win in 1985, I never experienced anything like it. I got in under the stand to be interviewed after the match, trying to get my breath back again.

'The next thing a security guy comes in and says, "Ciaran, you're going to have to go outside." And I said, "Serious – what for?" "You're going to have to go outside, Ciaran, because the crowd want you outside." I had never heard that one before at a rugby game. I remember going outside and up to that VIP place, standing up on the plastic chairs to just acknowledge the crowd and what they did. I nearly broke my neck because these chairs were flipping and I was wearing my big boots. You'd associate speaking to the crowd with Croke Park rather than Lansdowne. The crowd, the support, the ground, everything – I'll always especially remember that one.'

For someone who understood the importance of club, Fitzgerald fondly remembers St Mary's Leinster Senior Cup win over Lansdowne in 1987. Business commitments forced Fitzie to retire from international rugby, but Mary's filled the void. 'We were against a very fancied Lansdowne team who had beaten us in a league match by thirty-odd points three weeks beforehand. We had a team of kids playing against them. It was totally against form at the time. All the Mary's supporters went bananas afterwards. It was my last outing with them at Lansdowne and it meant a lot to me to be playing in the cup win. To win it at headquarters was extra special too.'

Fitzgerald was coach of the Irish team in 1991 and almost masterminded the greatest of all victories against Australia in that year's World Cup quarter-final at Lansdowne Road.

In his efforts to cultivate a lasting team spirit, Fitzgerald took the team out of the city centre to Finnstown House in Lucan for the duration of the tournament, and organised a weekend away in Kerry where the players even dabbled in hurling in Sneem GAA grounds. He recalls Kerry Radio trying to make a big deal out of it and stirring up some controversy that the Ireland team entered the field without getting permission. Fitzgerald says they got the go-ahead from Sneem GAA officials and the squad enjoyed a good game of rounders there.

'Everyone was up for the Australia match – I think silly mistakes cost us at the end. We didn't have a star-studded team from 1 to 15, but it was great squad, a great group of people. People were critical of Neil Francis in his ability to take pain and pressure but I thought that was one of his best matches for Ireland. There were guys like Donal [Lenihan] beside him and Dessie Fitzgerald in front of him and Philip Matthews behind and they were real winners in terms of being mean and hard and that's what you had to be.'

When Gordon Hamilton discovered untapped reserves of energy late in the second half to run in for what seemed to be a match winning try, Ireland looked safe. And then ... the restart. 'I said all we need to do is put this away. I knew the clock was ticking away. But Australia came down field and the rest is history.'

Hamilton's try was, however, one of the great Lansdowne moments. 'Gordon was a very good footballer. He came from a junior club. We picked him up and he came up to the standard very quickly. To score a try the way he did against an Australian side that had all the bells and whistles of running rugby was a great achievement. I couldn't believe it – to see this fellow passing down through the centre. I remember sitting in the stands and seeing this fellow going and saying, "Jesus Christ, we're going to score here!" I couldn't talk after that match. As a player, you'd always have something to say. It's worse as a coach. As a player, at least you're out there and you're doing it. When I went to the dressing room, I felt I had to say something though. As a coach, you have to be up for the guys, you're trying to get them back on their feet and give them credit where credit is due and all of that. I remember going to the after-match function at the Berkeley Court and Bob Dwyer was there. It was early afternoon and I couldn't eat. I was putting salad into a plate at this buffet knowing I wouldn't eat it and Dwyer comes over to me and starts talking about the match to me. I was in no mood to talk and was trying to be polite to him. But that's sport. He could not believe the performance of the Irish.

'After Gordon's try, he thought it was over and talking to [Michael] Lynagh afterwards, he couldn't believe it either. He was captain and he was trying to come up with a move. They didn't have a move. He couldn't think. Suddenly, the ball arrived in their hands and they played the skip which they usually do in training. They thought they were gone as well.'

Later, Fitzgerald worked as co-commentator for RTÉ Radio on international days at Lansdowne Road. He enjoys analysing but admits he used to have his hands full trying to keep animated commentator Michael Corcoran from jumping out of the broadcasting box during moments of high drama. 'Often, he belts somebody beside him with a microphone. Someday, I'll have to tie him down or else get him a parachute because when he does go over the side, he is going to have a big fall!'

Mick Galwey

Lock

1991–2002

It's every Kerry boy's dream to win an All-Ireland football medal and, at only nineteen, Mick Galwey was part of a Kingdom squad that annexed the 1986 title. Young and teeming with potential, it seemed Croke Park would become his field of dreams. But in little over five years, his attentions had switched to rugby and Gaillimh was running out at Lansdowne Road in an Ireland shirt.

When invited down to Castleisland RFC in his late teens to help shore up the lineout, the Currow native admits he developed an instant passion for the game. He was, what you might have then called, a Kerry dual player: torn between Gaelic football and rugby, but it wasn't unusual for lads in

Currow and Castleisland to mix their days between the round and oval balls. However, those whom he respected at the time advised him that, if he remained loyal to rugby, he'd play for Ireland.

He'd reached a crossroads in his young career and his head was spinning about which direction to take. For a Kerry lad so conscious of his GAA roots, he took the road less travelled.

Yet he needn't fear. He'd be following in the footsteps of his Currow neighbours Mick Doyle and Moss Keane, who had also represented Ireland in previous eras. 'Gaillimh' completed a trinity of players from this tiny parish in north Kerry to wear the green of Ireland. 'It was a very hard decision to make because, to be honest, a lot of the people would have felt I owed something back to the GAA because of the fact that I won an All-Ireland medal. But I felt I owed it to myself. Looking back, I certainly made the right decision. Kerry didn't win another All-Ireland for another eleven years – I doubt if I would have made any major difference! My rugby career, meanwhile, took off on a gradual rise.'

Mick Galwey earned his first cap for Ireland against France at Lansdowne Road on 2 February 1991. He was driving from Kilkenny to Kerry when he turned the radio dial to the 2fm news and learned that he had made the team. His heart pumping with excitement, he stopped the car in Clonmel to ring home and his friends at Castleisland RFC, but they, too, had all heard the news bulletin just like him.

He made his debut alongside five others: London Irish scrum-half Rob Saunders, Simon Geoghegan of Connacht, NIFC's Gordon Hamilton, Brian Rigney of Greystones and Brian Robinson of Ballymena.

The phone calls from well-wishers poured in during the week

but he particularly remembers the advice from his neighbour, Moss Keane, and only wished that Keane had played during his era, his easy humour and Kerry ways would have calmed Mick's nerves.

He got advice from other unexpected sources too. At a function in Ballymena the week before his debut, he and Brian Robinson got chatting to Syd Millar and Willie John McBride. He was in exalted company but Millar's words resonated with him afterwards. 'He said, "Best of luck next Saturday. Forget about the ball for the first ten minutes!" That's coming from a fellow who has been there and done everything. I would have known Syd Millar from what I saw and read – as a player for Ireland and the Lions and he coached and managed as well.'

The team stayed in the Westbury Hotel the weekend of his first cap and Galwey will never forget walking up Grafton Street towards St Stephen's Green and the crowd opening before them as the team made its way onto the bus. 'As a young fellow, I remember seeing the bus driving to the match and being on it this time was a great thrill. I roomed those couple of nights with John 'Packo' Fitzgerald – he was kind of a mentor to me at the time. In fairness, he looked after me.'

Beforehand in the dressing room, his nerves got the better of him. 'All these emotions were saying to me, "This is it, this is my chance, this is what it's all about. This is what I've been waiting to do for a long time."' It was more than a baptism of fire for Gaillimh, particularly against the notoriously abrasive French. In the 1980s, he had watched near anarchy break out at rucks and, the previous season, he had watched the intensity of the exchanges between Ireland and France on television. Galwey is not afraid to admit that forward exchanges in his early days were of the barbaric sort. 'Everything happened out there. Obviously, gouging and kicking fellows was unacceptable but it happened in some matches.'

He knew his debut would be a memory to stay with him for ever, but with French stud marks tattooed onto his back, these were decorations he did not expect to be living with for the next few weeks. At his first lineout, he put Millar's words into action. It was a case of getting your retaliation in first, he says. 'I remember France had this big brute of a fellow, Michel Tachdjian, and he did all kinds of damage in their previous match against Scotland in Paris. I remember the first lineout was going across the top. I just barely got him before he got me. It was just as well I went across because, otherwise, my head would have been taken off. It was a case of protecting yourself and laying down a marker. In fairness, the match carried on then. I remember getting a few right slaps during the match, serious slaps, like knees into the head or a boot into the back of the head. Remember this was a time when there were no video refs, no touch judges flagging for infringements, no citing commissioners. It was a hard game. You had to learn how to survive. It was the law of the jungle out there.'

Ireland took a surprise 10–6 lead in at half-time, but if they dared to dream, they were given a dose of reality when Serge Blanco, often described as an artist in motion, spoiled Galwey's Lansdowne debut. The Biarritz and French full-back set up the decisive try that consigned Ireland to a 13–21 defeat. 'We actually did very well against France that day. I know they beat us towards the end, but it was the norm at the time against such French sides. We certainly put up a great battle. But my biggest memory remains that it was a bloody hard game.'

Galwey was part of Ciaran Fitzgerald's World Cup squad in the autumn of 1991, but wasn't amongst the first-choice locks for the tournament. He played in Ireland's second group match against Japan at Lansdowne Road, a game Ireland won 32–16. 'Ralph [Keyes] gave as good a kicking display as I have seen in a long time. He kicked twenty points [four penalties and two conversions] while Noel Mannion scored two tries and Brian O'Hara got the other.' Donal Lenihan was picked at four in the lineout in the final pool game against Scotland and also in the World Cup quarter-final against Australia, but Gaillimh never felt excluded from team preparations. He noticed a great spirit developing within the squad, a bond that grew stronger even after a getaway trip to his native County Kerry. 'We came back from Scotland on a Sunday, flew to Dublin, and from there to Farranfore in Kerry. We checked into Parknasilla outside Kenmare for a bit of R and R, because, after the Murrayfield match, it took the lads about three days to recover. We also played a game of rounders in Sneem GAA pitch and I was saying to myself, "I was here three or four years ago playing Gaelic football for Currow." Then we went back up to Finnstown House in Lucan to prepare for the Australians.'

Ireland were within minutes of creating the biggest upset in world rugby after Gordon Hamilton ran in for a try that nudged Ireland 18–12 in front with only four minutes left on the clock. 'When Gordon Hamilton got his try, I was sitting on the bench. I wasn't subbing but I remember sitting alongside John Fitzgerald, and we were jumping up and down hugging each other because we felt we were going to have another three weeks of this. Unfortunately, Australia came back and got their try – a piece of Michael Lynagh magic – and it was one of the most disappointing atmospheres ever seen in Lansdowne Road. Would we have beaten New Zealand the following week or England in the final? I don't know. But some people were saying that, if we had beaten Australia, we would have won the World Cup.'

Galwey might never have worn a green jersey in Lansdowne Road again after suffering a serious neck injury in a club game in 1993. Six weeks before scoring a try in Currow Corner, he lay in a hospital bed in a neck brace. He was one of the first rugby players to have an MRI scan and was told by a doctor that he would never play rugby again. He was given the bad news on a Sunday morning but, five days later, was given the all clear and lined out for Shannon on the Saturday.

'I missed training that week but was straight out of the brace and into a match. There was no time to feel sorry for myself. It was a case of getting straight back into the action. And thankfully, with a bit of luck, I got back into the Irish team. That scare certainly made me appreciate the game even more. Being told that you won't play again because of an injury, well … that's your worst nightmare.'

He played against France at Number 8 but partnered Paddy Johns in the second-row against Wales. 'Eric Elwood had just made his debut a fortnight earlier against Wales in Cardiff where we won 19–14. Simon Geoghegan was at his best at the time, as were Philip Danaher, Vincent Cunningham and Michael Bradley, who was captain. We had a very good backline.' The Johns–Galwey partnership was renewed for the England match, but they were facing a formidable duo in Martin Bayfield and Wade Dooley.

'I wasn't an out and out lineout jumper – Paddy Johns was at two marking Bayfield, while I was at four on Dooley. They were big men, but, to put it mildly, we got stuck in.' There was also a strong Munster contingent in the pack and Galwey felt right at home. 'Terry Kingston was playing, Claw [Peter

Clohessy] was there, Pat O'Hara was there – what a great player O'Hara was. He was what I'd call 'a player's player'. He remembers O'Hara was involved in an accidental clash of heads with Peter Winterbottom, the latter getting umpteen stitches across his head. O'Hara just got up and played on. I'm not saying that incident defines O'Hara but that's the sort of fellow he was.'

Elwood was having one of those dream days for an out-half, Galwey remembers, and the Connacht man, with five minutes remaining, arched over a drop goal to push Ireland into a 12–3 lead. Then one of Galwey's favourite moments arrived when he notched a try to put the seal on an unexpected Irish victory. 'I remember there was a ball tapped back off a lineout. Phil Danaher was marking Will Carling in the middle of the field. Carling was trying to go around him, Danaher tackled him and turned over the ball. I remember Ritchie Wallace took it on, then one or two of the backs before I took it on and arrived at the next ruck. Michael Bradley decided to go down the blind, I just happened to be in right place at the right time. I took the pass, drove over and I remember Tony Underwood on top of me making a last ditch tackle.'

There was an outbreak of emotion from the touchline seats when supporters spilled onto the field to share in Galwey's moment. Amongst the giddy throng was his sister, Mary, who had flown in from New York that morning. She rushed over to give her brother a hug and, as it turned out, it was the closest Galwey got to having a conversation with his sister for another eight weeks. 'I didn't realise it but my sister was sitting near the corner. I left a ticket for her in the Berkeley Court – it would have been for the centre of the West Stand. Anyway, the ticket got mislaid or someone robbed it. Then she met someone on the street and bought a ticket off him at face value. She ended up down in the corner. She got so excited that, after I scored the try, she jumped out over the railing. She's embarrassed by it to this day but I thought it was a lovely moment.

'After beating England in 1993, I remember being carried off the pitch, some poor misfortunate under me. Eric Elwood was too. It doesn't happen anymore. That's the way it has gone and there will be no going back. I remember seeing Ireland winning Triple Crowns there and seeing Moss Keane being carried off the pitch.'

Mick Galwey has been dropped a total of fifteen times from various Ireland teams but, from 2000 to 2002, he featured more regularly and played a big part in helping Ronan O'Gara, Peter Stringer and Shane Horgan find their feet on their international debuts against Scotland in 2000. Galwey had been dropped again for the previous match against England but was recalled for the Scotland game a week later at Lansdowne Road. 'Thankfully, I never got bitter and, thankfully, I never threw in the towel. I look back on it now and at the time it was hard to take. It got to me, maybe I didn't show it but I was lucky to have Shannon and lucky to have Munster. Sometimes, there were players there who you felt you were better than them, sometimes there were things happening with Ireland you would love to have been involved in. The most important thing now is that I kept my dignity about me, I kept going and I got my chance again and I came back and, eventually, I was put out to grass. But my time was up at that stage. I was happy enough to walk away from it. I was thirty-five years of age and I had done my bit. Then, I knew I wasn't good enough to lead Ireland to the next World Cup.'

Gaillimh's recall for the Scotland Six Nations game in 2000

came on the back of sterling individual performances on a Munster side cutting a dash in the European Cup. 'Munster had done well, and Ronan, Peter and John Hayes got capped together against Scotland as well as Shane Horgan and Simon Easterby. At Twickenham, I came on at half-time, scored a try and was picked then for the next match. If we hadn't beaten Scotland, the likes of the O'Garas, the Stringers and these lads, including myself, would have suffered as well. Because I knew if we didn't win that day, I would never have played for Ireland again, but we did. We went 10–0 down and I thought, "here we go again".

'I was involved with Irish teams where you go 10–0 down and you wouldn't come back but there was something special about that team. We came back and we played well right to the end.'

It was thought that Ireland coach Warren Gatland had taken a major gamble in blooding so many new players, but it was a gamble that paid rich dividends. 'He often took gambles, some of them paid off, some of them didn't. But we all knew if we f****ed up that day, I knew I would never touch the grass of Lansdowne Road ever again. I was brought back because Munster were going well and the public were saying, "Bring Galwey back." That was putting fierce pressure on me. Thankfully, it worked out.'

Galwey took another metaphorical kick in the guts when he was dropped for Ireland's trip to Murrayfield in September 2001 in the Six Nations, a game rescheduled because of the outbreak of foot and mouth disease in Ireland and Great Britain earlier that year. 'At the start of the season, I was part of the teams that beat Italy and France and then for the next match against Scotland in Murrayfield, Warren Gatland dropped me. In fairness to him, he said he was planning for the next World Cup. Scotland won and then, the following weekend, Munster were playing Harlequins in England. I played well, Warren came up to me and shook my hand and said, "We'll see you at training next week." I said, "Fair enough, I'll be there." I admire him for saying what he said. He told me straight up that he got it wrong. No other Irish coach had ever done that. We played Wales in the Millennium Stadium and beat them, and the following week faced England at Lansdowne Road.'

This was another one of those momentous Irish occasions on a day when England were going for the Grand Slam. Ireland denied them. Galwey might not have got a try but he played an important part in the lineout that ended with Keith Wood charging over the line. 'It's one of those moments you do on the training ground over and over and over again. That it came off then was fantastic. It was an incredible try but a simple move. Keith Wood threw a long ball, I went up, passed it to Malcolm O'Kelly. Anthony Foley comes in and rips it, offloads to Keith Wood, David Wallace takes out the man at the back – illegally or whatever – and Keith goes in.' Ireland denied England the Grand Slam, Lansdowne erupted and Galwey was in the lap of honour that followed. He remembers England won the championship but they trooped off disconsolate.

The celebrations continued back in the dressing room when even Taoiseach Bertie Ahern popped in to congratulate the Ireland team. 'To see Bertie coming in, you know you were doing something right then. Ronan tried to drag him into the centre of the crowd – there was champagne and craic. They're great moments to have.'

Whether as player or coach, Galwey has been a central figure during many of Shannon's All-Ireland League campaigns. His steadfast leadership and motivational qualities were central to Shannon's historic four-in-a-row from 1995–1998, while, during his second coming as a provincial and international player, Gaillimh also helped the famous Limerick club to a further two titles in 2002 and 2004.

He took over the reins of coach at the start of the 2004–2005 season, and his influence over the next generation of Shannon players was instantaneous – one of Irish rugby's most iconic figures coached the Limerick club to two more AIL titles; a remarkable feat in anyone's language. 'Our biggest title win came in 1998 when we won the four-in-a-row and played against Garryowen, our biggest rivals, but the respect was very big between us. It was the first All-Ireland play-off final, and there were close to 25,000 people at Lansdowne for the game. Club rugby was still big because European Cup rugby was still in its infancy. For example, in 2005 when we won it, there were only 5,000 people at the match.'

As an assistant coach to Munster in 2004, he was in the stands when Wasps proved just too good in a memorable European Cup semi-final. Nobody understood or felt the heartbreak more than Gaillimh (who had captain in two European Cup finals in 2000 and 2002), but, as an occasion, he'll never forget the noise, the colour, the special atmosphere. He felt the old ground never felt more alive and vibrant as it did on that beautiful April afternoon in leafy Ballsbridge.

A few years later he was back in headquarters. Along with Peter Clohessy, the duo provided some half-time entertainment at the 2006 European Cup quarter-final between Munster and Perpignan. Two of the great characters of Munster and Irish rugby indulged in a spot of place-kicking for charity. 'Even taking penalties that day, it felt funny to be back there. You hear the noise, you see a kind of a blur of the crowd and it doesn't bother you – you actually get a good kick out of it. It was a nice moment for myself and Claw. I enjoyed it and it was fun. Let's put it this way: if I was to stand up on a tee box and there were five people looking at me taking my shot, I wouldn't say I'd be nervous but you'd realise they are there. Whereas, when I was in Lansdowne, it was normal; it was like I never left the place.

'There was always something special about the old Lansdowne. It just had a great name – L-A-N-S-D-O-W-N-E R-O-A-D. It was a great place when you were winning, but when you were losing it could be the loneliest place in the world. Nobody could tell you otherwise.'

Gavin Hastings

Full-Back, Scotland

1986–1995

Even before Lansdowne set eyes on Gavin Hastings, the old arena had seen some exciting Scottish full-backs. Andy Irvine immediately springs to mind, but Hastings, admittedly, was of a different mould, a giant of a full-back at six-foot two, his attacks from deep were characterised by a potent cocktail of power and aggression.

But his greatest attribute had to be his reliability under a garryowen, a much-loved tactic used by Irish kickers to unsettle a visiting full-back, particularly in the early stages of a test match. Hastings rarely fumbled one and, while it is easy to label him Mr Dependable, he was far from a one-dimensional player. The greats rarely are.

The taunts from the crowd as Hastings rose to gather a garryowen might unsettle some full-backs but Hastings had bottle and nerve in spades, to deal with the most unattractive of Lansdowne's 'executive high balls'.

But it was Hastings' metronomic place-kicking that impressed both Scottish and opposition fans alike. He kicked so consistently from place, drop and hand – often from the most acute of angles – that people figured if you blindfolded him, he'd still strike as dead-eyed as an arrow hitting its target.

'As soon as a garryowen was put up, I would know instinctively whether I was going to be inside my twenty-two or outside my twenty-two – in other words, would I be able to mark the ball?' Hastings says. 'But if I was inside my twenty-two, I instinctively knew whether or not the chasing attacking players would be able to get to me at roughly the same time as the ball. So, I worked out whether I had to jump up for the ball to catch it in order to secure the possession or whether I had time to make the mark.

'Now all this happened in a split second just because I instinctively or intuitively knew that that was the case. I just can't understand people today in the full-back position not knowing whether or not that is the case. Apparently, they don't have awareness of who is around them or what players might be following up from the opposition. Some people nowadays mark the ball when there is no one within fifteen yards of them. Quite why they mark the ball I have absolutely no idea. The only time I would ever mark was when an attacking player was coming on to me and was going to absolutely cream me. That all happened within a split second of the ball being kicked.

'With a swirling wind at Lansdowne Road, you had to be so focused on your surroundings – where you were, where the touchline was, where the posts were, where the twenty-two was and how much time you had. I was always pleased when I did get the response of the crowd having dealt with a kick positively and properly, and with a good kick to touch. The job of the goal-kicker, obviously, is to try and get the ball between the posts and you have to concentrate on that fact. Whether there is a host of catcalls and whistles or silence, you have to block all that out and concentrate on putting the ball between the sticks.'

Hastings settled in to becoming the darling of Scottish rugby quite comfortably. In some aspects of his play, he mirrored Irvine but, essentially, he was cut from a different cloth than the iconic figure of Scottish rugby in the 1970s.

An instant hero in Scotland on his debut after landing six penalties in an 18–19 win over France in Paris in the first round of the 1986 championship, Hastings was the one player on everyone's lips when he made his maiden Lansdowne appearance that March. Hastings and his team-mates arrived high on confidence; whle Ireland were stuttering into the last round of the championship with that most awful of millstones hanging around their necks – the prospect of picking up the mythical Wooden Spoon.

The first sighting of Hastings at Lansdowne brought as much giddy expectation as the return of Tony Ward to the Irish Number 10 position after an absence of two years. Footballing skill is always welcome at Lansdowne and both Hastings and Ward had the capacity to surprise and entertain. They didn't disappoint.

It appeared Ireland was set to avoid a whitewash having led 9–0 at half-time. But despite their best display of the season – and plenty of memorable Wardie cameos at out-half – Ireland couldn't close the deal. Scotland and Hastings could – although the latter felt a draw might have better reflected the evenness of the exchanges. 'We scored a try and I remember missing a fairly easy conversion. By rights, we should have gone 12–9 up then. Then, right at the death, Michael Kiernan had a penalty from a not dissimilar position to mine – obviously at the other end – and inexplicably he missed. We won the match 10–9, but I always felt I should have kicked mine to make it 12–9 and Michael should have kicked a goal and a draw would have been the correct result. I felt very relieved too, that my miss, which wasn't a difficult conversion, hadn't cost Scotland the match. And if I had scored, I would have bet on Michael Kiernan to put his over right at the death to level the match.'

When Ireland scored inside Lansdowne Road during those times, the decibel levels rose to a different level than in the final days of the old stadium, and Hastings believes the roar had a more 'throaty' texture than any of the stadia in which he had played around the world, particularly on his second visit to Lansdowne in 1988. 'When you ask my memories of playing at Lansdowne Road, it would be the noise and the passion of the crowd. When Ireland scored, for me, it was the noisiest place ever that you could play rugby in those days. The noise of the crowd when Ireland were running in some tries particularly that day was a sad noise to hear because it represented the strength of the Irish team but equally was something that was very, very strong and has remained with me to this day. Whilst we might have played a get-out-of-jail card in 1986, there was certainly no way we could play that in 1988. From my perspective, we did get well beaten on that occasion and deservedly so.'

Ireland put the Scots on the rocks with a 22–18 win, a day Ireland's pack subdued the opposition front eight. The back-row of Philip Matthews, Willie Sexton and Mike Gibson enjoyed their best afternoon as a unit opposite the Scottish trio of Iain Paxton, John Jeffrey and Finlay Calder. Ireland denied Scotland at source and, starved of primary possession, the Scottish backs, including Hastings, sparked only fleetingly. The full-back, as commentator Bill McLaren said afterwards, 'was made to move from one side of the field to the other. They [Ireland] blocked every porthole that was there.'

Ireland enacted their tactics to a tee. Indeed, afterwards, captain Donal Lenihan praised his coach, Jim Davidson, for his thoroughness in preparation for this test, and that the game-plan devised was hugely instrumental in beating the Scots.

But it was the two Irish tries that caught Hastings' eye, both a product of forward industry and backline magic. 'We started well and created some opportunities but the Irish defence put down markers early that day and I remember we were down inside ten minutes. The Number 8 [Mike] Gibson made the initial incision. Then that brilliant competitor Michael Bradley fed my good mate Brendan Mullin and it passed through [Paul] Dean's and [Michael] Kiernan's hands before Brendan took the last pass to dive over in the corner. I won't say where I was for that try! Paul Dean was really good that day, too, and set up the second brilliantly for Hugo MacNeill. I was very conscious of the fact that Ireland had very dangerous backs. People like Paul Dean, Brendan Mullin, Trevor Ringland and Keith Crossan and Hugo MacNeill at full-back were class players – a sort of golden generation. I always felt these guys were tremendously talented. I became extremely friendly with Brendan Mullin and Phil Matthews, who was a great blindside flank for Ireland over many years. Indeed, I always looked forward to the nights out in Dublin with these guys!'

Even though Hastings enjoyed the post-match drinks and a (self-professed) love of Guinness, the idea of coming to Lansdowne Road biannually applead hugely to him. As amateurs, these opposing players only had a single chance to play against each other every season, but in a strange sort of way, the bonds became tighter.

Professionalism, and the familiarity built up between opposing players through Celtic League and European Cup ties, has severely weakened the bonds that once held in the amateur era. 'We didn't have the European Cup matches. Remember, it was still a time when most guys only played rugby in their respective countries. There were a few guys who were playing for London Irish and I might have come up against them during my time with London Scottish. However, it was only a result of visiting these places – and coming to Lansdowne Road once every two years – that that's what made them so unique, so different and so special to play at. It was so different and that was why I think you could create a fortress at your home ground because the players from other countries didn't play you there, apart from when they played for their country. In a way, one of the aspects of modern-day professional rugby is that everything is very much too familiar than it was in the past, and when you have familiarity you're not so frightened as you would be with going to some absolutely brand-new ground for the first time.'

In Hastings' early year career, the cult of the out-half gained a lot more news space, particularly in Ireland where the Campbell–Ward contest for the Number 10 shirt was discussed ad nauseum from the beginning of the 1980s. But Ireland was never short of a progressive pivot, one to cajole and orchestrate the game at stand-off and Paul Dean is someone Hastings rates very highly in the pantheon of great Ireland Number 10s. 'I found Paul [Dean] to be a cross between Tony Ward and Ollie Campbell – not quite the flair of Tony Ward, but he was certainly very, very dependable and he was capable of making a break in a way Ollie wasn't. But Ollie remains a legend of Irish rugby. I remember Paul deservedly winning a place in the 1989 Lions tour, alongside Craig Chalmers of Scotland. I always felt Paul was an astute tactical kicker – he was always capable of making a very good break, had some excellent players outside him and I always felt the Irish three-quarter line in those days was very, very dangerous.'

He also admired the qualities of then Ireland scrum-half Michael Bradley. 'Bradley was a tremendously competitive player, in the mould of Gary Armstrong [of Scotland]. For me, they were both very combative players, had great energy and enthusiasm and their performances were tireless on the field. They engaged each other to raise their games to the levels they had set. That's what you need from team-mates – you need team-mates to stick their head above the parapet.'

As testament to the demands placed on rugby players six years before the onset of professionalism, the plight of Armstrong is worth telling. Armstrong retired early from rugby in 1989, though returned to the game again in 1994. 'Coming from a border town, he just really couldn't afford to take time off work,' says Hastings. 'In those days, I think latterly certainly, you are likely to get compensated by your employers or the SRU would compensate for any loss of earnings. I think in those very early days Gary Armstrong was struggling getting away from his business and just taking the time off that was necessary. It's extraordinary to think now that one of the greatest players of his generation was struggling to get time off work to play international rugby. It's unthinkable in terms of what happens nowadays.'

Hastings returned from the 1989 Lions tour to Australia a hero, but, at home, strangely was relieved of kicking duties in what turned out to be Scotland's Grand Slam season. When they came to Lansdowne in 1990, Scotland met a formidable Ireland team up front but one that was bereft in the backline.

With no spark in the Irish backline, Scotland capitalised and won 13–10 thanks to two tries from Derek White.

'I didn't kick in 1990 for whatever reason and I don't know quite why. I went on tour with the Lions in 1989 as first choice goal-kicker, and in 1990 I wasn't first-choice kicker for my country. I think I only took a couple of kicks that whole season. I was living in London at the time and playing for London Scottish and Craig was playing in Scotland for Melrose – perhaps he was more in the public eye and it was decided that Craig should take the kicks. Anyway, I was struggling a wee bit with my kicks. I don't recall exactly the reasons behind it but I didn't really kick at all during that whole Five Nations Grand Slam winning year. Maybe that's one of reasons we won the Grand Slam!

'We came over to Ireland for our first championship game. We had a bye in the first round of championship but we played then on four consecutive fortnights. We had a very strong back-row with Finlay Calder, John Jeffrey and Derek White. For me, they were the epitome of Scottish breakaway forward play – they were always scampering around the field, really just generating mayhem and causing havoc in opposition defences. I think for one of White's tries – it might have started with a break from Sean Lineen in the centre – he passed inside to White, who was always there in support and he went over close to the posts. Amazingly, we always seemed to leave Lansdowne Road with a sneaky little victory – in 1986 it was 10–9 and, in 1990, we squeezed a very close victory.

'We were content as always in those days just to get off the mark, and playing away from home was never easy – it's not easy today and wasn't easy then. To get your campaign off and running was a good start for us.'

Some of Irish rugby's darkest days came during Hastings' next two visits to Lansdowne Road in 1992 and 1994. In the '92 match, it was a grim afternoon to be an Irish supporter and most unpleasant for the Ireland players who absorbed a barrage of abuse near the end from the home crowd. Jeering and slow hand-clapping were ways the home 'support' vented their frustration at Ireland's inept display. But this was a strong Scotland side that put Ireland to the sword with an 18–10 victory.

Hastings gave an exhibition of place kicking, arching over two touchline conversions following tries from Tony Stanger and Andy Nicol. 'Again, as ever, it seemed to be always damn windy,' says Hastings of the day.

The 1994 game between the sides ended all square (6–6), a poor return from Ireland especially as it came so soon after their thrilling 13–12 win in Twickenham. Conditions, however, were horrible. Indeed, the ferocity of the wind led some commentators to write that age-old regulars at Lansdowne could not recall the last time a game had to be played under the same conditions. The game was a non-event – except for an injury Hastings is likely to remember for a long time yet.

'My abiding memory of that whole day is I got some staples put in my forehead and I think I went off before half-time and came back on with the head all bandaged up. I went out to have a couple of pints of Guinness after the game, and it was probably ten o'clock when I was delivering my post-match speech at the dinner. I could feel the staples coming out of my head because it was so damn hot in the room.

'There was blood and sweat dripping down onto my nose. I finished my speech anyway, and I went over to see the team doctor explaining that these staples were coming halfway out my head. So we both had to return to the team hotel and he had to stitch me up. I'm grateful to him because I don't have a big scar. That was my abiding memory of that 6–6 draw!'

Hastings was always very grateful to get a victory at Lansdowne Road. 'The Irish might say that if we're going to lose to anyone, they'd probably feel happier losing to the Scots, but it became a bit of happy hunting ground for us.'

Yet, like so many visiting players, Hastings was sad to learn that the old Lansdowne was to be demolished and replaced by the new Aviva Stadium. 'It's a shame in a way a ground as graceful an old lady as Lansdowne Road had to come to an end. In every sport, as in life, a mixture of the old and the new is what is best and I think that is what makes Ireland and Lansdowne Road so unique. Logistically and health and safety wise, the thought of building a railway line under it so that every time the train comes along the whole stand shakes, all this stuff, you could argue it is a disaster waiting to happen, but equally that's the Irish for you – it could only ever happen in Ireland. I say that as a compliment, not as a criticism and that's what made Lansdowne so unique and wonderful in the eyes of so many people – myself included.'

Denis Hickie

Winger
1997–2007

As a schoolboy, Denis Hickie played before 20,000 people at Lansdowne Road, captaining St Mary's College to victory over Clongowes in the 1994 Leinster Schools Senior Cup final. That year it took two matches to produce a winner but, in the replay, Hickie, a quality full-back in his schooldays, proudly walked up the steps of the West Stand to accept the college's first title in twenty-five years.

'We drew the final on St Patrick's Day, and then we had the replay the following Wednesday which added to the sense of drama and atmosphere. It was certainly my first big final and we were playing a very well-matched team in Clongowes. It was like winning the World Cup. Father Flavin was our manager and Brian Cotter and my Uncle Denis (who played for Ireland in the late 1960s/early 1970s) were coaches. We were very happy to have won but they instilled in us a sense of modesty, and we celebrated accordingly. That was Fr Flavin's way, something cultivated within the school as a whole.'

As a kid, he was taken to Lansdowne many times, Mick Doyle's Triple Crown winning team of 1985 making a strong impression on the then ten-year-old. That year, Ireland drew their opening game against France (15–15) before going on to record wins over Wales, Scotland and England.

The French teams of the 1980s, says Hickie, built up a tough-guy image, something that disappointed him as he generally admired their attacking philosophy. Meanwhile Doyle's team, that had promised free expression all week, had to go fighting in the trenches against the French before Ireland displayed a more explosive approach in wins away to Scotland and Wales before returning to Lansdowne for the Triple Crown victory over England.

After Mary's, Hickie attended UCD where he was on a dual scholarship for rugby and athletics. He played there as a full-back, but it wasn't long before Leinster senior management came calling. They moved him onto the wing, believing his blistering pace might be better served in this position. And if he wasn't playing rugby, Hickie might just have taken up an athletics career. At St Mary's, for example, he represented the college at all-Ireland meets alongside class-mate and future club, provincial and Ireland team-mate, John McWeeney.

As for his Lansdowne Road debut as an Ireland senior player, that came on another black day for Irish rugby, against England in February 1997. He'd just marked his first cap with a try against Wales in Cardiff that helped Ireland to a morale-boosting 26–25 win. But against England, any thoughts of an Irish revival were quickly dispelled in a crushing 46–6 defeat. 'After my opening game, a win in the old Cardiff Arms Park, I thought all these international weekends were fantastic. Then we played a very, very good England team. Will Carling and Jeremy Guscott were in their pomp and I was opposite Tony Underwood. It was a heavy defeat, and this came in a time when we were losing a lot more games than we were winning, no matter where we played. Still, it was great to play my first game for Ireland in Lansdowne Road. I enjoyed that aspect of it, but when the final whistle went, I tell you there wasn't much to enjoy.'

Hickie's senior international career began during the Brian Ashton era. The Englishman later made a name for himself as a backs coach under Clive Woodward, his ideas sparking the right responses in Woodward's England three-quarter line. In Ireland, however, he just couldn't find the right formula to ignite the Irish.

During that 1997–1998 season, Ashton attempted but could not revitalise an Irish side low on confidence; instead, he grew flummoxed and frustrated as his ideas were reportedly not washing with the players, and after the visit of Scotland to Lansdowne in 1998, when Ireland lost 16–17, Ashton's patience finally ran out.

With twenty minutes to go, Ireland led 16–11, but the team had neither the imagination nor the tactical nous to capitalise when opportunities arose out wide. And at one stage, Ireland had six scrums on the Scottish line but failed to fashion a try. Two Craig Chalmers penalties eventually won the game for Scotland and the one point loss pushed Ashton's nerve to the edge, prompting this famous line in his post-match press conference: 'I do not know whose game-plan that was, but it most certainly was not mine.'

Two weeks later, Ashton resigned his position as Ireland head coach, citing an "attack of shingles" as the reason for his departure. 'You could say his methods were very different at the time and, yes, he was ahead of his time,' admits Hickie today. 'Looking back, his approach would be pretty standard to what coaches are doing now, but, at the time, Ashton's ways were certainly different to what everyone else was doing. I think everyone enjoyed his coaching, but the reality was we didn't have the type of players to implement the type of game he wanted to play. I think that is why he left. And there was plenty of frustration underlying it all. A lot of other stuff was said, and I'm sure there were other small reasons too. But if we'd had the type of players that he wanted us to have, the type of skills that he wanted us to have, he would have stayed.'

In November 1997, three months before Ashton's resignation, Ireland faced the All Blacks in Lansdowne Road. Ashton, impressed by what he had seen in the European Cup and in the inter-provincial competition, included five new caps in his team – three from Hickie's club, St Mary's College, including full-back Kevin Nowlan, wing John McWeeney and scrum-half Conor McGuinness while London Irish duo Malcolm O'Kelly (lock) and Kieron Dawson (flanker) completed the five.

Hickie played opposite Glen Osborne while McWeeney shadowed no less a player than the then darling of New Zealand rugby, Jeff Wilson, and the two All Blacks wingers had a field day, scoring two tries apiece in a stunning 63–15 win. Though Hickie remained on until the end, McWeeney was called ashore in the fifty-fourth minute to be replaced by Kevin Maggs.

'There were a lot of new players playing that day but it was a different sort of time in Irish rugby: there just seemed to be a lot of chopping and changing on the Irish team in those days because results weren't great. Guys were getting played for one match and then dropped for the next. It was a tough old time really, and John, for example, was up against Jeff Wilson that day which wasn't an easy task.

'In that era, you could make up a one-cap wonder team – people who played one game and you'd never hear of them again. That is something that's changed a lot over the past few years; there's a lot more consistency in selection now and guys are given a chance to prove themselves. There was just so much uncertainty with the new professional game: so many new coaches and some guys on professional contracts, some guys on part-time ones and some guys who just remained amateur. It was probably bad luck for a lot of guys to get their first cap during that time. John [McWeeney] certainly wouldn't have been the first or the last around that time to have played one game and not play for his country again.'

The All Blacks game whistled by very quickly in Hickie's eyes, and Ireland's attempts to keep the score respectable died a slow death as probably the most-talented All Blacks team of all time overpowered an Irish team still grappling with the new professional era – as well as trying to get to grips with Ashton's ways. In terms of professionalism, the All Blacks were aeons ahead, though Hickie says there was one character in the Irish dressing room beating down the door of amateurism in Ireland and crying for everyone else to follow suit – Keith Wood, scorer of two tries in an afternoon of mostly forgettable memories. 'I don't think too many people get two tries against the All Blacks, certainly not in those days and certainly not playing for Ireland. Woodie at this stage was head and shoulders above anything Ireland had. In the 2003 World Cup, I think he was in a team that suited him a bit more, and surrounded by a lot more players that, you could say, complemented him. But he was so far ahead of everyone else even to the day he retired. He was a real world-class player and always will be regarded as a world-class player. Up to the time he finished, he could have got into any team in the world and that's the sign of a world-class player. Ireland never had that many players at that level.'

After Ashton resigned, Warren Gatland was parachuted in from Connacht (where he enjoyed huge success) and for the remaining three games in the 1998 Six Nations against France, Wales and England, Hickie retained his place on the wing. Ireland may have lost all three but Hickie's emergence as a genuine talent gave hope for the future of Irish rugby. The St Mary's man ran in a memorable try in Paris – a game Ireland came desperately close to winning – and two against England in Twickenham. Alas, Ireland picked up the Wooden Spoon once again.

'As a team, the confidence probably wasn't there. It's there in spades now, but back then there were a many different reasons for our run of poor results: a lot of uncertainty, a lot of changing in selection and many players remaining in amateur rugby but trying to play in a professional game.'

Following, the summer tour to South Africa in 1998, Hickie remained out of the picture for two years; loss of form an excuse cited by many selectors, but the Leinster man returned in style when Irish rugby fortunes took a turn for the better against Scotland in February 2000. 'That would have been our first Six Nations win in quite a while. For example, I don't remember winning a Six Nations game really in between my first Six Nations game and that one.

'Eddie [O'Sullivan] had come in as an assistant coach to Warren Gatland at that stage. He'd coached a lot of us at under-21 level – Ronan [O'Gara], Peter [Stringer], Shane Horgan, myself – and after a defeat like the one we experienced at Twickenham (Ireland had lost their opening 2000 Six Nations game 50–18) sometimes you need to have a free hand to make those changes.'

Hickie, for one, never played in an era when the sound of slow hand-clapping or booing from the Lansdowne stands were the signs of a crowd frustrated with the Irish team; instead his overall experiences of the Lansdowne crowd have been largely positive ones. 'One thing I must say about Lansdowne Road – even in the games where we weren't winning – we always had massive support; there was always a lot of noise. Because we hadn't won many games there, I'd always been impressed with the level of support whether we won or lost. It was amazing to see it increase even more when we started winning. You'd always depend on the crowd to give you a level of noise that's as good as anywhere. Even the bottom level of noise in Dublin is as good as you're going to get anywhere.'

His first international try at Lansdowne Road came against South Africa in November 2000, a game of scorching intensity but where a somewhat liberated Irish three-quarters line conjured up some moments of magic that even took the visitors by surprise.

Tyrone Howe's try signified Ireland's new-found confidence, but Hickie says his own try in the first half remains his all-time favourite. 'I haven't scored a massive number of tries at Lansdowne Road – a lot of my international tries have been away from there – but one of my favourites came in the match against South Africa. I'd come back into the team after being out for a while and to get man of the match that day capped off a personally satisfying day, too. It wasn't the most spectacular try I ever scored but, in terms of who we were playing, I was thrilled with it. Rob Henderson chipped it through for me and I came up in the inside and beat him to it as he reminded me at the time. He insists he would have got there ... but I wouldn't be so sure!'

Hickie was also at the centre of one of the best tries ever scored at Lansdowne, a stirring move initiated by replacement out-half David Humphreys. Humphreys, standing on the halfway line, passed a long ball to O'Driscoll. The centre then jinked, pretending to go inside, but instead flipped up a ball on his left to Hickie. Hickie had come around on the burst and the jet-heeled winger skipped out of Braam van Straaten's tackle before putting Howe over on the left.

It was a wonderful try that helped level matters, though the Springboks saw off Ireland on the end of an 18–28 final scoreline. 'We went out and attacked from the start; we kind of caught them on the hop in that regard,' remembers Hickie of that day. 'We probably didn't have the defensive organisation that Ireland teams have now and that's what probably cost us the game. With ten minutes to go, we weren't sure we would win, even though we could have won – again it's a stage teams have to go through before they start winning.'

Hickie was part of the Ireland team that beat England in a rescheduled 2001 Six Nations fixture following the outbreak of foot-and-mouth earlier that year. That day, Ireland did what Ireland do best at Lansdowne Road – they emerged breathing fire and played with incredible passion and took the shortest, most direct and simplest options. David Humphreys might have been inconsistent from his place-kicks, but the Ulster Number 10 hammered England with his kicking out of hand and, as Hickie recalls, the forwards loved him for it!

A neutral observer might have summed up that England allowed themselves be sucked into a frantic harum-scarum game which suited the Irish. 'There had been two very famous wins against England [1993 and 1994] before I made the Ireland team, but there was never any consistency either before or after those wins. We got to a stage where we did well against South Africa, were going well against a few different teams but we never were able to drive the nail home against a really top nation. We needed to make that step. We got on top of the other Six Nations teams – Scotland and Italy – but we couldn't make the breakthrough against the likes of France or England. I think when we beat England in that rescheduled game in Lansdowne Road, it was a big confident step for everyone, individually and collectively, as a team.'

Hickie's best moments in the win over England were his defensive cameos, leaping confidently to fetch garryowens, calling for marks, which were all a throwback to his days as a full-back at school. Wood's try, Stringer's famous ankle trip on Dan Luger and Ireland's defensive heroics made the headlines the following morning, but Hickie prefers to read into the little details on days like that. No one stood taller, he said, than Eric Miller, a player who was striving to return to the form of 1997, the year he was made a British and Irish Lion. 'I think Eric was a real stand-out player that day. He got a lot of flack over the years because he was injured a fair bit, but when Eric was fit and when he was at his best, he was probably the best Number 6 Ireland had produced in many years. He's a most natural footballer, extremely aggressive, possesses great skills, and, when he's at his best, he's a match for anyone.

'You get a win like that and if you went down through the team [ratings] afterwards, you'd find everyone played well. In the past, you had Woodie, who was too far in front of everyone. But to beat a team like England, especially the team they were at the time, you needed everyone to play well. And we all did, I thought.'

Buoyed by this heartening victory over the English, Ireland's new-found confidence found full expression against the touring All Blacks in the autumn internationals. A five o'clock kick-off under floodlights ensured a raucous din reverberated around the old ground for what is always a glamour rugby fixture in Ireland. Hickie scored that day, diving over two minutes after half-time to push Ireland 21–7 ahead.

Lansdowne Road erupted and a first win over the All Blacks in fifteen attempts seemed within reach. But the visitors showed why they still are one of the best sides in the world, and in a devastating show of attacking rugby, they ran in four tries during a twenty-minute spell. It finished 40–24, Ireland's lack of a defensive system proving their Achilles heel once again.

'We didn't have the defensive organisation that we have now. Mike Ford wouldn't have been brought in at that stage, so we were defending on our wits. Certainly, against a team like that, we let in some soft tries that, two years later, we wouldn't have conceded. Still, I thought it was an opportunity missed. Again, some guys had fantastic games. I remember Shane Horgan got a bad ankle injury before the game, or during the game, and managed to play up to the last six minutes and did a fantastic job on Jonah Lomu. Again, at the time, Shane would have been under a huge amount of pressure. I remember going into the game, there was a lot of noise that he wasn't going to make it as winger and I think he made the step up that day and the nation relaxed about him after that – he really proved himself against the best team in the world.'

Hickie's try two minutes into the second half pushed Ireland into a dream position and the build-up is still fresh in his mind today. 'Miller first went wide, we recycled, Humps [David Humphreys] took it into the twenty-two, Drico [Brian O'Driscoll] went close and fed me and I dived over in the corner.'

Not long after the dust had settled on the autumn series, there was another changing of the guard when Eddie O'Sullivan replaced Gatland as Ireland head coach. This was Hickie's third coach since 1997, but the momentum Ireland had built up since the autumn didn't break. Going into the following year's Six Nations, hopes were high that Ireland could finish high up the table and the opening day win over Wales underlined those aspirations. Hickie was one of six try scorers in a stunning 54–10 over Wales in Lansdowne Road.

The game was well wrapped up by the time Hickie cantered over the line, but the move is worth retelling. Simon Easterby took the ball into the twenty-two, O'Driscoll was involved but after being brought down, Humphreys took possession and fed Hickie for the easiest of run-ins.

Despite the confidence generated by that victory, a mixed Six Nations followed: a heavy loss in Twickenham, wins at home to Scotland and Italy before the French ran riot once again in Paris.

But better lay ahead, especially in the 2002 autumn series.

World champions Australia arrived in Lansdowne confident of turning over the Irish as they'd done so often in the past. Hickie retired concussed before the break, at which stage Ireland had sailed into a 12–3 lead. 'I actually got knocked out and was taken off just before the end of the first half. I think I put my head on the wrong side of a tackle with Wendell Sailor, who is not a small guy, and got a knee in the side of the head. I can't even remember when they took me off. The next thing I do remember is the end of the game and celebrating with the rest of the lads. I don't remember any of the game to be honest.'

Hickie viewed a video later and remembers it now for many reasons: Brian O'Driscoll's first game as captain, Ronan O'Gara's flawless kicking display, landing all of Ireland's eighteen points, and the re-emergence of Victor Costello on the international stage after a four-year absence. 'Woodie was injured at the time so Brian was brought in as a captain. We played in pretty horrific conditions, but Ronan pretty much won that game for us – he scored all our points in a masterful display. Other guys also played well like Shane Byrne, throwing in not only torrential rain but unbelievable wind, but he hit the lineout every time. I believe we got a 100 per cent record in the lineout. Victor also came in at Number 6 after being in the wilderness for quite a while. He [Costello] was man of the match that day; himself and Anthony Foley worked very well at 6 and 8. They swapped around positions having been on opposite teams and adversaries for so long. A lot of people didn't realise how well the swapping worked – and it worked well for us in the next few games as well. That win was a big step – our first southern hemisphere scalp as a group.'

Ireland remained unbeaten until the Grand Slam decider

against England in March 2003. 'We'd beaten England in 2001 and expectations were high. But we were beaten by the side that effectively went on to win the World Cup. You'd guys like Dallaglio, Johnson and Hill in their prime, Leonard was on top of his game as were Jonny Wilkinson and Mike Tindall. I remember everyone being disappointed after that game, but there was a sense that we could have no complaints; we were beaten by the better side and they proved that when they went on to win the World Cup.'

Injury at the 2003 World Cup against Argentina deprived Hickie of a chance to play in the 2004 Six Nations campaign – and a Triple Crown win. He did, however, return for the 2004 autumn internationals against South Africa and Argentina. 'The win over South Africa was another great scalp. Ronan [O'Gara] got all the points and the man of the match award. Again, it was a performance where everyone needed to play well, and did play well. Ireland had gone to South Africa that summer full of confidence, but our confidence might have been misinterpreted. You go to a southern hemisphere team and, irrespective of what they say, they'll always expect to beat Ireland. For us to win a game out there, we need to go there believing we can win. If we don't think we're going to win, we're not going to win. They beat us 2–0 in the series. Then South Africa were making the noises of a Grand Slam tour in the autumn internationals, all that sort of stuff, but we were keen to get one back on them.' And Ireland did, beating the Springboks.

With Leinster, Hickie also enjoyed great moments in Lansdowne Road, European Cup days, especially. Against Bath in October 2004, Leinster's New Zealand import, out-half David Holwell, gave a man of the match display and

Hickie scored a gem of a try himself after twenty-five minutes, dancing down the left wing to beat two men in a twenty-five-metre dash to the corner. That's tempered, he adds, by two gut-wrenching defeats there to Perpignan (2004) and Munster (2006).

The highlight of his Leinster career came in the inaugural Celtic League final against Munster in 2001 – a game that drew 30,000 spectators to Lansdowne Road and one where the Leinster coaching ticket of Matt Williams and Alan Gaffney saw their vision of total rugby realised. 'A great occasion, a lot of drama,' he remembers. 'We had a guy sent off early and were down to fourteen men. The Celtic League is not the European Cup but, in terms of important wins, it was huge to us at the time; it was the start of provincial rugby getting big. Having 30,000 there in Lansdowne Road where two Irish provinces were playing had never been done before up until that point. It was a great final. They [Gaffney and Williams] were trying to take us to a different level and, at that time, it was as big a game as we played.

'Lansdowne could be the greatest ground in the world it was that night. I've good memories and heartbreaking ones as well, but that's what endears me to the place even more.'

His biggest heartbreak came against Munster in the 2006 European Cup semi-final when Leinster's backline was denied the freedom of the park by a superbly motivated and defensive Munster side. Around then a lot was made between the two sets of backs, but Munster's backs played very well that day. I almost got in for a try at a stage when we really did need to get ahead, but we never got there.'

Pride of place for Hickie, however, are the brace of tries he posted in Lansdowne's final days. Against Australia in the 2006

Eye on the ball: Watched by Phil Orr (centre) and Willie Duggan (right) Ollie Campbell, one of Ireland's greatest out-halves, finds touch in Lansdowne Road's West Stand during Ireland's Triple Crown win over Scotland in 1982.

Father-figure: In this iconic shot, Mick Galwey helps settle the nerves of Peter Stringer (left) and Ronan O'Gara (right) as the trio line up for the national anthems prior to Ireland's 2000 Six Nations clash with Italy at Lansdowne Road. Both Stringer and O'Gara were winning only their second Ireland caps.

Tom Kiernan, a quality full-back and an inspirational captain for his country, is shouldered from the field after Ireland recorded a 14–0 win over Wales in 1970 at Lansdowne Road.

Willie John McBride tackles France's Paul Biermouret during Ireland's narrow 6–4 win over *Les bleus* in the 1973 Five Nations clash between the sides at Lansdowne Road.

The Jackie Kyle show: Ireland's greatest Number 10, Jack Kyle, clears to touch during Ireland's 22–0 win over England in the 1947 Five Nations championship at Lansdowne Road. Kyle was earning just his second Ireland cap while both Bertie O'Hanlon and Barney Mullan notched two tries apiece on an historic afternoon in Dublin 4.

Bertie O'Hanlon, winning his first cap, fends off David Swarbrick (England) and heads for his second try in the 1947 Five Nations.

In his debut match against Scotland, Tony Ward (centre of shot) makes no secret of his delight after Stewart McKinney crossed the line for the only try of the game in the 1978 Five Nations championship.

Tripped up: One of the great Lansdowne moments. Peter Stringer (on ground) after catching Dan Luger's (14, England) ankle, an action that helped prevent a certain England try in the delayed 2001 Six Nations Championship (Ireland won 20–14). Also pictured are David Humphreys (10, Ireland) and Jason Robinson (11, England).

Happy days: Euphoria beaks out in the lower West Stand as Ireland captain, Ciaran Fitzgerald, and Moss Finn make their way down the steps to the dressing room after clinching the Triple Crown in 1982. Ireland defeated Scotland 21–12 thanks to Ollie Campbell's six penalties and drop goal.

That winning feeling: Keith Wood, former Ireland captain, holds his hands aloft following his side's rollercoaster 20–14 win over England in the delayed 2001 Six Nations clash at Lansdowne Road. Wood describes this famous October day as his greatest in a green jersey.

Triple cheer: Eddie O'Sullivan, head coach, (kneeling, far right) celebrates in front o
Tries from Gordon D'Arcy (two), Geordan Murphy, David Wallace and Peter Stringer pro

Squad (*back row, l-r*): Marcus Horan, Brian O'Driscoll, Paul O'C
Gordon D'Arcy, Victor Costello, Anthony Foley, Da
(*front row, l-r*): Geordan Murphy, Shane Byrne, Peter Stringe
Missing from photo are Donn

...th Terrace with his players following Ireland's first Triple Crown in nineteen years.
...imental in this 37–16 victory over a Matt Williams-coached Scotland at Lansdowne Road.

...hane Horgan, Guy Easterby, Malcolm O'Kelly, Reggie Corrigan,
...phreys, John Hayes, Ronan O'Gara, David Wallace.
...Easterby, Kevin Maggs, Girvan Dempsey, Eddie O'Sullivan.
...llaghan and Frankie Sheahan.

Gordon Hamilton is tackled by Rob Egerton (14, Australia) but manages to cross the tryline and push Ireland into the lead against Australia during the epic 1991 Rugby World Cup quarter-final clash in Lansdowne Road. The great David Campese (11, Australia) is also pictured.

autumn internationals, a game where Ireland played some sparkling rugby in a 21–6 win, Hickie showed his quiet brilliance as a finisher, notching a fine try in the Lansdowne Road/East Stand corner of the ground. And then, over a month later, on 31 December to be precise, in a game billed aptly as 'The Last Stand' (Lansdowne's last ever game), he was one of three Leinster try scorers, along with Owen Finegan and Jamie Heaslip, in a Magners League win over Ulster.

Ask him his best memory of Lansdowne, and he'll say that feeling of running down the touchline with those nearest leaning out over their seats, willing him towards the tryline. 'Nothing beats that feeling. Having everyone so close to the pitch, you could see the whites of people's eyes. And, when you looked up after grounding the ball, people could be smiling at you from only ten feet away. It was the only international ground in the world where that could happen and you could nearly go in and give someone a high-five.

'Not too many grounds are that close to the crowd. The old Lansdowne had a pretty good innings – everyone was glad to see it go, but I think there are enough good memories in it. I don't think the old ground will be forgotten that quickly.'

Martin Johnson

Lock, England

1995–2005

Between 1995 and 2005, Martin Johnson played four times for his country and twice for Leicester at Lansdowne Road and he never lost a game there. Famously, in 2001, he was unable to play because of injury; instead the giant lock was confined to a seat in the West Stand nursing a broken wrist suffered in a club game seven days earlier. The image of Johnson that afternoon is of a restless giant, often frowning with head in hands as England allowed another Grand Slam to slip from their grasp – their third in three seasons.

He admits he felt the stadium shudder that afternoon when Keith Wood, his former Lions team-mate, crashed through Neil Back for a decisive first-half try and, when the final whistle went, Johnson just wanted to get the hell out of Dublin. Instead, protocol dictated he head to the presentation rostrum to accept the championship trophy, which England had won by topping the Six Nations table.

Johnson has said that England always perform best with a healthy dose of fear, and he certainly must have felt a healthy measure of anxiety and anticipation before playing his first England game at Lansdowne Road in January 1995. If he felt he was entering the eye of the storm, he didn't think he'd be literally entering it. During the national anthems, the hulking six-foot six-inch lock from the midlands experienced a bit of trouble keeping his balance while belting out 'God Save the Queen'. 'It was one of the windiest days I can ever remember,' he says. 'We were getting blown sideways in the anthems!'

If the wind was an irritant, England's game-plan, nevertheless, ran ever so smoothly, almost in defiance to the prevailing weather conditions. Opting to play against the elements, the visitors eschewed their kicking game; instead quick-tap penalties were the order of the day as the English forwards rucked and mauled and ploughed their way through a physically inferior Ireland. This England team was built in the image of their coach Jack Rowell – big, grizzled warriors, who guaranteed their wide men quick and clean possession. In that first half, England buckled down and adopted the correct tactics against the breeze and went in at the break leading 12–3.

Essentially, it was game over at that stage and, for Johnson, the pre-match nerves had dissipated. 'We were playing into the wind in the first half. Kyran Bracken was scrum-half and he said, "We can't kick a penalty into touch, we should just tap and go and keep hold of the ball, and keep the ball away from Ireland because as soon as we lost the ball they could kick it

virtually seventy or eighty yards down the field if they wanted."
We got right into the game and took Ireland on up front. We
had a good pack, which included Dean Richards.'

In that team, Richards was a colossus and his performance
in the back-row that day alongside Tim Rodber and Ben
Clarke was immense. This trio, especially, rarely allowed
Ireland break the gain-line and the home side were obliterated
in the first half.

Even Ireland manager Noel Murphy, himself a useful back-
row operator in the 1960s, took time out afterwards to lavish
praise on Richards. 'Dean Richards was great for England; he
is the kind of man you need on a day like this,' he said in his
post-match press conference.

'We just drove it and mauled it,' continues Johnson, 'and
because we had the urgency of having to play into the wind, it
actually worked in our favour. It was one of the best first halves
I had with England.'

Wave after wave of concerted English pressure yielded two
tries during the opening forty minutes. Lansdowne could
scarcely believe the might and force of England as Johnson and
company moved relentlessly down the field with Will Carling
and Ben Clarke each running in tries. 'Early on, we just tapped
and went. It gave us the sort of initiative to try and get into the
game. When I think back, if our game-plan had backfired, we
could have been twenty points down in those sort of
conditions.'

The lineouts would prove crucial in the first half. Ireland
were willing to kick to touch with a boot-the-ball policy, the
most sensible option you'd think with a gale to their backs. But
whatever lineout play there was in the first forty minutes,
England dominated. The two Martins – Bayfield and Johnson

– were imperious. And a problem area for the Irish was compounded with the forced retirement on half-time of Neil Francis who sustained a rib cartilage injury. It's something Johnson remembers. 'Neil Francis' injury was a big blow for Ireland; I thought he was a very good player, a very athletic guy.'

At the break, England knew they had Ireland by the throat but the expected squeeze and follow-on humiliation of the Irish never materialised. Still, Ireland continued to suffer in the lineouts with Bayfield and Johnson stealing and making themselves a right nuisance on Ireland's throw. In the loose, Anthony Foley and Keith Wood did their best to stem the ferocity of England's power-play – emanating particularly from the sustained driving from the back-row triumvirate of Rodber, Clarke and Richards.

Ireland braved it out in the second half; and Anthony Foley notched a late try on his first Ireland outing to keep the final score somewhat respectable at 21–8.

In an era when Irish teams were known to fall away dramatically in the last twenty minutes, it was during this period that the home team's truer side came to light. And if Ireland had performed like that for the previous hour, they might have been closer at full-time.

That afternoon, Johnson's colossal shadow was cast across Lansdowne for the first time in a masterful second-row display. Lansdowne might not have known it then, but his giant silhouette was to haunt many Irish performances over the next ten years. 'With the wind, we didn't play any bit near as well; in fact we then changed the way we played and weren't anywhere near as successful. The only points we scored came from one more try. But we really killed the game off. If Ireland came at us, we were able to turn it over and go fifty or sixty yards down the field with the breeze. That was crucial.'

England took the Grand Slam that year – big players and big characters helping them along their road to glory. 'That was our first game of the tournament and, the thing was, we hadn't played any major side the previous autumn. Yes, we put big points up against Canada and Romania – but they weren't top-flight opposition. In fact, we hadn't had a tough game since the tour to South Africa the previous year. It was a new side, too, and the win gave us huge confidence. I'll forever remember that first forty minutes. We knew also that Ireland were going for a hat-trick of wins over us. We had to be mentally tough because Lansdowne could be a real cauldron but I always felt it was a great place in which to play.'

Keith Wood's words in the aftermath of the 1997 Five Nations match at Lansdowne Road succinctly sum up the reasons behind Ireland's 46–6 pummelling at the hands of the old enemy. Wood was injured for the game but writing in *The Examiner* he pointed to the power of the English forwards, with Johnson in the engine room, as the catalyst to Ireland's dramatic collapse: 'They overpowered us; they pummelled us,' he wrote. 'They were much heavier and never relented. Normally, a team picks certain scrums to give a special effort and attack. Not so England, not for a second. I remember a scrum with about ten minutes to go, it seemed to be of little consequence but they gave it everything.'

Wood added that the superior weight of the English took its toll and Ireland ended up doing an awful lot of defending which, consequently, sapped the energy from his team-mates. 'It wasn't a lack of fitness; it's just that the huge men in the back five of the English scrum took the heart and soul out of our men. They concentrated on taking every ounce of resistance out of the Irish. It's not nice to look at, it's not pretty but it's bloody effective and enabled them to finally turn on the style in the last few minutes. It's easy to become downhearted in those circumstances. You have to be fair and say England played great rugby in the closing stages.'

England's backs paraded their wares to stunning effect running in five of their six tries over the eighty minutes, five tries arriving in the last seventeen minutes.

It could have been so different had Ireland taken their chances, says Johnson. 'After seventeen minutes, Ireland were leading 6–3 and then Denis Hickie beat a couple of our boys, space opened up and he could have reached our line. But, somehow, he slipped or tripped over and we escaped. Eric Miller got badly concussed early on, too, which worked for us because he was in the best form of his life at that point. I remember it being fairly even in the first half, then Johnny Sleightholme scored to give us a bit of an advantage going into the second half.'

Johnson admits that a new-look England could not get into any discernable rhythm in the first half, as they either knocked the ball on or made fundamental errors and conceded a succession of needless penalties. Ireland were 6–11 in arrears at half-time but the loss of Miller and Eric Elwood (who had departed two minutes after Miller) proved hugely detrimental to the Irish game-plan. Their chain of creativity was broken. As Wood says, 'It is unsettling to lose two key decision-makers. We were relying on Miller's speed and Elwood's experience and to miss both was a major handicap.'

Once Andy Gomarsall sauntered over in the sixty-fourth

minute, England turned up the heat and Ireland melted. England played champagne rugby, fizzing in attack as Ireland were flattened by the chariot. 'The last fifteen minutes was when the damage was done,' says Johnson. 'Ireland tried to run it, but we just picked up the pieces. At the end, they were playing catch-up rugby and that's no easy thing when you're under the cosh.'

It was a demolition, a humiliation that signalled massive regression for Irish rugby still grappling tenuously with professionalism. England appeared to be light years ahead in every respect. But who was there to shout stop? Ireland looked to coach Brian Ashton, who took the flak for the shambles all around him. Afterwards, in an effort to conceal the cracks behind another public humiliation, he stated, 'There is no quick fix for the ills of Irish rugby. It could take two or three years, not two or three weeks to put things right.'

It wasn't such a bad diagnosis. In 2000, though under a different coach (Warren Gatland), Ireland won three consecutive Six Nations games, including a win against France in Paris, all of which marked a turn in Irish rugby's fortunes.

'I didn't know Brian at all at that point [in 1997],' says Johnson. 'All I knew is that he was associated with backs. He was on the television the week before talking about being involved with England at various other levels. He said that he wanted Ireland to win; obviously he was coaching against his home country and he felt quite mischievous about it. Brian just wanted to coach – being a head coach is just an entirely different thing. He maybe got that feeling with Ireland when things started to go a little bit wrong for him, they didn't really have that belief in themselves. The game turned into a rout, but we weren't forty points better than Ireland. There was real silence in the crowd especially near the end. They started to leave early. But as the away team, to come and play the way we did, was a great feeling. We even had Jeremy Guscott on the bench and Austin Healy came on as a replacement to win his first cap. I thought we had a pretty strong squad then: it was Hilly's [Richard Hill] debut season in the Six Nations, Lawrence's [Dallaglio] second season, Shawsey's [Simon Shaw] first season. It was a fairly exciting time for us. There was almost a changing of the guard from two years ago. No [Brian] Moore, Richards, Bayfield, no Rob Andrew. We should have won the Grand Slam – we lost a hell of a lead against France in Twickenham afterwards.'

The British and Irish media reasoned before England's visit to Lansdowne Road in 1999 that Ireland had the best tight five in the northern hemisphere and their deduction seemed rational enough given Ireland's exciting win over Wales in Wembley and England's travails against Scotland. The big question was whether Ireland could actually do it? In the Lansdowne press box, there was a pool organised in which predictions were made on the final outcome. Most journalists – both British and Irish – went for a home win.

The pre-match predictions and newspaper headlines suggesting frailties in the tight five seemed to galvanise England's pack, and they ran roughshod over Ireland almost in ruthless defiance to the soothsayers. Richard Cockerill, Tim Rodber, Martin Johnson, and a back-row of Richard Hill, Neil Back and man of the match Lawrence Dallaglio beasted the Irish pack while there appeared such easy and smooth cohesion between England's backs and forwards. 'We got a rugby lesson today,' said Ireland coach, Warren Gatland afterwards.

England elected to play against the wind in the first half

and, Johnson says, 'We laid the foundations for our victory down in the first twenty minutes.' England retained possession superbly against the elements. 'I think we got the tactics right again. Even against the wind, we were dominating possession which frustrated the Irish. They were still very good defensively and, perhaps, we should have got a few more points inside their half.'

Indeed they should. During this opening period, Ireland had a mere 20 per cent of possession and their lineout imploded – England took possession from four of Ireland's throws in the first half. Tim Rodber and Johnson were claiming ball at will, and gave them another platform to drive at an Irish pack already under pressure. 'Lansdowne was very quiet during the opening twenty minutes. I suppose there was a lot of pre-match hype around Dublin after Ireland's impressive victory over Wales but the noise quickly subsided when we took charge up front. I think the Matt Perry try showed us at our best – forwards driving up the middle and the backs forming good lines behind which enabled Perry to finish off in style for the first try. Still, there was only two points between the sides at the break.'

Johnson points to the influence his one-time Leicester team-mate Eric Miller had on proceedings following his introduction in the second half. 'When Eric came on, there was more purpose to the Irish play and I think his sense of urgency was one of the factors in Ireland bringing the score back to 15–12 with about ten minutes left on the clock. Ireland displayed typical fervour and passion but our defence did really well.'

A young man named Jonny Wilkinson lined out in the centre for England and, though only nineteen, the teenager showed maturity beyond his years landing his fourth penalty in the sixty-third minute to push England 20–12 in front. Though David Humphreys replied with a penalty, England's forwards – Johnson, Dallaglio and Back, in particular – helped settle the game when Tim Rodber scored a try in injury-time. The overwhelming feeling around Dublin that evening was that Ireland were lucky to keep the final score so respectable given England's powerful demonstration in the rudiments of forward play.

The game, however, wasn't without its controversial moments. There was a suggestion afterwards that Cockerill had taunted spectators at Lansdowne at the final whistle. He ran down the touchline giving what he recalled later as a 'routine victory gesture'. Cockerill pleaded innocence afterwards, 'I don't want my action to be misinterpreted,' he said. 'England have been criticised all week and, when we scored, it was clear we had won the match. I gave the spectators a routine victory gesture – with two fingers held up showing that we had won.'

The sense of relief for England at this victory was echoed at the time by their coach Clive Woodward, 'That was the biggest game since I became coach – bigger than New Zealand, Australia or South Africa. It put them all in the shade because we simply had to win.'

'It was a pretty tough game. It wasn't over till it was over,' admits Johnson now. 'It was a hard slog. This was Lansdowne Road and any win there had to be savoured. It was a transitional England team and a good team. Again, a team that should have won the Grand Slam but lost to Wales.'

In the spring of 2001, England were playing an all-singing, all-dancing brand of rugby, and looked shoo-ins for a Grand

Slam. Those plans, however, were disrupted after an outbreak of foot-and-mouth disease across Britain, and their Lansdowne date was pushed back to late October. In a rugby players' mind that constitutes a new season and, after a disappointing Lions series in Australia, many England players had lost form – and, in Dallaglio's case, picked up injuries. Momentum can be difficult to carry over from one season to the next and, if you factored in their catalogue of injuries to key players, England's chances of a Grand Slam win in Dublin diminished by the day.

All week the key mnemonic preached by Woodward had been his famous T-CUP expression – think clearly under pressure – but how could their minds be right as heading into their first international of the new season without so many key players? 'In spring 2001, we'd beaten everyone out of sight. I think we broke a record for most number of tries or points scored. We had a really quick and fit team. Iain Balshaw played at full-back and we were bringing Jason Robinson off the bench for those spring games. That's how strong we were. We just ran teams off their feet really.'

Fate seemed to be conspiring against Woodward and his team, as three pillars in their Grand Slam assault – Lawrence Dallaglio, Johnson and Phil Vickery – missed their biggest game of 2001. The sight of Johnson confined to a seat in the West Stand as his team crumbled under a fired-up Ireland remains a lasting image. All he could do was close his eyes and wish matters on the field would resolve themselves, but that didn't happen. The biggest and most impressive figure in English rugby was powerless. 'I broke my hand the week before playing for Leicester. It happened after about twenty minutes, but I played up to half-time. It's not a ridiculously painful injury, and I remember the physio saying, "You'll be all right", but you could feel the bone rattling in my hand. Lawrence got hurt, I broke my hand, Phil Vickery was out, Balsh had lost a bit of form during the Lions tour, so it was difficult before we even hit the field.

'We probably even made more breaks in that game than we did in the previous two, but I was very frustrated watching it. We tried to play some beautifully attractive rugby in our own half of the field and we kept turning the ball over. When you go away and you concede the first try – which we did – it makes it an awful lot harder and Ireland scored a really well-worked try. Then we had five opportunities in that game late in the second half but the referee penalised us a few times. Even at the end, I remember saying to Clive, "If we keep hold of the ball here, we'll score a try." I was sure of it. Ireland defended well, but we tried to play too much rugby in our half, which was crazy.'

Ireland's win precipitated unforgettable celectrations on and off the field. The irony of it all was amazing. A dejected England team had just won the Six Nations Championship but they only spoke in terms of Grand Slams. Then, reluctantly Johnson along with captain for the day, Matt Dawson, accepted the RBS Six Nations trophy and trooped off disconsolately. Ireland, on the other hand, did a lap of honour. 'For Ireland it was real big, emotional win. I said if we won, I'd go on the field. If we lost, I was saying to Clive I'd rather not go down and collect the trophy. In fact, when we lost, I'd rather not have won anything. I don't think the preparation was right either. The guys were in Ireland all week which I thought was a mistake. I think the best way to prepare for those games is to fly in on the Thursday afternoon. Then you've two days to get ready for it. I think we made the mistakes off the field.

'But it's all about who wins the game – and we didn't win the game, Ireland won the game. We would have much rather given them a clap and walked off because it was as flat as it could have been in our camp. We'd lost another Grand Slam – it was getting beyond a joke at that point really.'

At a press conference the week of the Grand Slam showdown in Lansdowne Road in 2003, you could really sense England were ready to close this Grand Slam deal. In one-to-one interviews, there was a cold steeliness to their carefully chosen words. The pressure was on them to deliver but they were used to that and, once and for all, they wanted to break down the barriers of underachievement, which, in their vocabulary, amounted simply to their inability to win Grand Slams. Even Neil Back was not going to allow heckling from the Munster contingent in the Irish crowd (the 'back-hander' controversy from the 2002 European Cup final from Cardiff was still fresh in Irish minds) distract him from the task in hand. The rugged flanker delivered his words with a determined delivery, no cadence, each word emphasised flatly for optimum effect. 'No amount of intimidation from any fan in any stadium in the world has affected my performance in a negative way.'

The message was clear: England were on a mission.

As for the match, England dominated in every sector. Their forwards crucified their counterparts in open play and the Lansdowne crowd was silenced. England won 42–6 and Johnson, at last, could lift the Six Nations trophy, this time as Grand Slam champions.

Johnson believes that the final scoreline didn't reflect a fine Irish performance ('better than 2001') but Ireland caught England in a mean mood. It seemed the years of hurt that had built up inside them made 2003 a crusade to lift a Grand Slam. 'Ireland probably played better than they had two years before in many ways. It was just opportunity taken. We played into the breeze and, early on, we were under a lot of pressure. I remember Geordan [Murphy] playing very well – I thought he was Ireland's best player that day. For the first try, we put them under pressure in a scrum, won the turnover and Lawrence scored a try. Jonny then dropped two goals to make it 13–6. In a way, the game was a reverse of 2001 because Ireland were creating opportunities and were counter- and counter-attacking and playing a very wide game as we had done two years earlier. We defended very well and got a couple of chances and scored. Jonny's tackle on Maggs, for instance, was a key moment in the first half and there were a couple of other occasions as well. We could have been 13–3 down at half-time.'

With the pack in control, Jonny Wilkinson came into his own at out-half and, before half-time, dropped two goals with his so-called weaker right foot. 'Jonny dropped one just before the half, to bring it from 10–6 to 13–6, which is quite a big stretch. We just took points at key moments.'

When the second half rolled around, England started making mistakes and failed to build on their score. 'We made a few mistakes, the referee penalised us and we were getting a bit frustrated with things. There was no score for the first twenty minutes in the second half and then [Mike] Tindall broke through two tackles to score. Before Mikey's try, Ireland were pushing to get back into the game and, if they had even got three points at that time, the game would have had a very different feel about it. But with Mikey's try, you suddenly had a fourteen-point gap and that's a long way back in the modern game. Will [Greenwood] then intercepted Geordan who was trying to force the game and Will was helped over the line by most of the England pack. Really, we got on the back of Ireland chasing the game. It was one of those games where the score didn't reflect the pattern of the game; but, then again, we didn't think the score reflected the game in 2001. The most important thing was our attitude. We would have taken a one-point win and everyone would have been happy in the England camp, and outside the England camp. There were no illusions of playing attractive rugby and sometimes it gets into people's heads about how they play. I say, "Just win at all costs, however you have to." We played a lot less rugby than we did in 2001 but we just happened to score tries and get points.'

The day, however, will be remembered for Johnson's refusal to move to Engalnd's appointed side of the red carpet for the arrival of President Mary McAleese. England positioned themselves on the left-hand side of the pitch (as you looked from the West Stand) where Ireland usually line up for internationals. When Johnson was asked to move his players twenty metres to the other side, he refused point-blank. 'We were getting a lot of grief from the Irish fans because, obviously, they were up for the Slam as well. But we had our heads on; we weren't taking any rubbish. I walked out to the side where we were going to play from and I didn't know anything about it being Ireland's lucky side. I just walked out to the side I was going to play, lined up and I remember seeing the Irish boys walk down behind me and the team. I wondered what they were doing. I thought they were going down to the North Terrace end of stadium to gee the crowd up. Then this guy came out and said to me, "You gotta move." I said, "I'm not moving anywhere mate. Just get on with the game." And then the crowd went crazy because I obviously gesticulated at the guy. The crowd was getting noisier and noisier and it became a stand-off. Then, I thought we couldn't, and shouldn't, move. It would have looked like we were backing down. If they'd been clever, they would have got the referee to ask us to move – I would never have refused to do it for the referee because that's before the game kicks off. Then they sent someone else out and he said you got to move and I repeated, "I'm not moving anywhere, just get on with the game."'

It appears England were not informed about correct Lansdowne protocol. 'We don't even think about it,' says Johnson. 'In most stadia the changing rooms are on either side of the tunnel and you naturally go to your side. In Twickenham, if you're on the left-hand side, you walk onto the pitch on the left-hand side. In Lansdowne, it wasn't like that because the changing rooms were next to each other down the same corridor so there was no natural way for the teams to walk out. I've seen it on video afterwards and the whole red carpet controversy looks like a pause where nothing happens. The president then came out and we got on with the game. Irish people said to me, "You made the president walk on the grass", but we had red carpet in front of us.'

Johnson returned for his final game in Lansdowne Road in 2005 when Leicester Tigers defeated Leinster in the European Cup quarter-final. It was a game Leinster were expected to win but, with Johnson at the helm, the Tigers smothered the Irish province's free-wheeling style and one of the most iconic figures of world rugby maintained his winning record as a player at the ground. 'I was thrilled with the response from the players. It was a great occasion too – to fill a stadium like Lansdowne for a European Cup game was brilliant. It went right for us that day but all wrong for us in the semi-final afterwards. I remember I came over as well in 1997 for a European Cup game against Leinster and really snuffed a win against a really good Leinster team in our very first midweek European Cup game at Lansdowne. It was a good win against a Leinster team that included Paul Wallace, Malcolm O'Kelly and Neil Francis.'

Tom Kiernan

Full-Back

1960–1973

One could not but be envious of Irish rugby followers of the 1960s. Even for the talent of the modern era's Holy Trinity of Brian O'Driscoll, Paul O'Connell and Ronan O'Gara, the mighty triumvirate of Tom Kiernan, Willie John McBride and Mike Gibson dominated the Irish rugby landscape during a prosperous enough time for the union game in Ireland, albeit one where neither a Triple Crown, Grand Slam nor Championship rested on these shores.

Yet, powered by the Kiernan–McBride–Gibson axis, two of the southern hemisphere big guns were thwarted at Lansdowne Road, in much the same way that O'Driscoll, O'Connell and O'Gara have been hugely instrumental in helping topple some of the SANZAR nations throughout the noughties.

For example, the Aussies regularly came unstuck in Lansdowne during the 1960s, as did the South Africans, while the All Blacks just about sneaked home by the skin of their teeth in the oft-mentioned 1963 game, thanks in the main to Donald Clarke's tornado-boot.

At the centre of all this was Kiernan, the very essence of consistency, who has since been variously included in 'Greatest British and Irish Lions' selections to have donned the Number 15 shirt. According to those lucky enough to have seen him play, Kiernan was endowed with some of the best attributes of a full-back: a huge boot, a coolness under the high ball and he was teak-tough defensively. He remains up there in the pantheon of many Lions Number 15 immortals such as J.P.R. Williams, Andy Irvine, Gavin Hastings, Neil Jenkins and even Ireland's own 2009 Lions revelation, Rob Kearney.

And like any good full-back, shouldering responsibility rested easily with the Cork man. As a place-kicker, he had few peers to match his level of consistency during this era. And while there've been players down through the years who've found the art of place-kicking at Lansdowne taxing, Kiernan admits he found kicking difficult in all stadia.

'I would have gone to Lansdowne as a schoolboy, and it was always a big occasion. I was there three times and saw the likes of Jackie Kyle, John O'Meara and Mick Lane. I first played there against Leinster in a pre-Christmas inter-pro in 1959. When I left college in 1963, I joined Con, and we used to play friendly matches against Wanderers and Lansdowne FC, both tenants at Lansdowne Road, and those matches were played every year in the stadium. It was great to get that kind of experience there. You'd one match up there at least every year because Wanderers would be down here [in Cork] one year and we'd be up at Lansdowne FC, and then the following year it'd switch. And all Munster matches against Leinster were played there every second year.'

Kiernan, a member of a Cork rugby family with a long tradition in the game, made his Ireland debut against England in Twickenham in 1960, and went on to play fifty-four matches (twenty-four as captain) for his country before bowing out at Murrayfield in 1973, retiring then as the most capped full-back in international history – and this at a time when there was nowhere near as many opportunities to win caps.

Famed for his ability as a calming and sensible captain, Kiernan was also a prolific kicker, and landed some very important points throughout his career at Lansdowne, notably in wins over South Africa (1965) and Australia (1967).

Before all that there was his first Irish trial at Lansdowne, which could not have gone better for the ex-Presentation Brothers College student and then UCC and Munster player.

'I remember playing for the Irish Universities in December 1959 and was picked for my first Irish trial – on the Possibles – in January 1960. I was picked at full-back even though, at the time, I lined out at centre for Munster. Both Ray Hennessy and my brother would have been Munster's Number 15s. Anyway, Ray happened to be picked on the Probables at my first national trial.

'I was picked on the Irish Universities at the end of December at full-back. I had a fairly OK game, and was subsequently picked for the Possibles. I wasn't seen by anyone, maybe a few University selectors, that's all. So, it was a certainty that Ray would be picked for Ireland. But the night before, Ray cried off with an injury and I then got on to the Probables, and someone else was chosen for the Possibles. The day could not have gone any better for me. Everything I kicked went to the right places. If I closed my eyes that same day, the ball would have gone over the bar. If I back-heeled the ball, it would probably have gone over, too! One kick, I remember, hit the post, hit the crossbar and bounced over!

'The Irish selectors then picked the Probables team en bloc for the England match, and Ray never got a cap thereafter, though he would have got three Irish trials during his career.'

For a young man coming onto the Irish team, nothing could have been more daunting than the prospect of facing into an away fixture at a packed Twickenham. But Kiernan took it all in his stride. 'I would have got to know some of the players through the inter-provincial series of games. However, the players did not get an opportunity to meet up and train as often as they do today. You'd travel by train to Dublin on a Friday, have a light training session in Trinity, play on Saturday and go back home on Sunday.

'The difficulty was getting half-backs to click. For example, if they came from separate provinces, it might have been difficult to get an understanding going; the wing three-quarter used throw in from touch, so getting the timing right for second rows and signals was difficult. But other than that, it was fine as you went on from year to year. And there used be few changes every year – maybe three or four – so most people knew each other pretty well anyhow.

'We were beaten 8–5 in a close match in Twickenham. I remember it being a tense atmosphere. We had lost Ronnie Dawson that year – he'd injured himself after coming back from captaining the Lions and Andy Mulligan was captain instead. He was in Oxford at the time, and I remember being very impressed with his knowledge of the game and his knowledge of the English.

'I was kicking that day – we had just one kick which thankfully was under the post.'

Kiernan's kicking style also caught the eye, a method somewhat different and removed from the techniques employed by the modern-day kicker. However, his 'through toe-punt' kick proved hugely reliable on countless occasions.

'I just wonder how they kick the ball today. But they seem to be very accurate. Mine was a completely different technique. I'd firstly make a mound – we didn't have kicking tees – place the ball diagonally towards the posts, and the line going through the middle of the ball you set to split the posts. I toed the ball – ran straight into it, kicked through and followed through.

'There were round-the-corner kickers during my days, too. Now they all seem to kick around the corner but with their instep. And I find that strange but obviously it's no problem to them. They're largely very accurate with their kicks.'

One of his favourite Lansdowne memories came against South Africa in 1965, Ireland's first win over the Springboks. Conditions, he says, weren't ideal even though it took place in mid-April, and he remembers a strong wind and sporadic showers making control and ball handling difficult.

'We took the lead. Pat McGrath, our winger, did very well to get his hand to the ball after Roger Young kicked it over the South Africa line. It was a huge defensive display by us. Our line wasn't breached during the first half, even though the Boks did get a penalty to leave it stand 3–3 at half-time.

'We had the wind to our backs in the second half and half-expected to dominate territory as they did in the first but their centre [W.J.] Mans got a try. It went unconverted but then I landed a penalty before Mike [Gibson] went over for a try which was subsequently disallowed for an apparent infringement.

'That was a blow, sure, but Lansdowne was now at full voice. We sensed victory, a South African scalp which would have been huge for us. I kicked the winning score, though I actually mis-kicked it; topped it in fact. And Bill Twomey, who was commentating that day, said at one point, "He's missed it; it's gone under." But the height of the ball was just at the height of the bar. Thankfully the ball went over, and the Boks were beaten for the second time in five days. On the previous Tuesday at Thomond Park, a Combined Universities side beat them as well, so it was a good couple of days for Irish rugby.'

When the Fifth Wallabies toured these shores in 1967, Ireland once more registered a win over a southern hemisphere giant. 'We managed to beat Australia in Dublin, and again out in Sydney in May. This was the first time Australia had been beaten by a northern hemisphere side in Australia – that was fairly special. In Dublin Mike [Gibson] dropped two goals, Dixie Duggan got the first of his eleven tries for Ireland and I managed to get a penalty goal. And I remember lining out for Munster four days later at Musgrave Park and beating them 11–8, so Irish rugby once more was on a bit of high going into the 1967 Five Nations.'

When sport and politics mix, it can sometimes become a dangerous and explosive combination. For example, when Kiernan played against the touring Boks in 1970, the game was marked by huge demonstrations outside the stadium. Then, in 1972, Ireland was scheduled to play England in Twickenham the week after the Bloody Sunday shootings in Derry.

'It was a strange time,' admits Kiernan. 'There was huge tension in the country at the time. I suspect people might have been under pressure in travelling to Twickenham in 1972. Fortunately, the Rugby Union and the people who ran it seemed to accept they could divorce rugby from what was going on around them.

'We travelled and won that match in the last play of the game which made it more pleasing. Kevin Flynn got the try. It was a dramatic finale: I remember he scored under the posts which meant we went one point ahead. As I was going to take the convert, I asked the referee, how much time was left and he said it was all over. I always regretted not putting the ball under my jersey and walking off without taking the convert: But, I never saw the ball again!'

Kiernan bade farewell to international rugby in Murrayfield in 1973. Scotland won a 19–15 thriller, thanks mainly to the boot of Douglas Miller, but not before Kiernan, Ireland's full-back, was awarded a dubious try after having been knocked into the corner post.

'I wouldn't say he was off the pitch,' said Tony O'Reilly, a spectator that day in Murrayfield, 'but I was sitting in the front row of the stand, and he went round outside me!'

One of Kiernan's last acts in an Irish jersey was to wave his right arm in the air to signal that the final Scottish drop at goal was good. It was farewell from a great player and a great captain.

His peers still rate him highly. 'As captain, he was very good, very solid and also very respected by the players,' admits his team-mate, Willie John McBride. 'He was a calming influence and always took the sensible attitude to things. He wouldn't expect impossible things from players and he was very much in favour of the fifteen-man game. He used to say, "We're all going to make mistakes so it's up to us to help each other", that sort of thing.'

To this day, he continues to have a close attachment to his beloved Cork Con, and makes it his business to attend all their home games at Temple Hill, and still admits to bouts of nervous tension when watching his beloved Munster.

However, since retiring, Kiernan's role in rugby union's development has been monumental. As a top administrator within the committee rooms of the IRFU, IRB and ERC, Kiernan's legacy will forever remain intact. He was a key figure when the game went 'open' in 1995. Along with Vernon Pugh, Kiernan helped co-found the ERC (European Rugby Cup) in 1995, the body which organises both the Heineken Cup and its sister competition, the Challenge Cup, cups that that have captured the imagination of the rugby public, especially in Ireland.

As a coach, he was at the helm when Munster defeated the All Blacks in 1978, and in his capacity as Ireland national team coach, guided his country to Triple Crown success for the first time in thirty-three years in 1982.

All in all, Kiernan remains a legend of the game, and one of greatest players to have ever graced Lansdowne Road.

Jack Kyle

Fly-Half

1947–1959

In the late 1940s and 1950s there was no one with whom the gathered crowd wanted to identify more than with a slim Ulster fly-half named Jack Kyle. A terrifcly gifted Number 10, Kyle was the consummate artist of his time and the poster boy of Ireland's golden generation between 1948 and 1951, and the inspiration during one of Irish rugby's most successful eras.

Those lucky enough to have seen Kyle play say some of his best attributes included his elusiveness, fleet-footedness and his judgement to touch when kicking out of hand. He was a linebreaker and a playmaker of the highest quality too, and though slightly built, packed a heavyweight tackle. He also had a knack of waiting for the right moment to pounce – when you expected him to kick, he passed, and when you expected him to pass, he kicked – and he had what Ronan O'Gara possesses today, a most astonishing diagonal kick.

It's said Jackie mightn't do too much for an hour, but genius, we know, strikes at the most unexpected and opportune times. Above all, records show that Kyle was the one reason Ireland were to the fore in world rugby during what are now termed, in reverence to the Belfast boy, the 'Jackie Kyle years'.

Lansdowne Road was not home to his most striking cameo in test rugby – that was at Ravenhill against France in 1953 where he took off on a thirty-yard mazy dash for the tryline, leaving six French defenders in his wake to touch down almost apologetically. *The Times* rugby writer A.A. Thomson wrote at the time: 'He has an extraordinary deceptive way of persuading opponents that he was about to do something wholly different from what in fact he did … if you hesitated, he would dart by like a trout in a pool and either score a dazzling try on his own or put in a curling, puzzling cross kick which one of his wingers would eventually touch down.'

Jack Kyle, the pale-faced, freckled, flame-haired, Queen's University medical student, made his debut at Lansdowne Road when Ireland played the first of its 'Victory Internationals' against England. On that day in 1946, nineteen-year-old Kyle introduced himself to the rugby world. Even the match programme that afternoon carried a biography of the teenager, stressing his strengths and burgeoning reputation. It read: 'The discovery of the season, John Wilson Kyle was on the Ulster Schools XV two years ago and proved himself to be in the top class by his great display for Ulster against the Kiwi Servicemen in November, subsequently confirming that form against the army. A particularly straight strong runner, he looks to have a brilliant future.'

Kyle remembers travelling to Dublin with the Ulster Schools team for an inter-provincial against Leinster in 1943. Not only was he chirpy about the prospect of visiting the Irish capital, but relished the chance of running out at Lansdowne Road. 'My earliest memory of Lansdowne Road is being picked at out-half to play for Ulster schoolboys against Leinster in 1943. It's hard to believe it now with the world of travel we have, but at that time I'd never been outside Ireland. I was about seventeen at the time. I think, as a child, I had been to Dublin with my mother and father at some stage when I was old enough to appreciate a major city. I remember getting brochures and reading all about what I should see in Dublin – Trinity College, *The Book of Kells* – but the excitement of being picked on an Ulster schoolboys side to play at Lansdowne Road topped it all. One of the perks of representative rugby was that when your school team [Belfast Royal Academy] photograph was taken, you wore your Ulster jersey so you stood out from the rest of the side.

'We travelled by train and we went to the hotel of Freddie Moran's father Pa Moran, up from Amiens Street [now Connolly] Station, and had a lunch there. Freddie Moran, who was a sprinter, played for Ireland many times before the outbreak of the Second World War. We played the game and won 16–3. My old headmaster at Belfast Royal Academy, Alex Foster, had played and captained Ireland in 1910, 1911 and 1912 – he had also gone with the Lions to South Africa in 1910 and had introduced rugby to the Royal Academy. Alex was a wonderful man and a great influence on many of us.'

The match programme may have introduced Kyle as the

player to look out for in the match against England in 1946 – the year of unofficial internationals when no caps were awarded – but Kyle picked up a serious foot injury that day and didn't play again for the rest of the season. Although he hoped to make a quick comeback, his return was halted by a doctor in Queen's who had attended the match and was aware of his injury. In hindsight, Kyle is thankful for his medical intervention.

'When I look back, I give thanks to that man who got hold of me. He was head of the fracture clinic and had been at the game and told somebody in the anatomy department that he wanted to see me.' Kyle arrived at the clinic in the hope of getting the plaster off, but the doctor had other ideas. '"What are you here for?" he said to me. I replied that I was here to get my plaster off. "How long is it on?" "Four weeks," I said. "I think the plaster needs strengthening! And come back then in four weeks' time!" Looking back, it was the best thing that ever happened to me because a lateral ligament tear can be worse than a fracture of the outside bone of the leg in that area of the foot. I strapped it up for a season or two and never had really any trouble with it after that.

'I remember that day in Lansdowne – and the injury – well. It happened to my right foot. Another player on the Irish side and I were both going for the ball at the same time and he took a dive and hit me in the ankle. I couldn't run anymore but you often didn't go off in those days. I went onto the wing, and hobbled around for the remainder of the game. It was the only time I ever played wing.'

But, thankfully, Kyle returned to Lansdowne in 1947 when Ireland defeated England 22–0 (a then record margin against the old enemy which stood until 2007, the evening Ireland beat England 43–13 at Croke Park).

'I remember it being a windy day in 1947. Con Murphy of Lansdowne, who had played with Ireland before the war, was captain and I think he was dropped after the game. We couldn't understand why – we won twenty-two points to nil after all! It was quite a good England side with Dickie Guest and Jack Heaton in their ranks. After beating England, we then overcame Scotland before losing 6–0 to Wales in Swansea in a Triple Crown match.'

Kyle could be quite a laid-back character and apocryphal tales abound of him arriving at training sessions with only one boot or of falling fast asleep on the bus before it pulled up outside the old Lansdowne Pavilion before internationals.

'Ahead of internationals, we took the train down to Dublin on the Friday morning, transferred to the Shelbourne Hotel where we lunched, and then had a run out in Trinity College or Bective. We'd then come back and usually have a team meeting. The training itself was always a casual affair. You didn't do too much because the match was the next day, while the team meetings were quite informal gatherings. You'd have the captain sitting on a table and everyone gathered around him. Usually, it was a case of, "Anyone have any ideas for tomorrow?" Compared with what the guys go with today...'

Then players were tied to a very strict amateur code. Even the jerseys they wore for internationals had to be returned after games. Kyle remembers a time when the players turned up in their club socks, Barbarian-like. There would be Jim Nelson in Malone's complete red socks, whilst Kyle wore the black, blue and green of Queen's. 'Later, the union decided they could afford to give us socks, but players still had to bring their own shorts and boots. The jersey had to be returned after a match. Dear old Billy Jeffers would be in the pavilion after the game saying, "Jersey, jersey!" But after the last game of the season, we were allowed to keep the jersey.

'The late Robin Thompson told me this story once. In the first game, we usually played France. He exchanged his jersey with a French guy, went into the pavilion, but who did he meet first but Jeffers. "Where's your jersey, pal?" "I exchanged it," said Robin. "Well, get it back. Quick." Robin says he was very keen to have it and said he would give him the cheque for it. "No," Jeffers went on, "that was meant to be the jersey for your position during the season." Robert then had to go to this French guy and ask him for the jersey back. The French guy wasn't at all pleased because he probably got a jersey for every game.'

Other rituals needed to be fulfilled too. 'We'd be called out before the game to have a photograph. There would be different photographers around and then we would get back into the pavilion again. We'd get a few words of encouragement from the captain before we ran out onto the ground to play the match. The one thing I liked about Lansdowne Road was I felt the turf had a certain spring about it compared with some other grounds which were heavy. Take the Mardyke, in Cork, for example, which could be flooded at times. Lansdowne, I think, drained very well.'

In 1947, fourteen new caps were introduced for the first official post-war international against France. There was a vibrancy to the Irish play, something, says Kyle, not too dissimilar to the jauntiness of the New Ireland that rang in the new millennium in February 2000 against Scotland.

Going into 1948, confidence was high in the Irish camp despite the Triple Crown loss to Wales the previous season. The season started with an international against the visiting

Australians in December 1947. There were eight new caps introduced, but Ireland shipped a heavy loss to the Wallabies – 16–3 – but then began a run of four matches that ended with Ireland's first Grand Slam.

At the centre of this team, steadfast, steady and unwavering was Jackie Kyle. As a stand-off, he was described as the ultimate improviser, the orchestrator-in-chief, who, with a shimmy of those hips, could create something out of nothing. 'What we reckoned was that the game of rugby was a game of spontaneity. When the chance is there, you had to take your opportunity. And as I mentioned to you, there was no game-plan – if you saw the gap, you went for it. Some days, you went out and you just couldn't see them. We'd have those days where you'd look, having to pass the ball out or kick the ball, you were well covered so you depended a lot on your scrum-half to give you a good pass, a pass that you could pick out of the air and keep going. The 9 and 10 combination was important. Like Johnny O'Meara who I played with for years. Because we didn't see each other very frequently, we would work out uncomplicated signals. When I met him, I'd say, "Nothing too complicated, Johnny. If I'm going to the right, I will tap my right leg and if I'm going left, I'll tap my left leg."'

Kyle distinguished himself against France in Stade Colombes in 1948, scored a try against England in Twickenham and notched another against Scotland at Lansdowne Road – and as it turned out the only score – in a 3–0 win. 'I remember running towards the old Lansdowne Road Pavilion where we togged out. I got one of those lovely passes outside the twenty-five [twenty-two today], one of those wee beauties that fall into your hands. Then a gap appeared in front of me and I was able to get through it. The timing was everything. If you take a three-quarter who can run a hundred yards in thirteen seconds – which isn't great – but if you get half a second, you've got four yards on your marker. Also a good pass makes all the difference between scoring a try and your marker catching you.'

In the Grand Slam match in Ravenhill, Ireland triumphed 6–3 – Barney Mullan and John Christopher Daly getting the tries but the legend of Kyle was growing by the day. Indeed, many went as far as to say that Kyle carried the Irish backline, which was reputed to be only able to defend well. 'I wouldn't agree with that at all,' argues Kyle, 'because you had Bertie O'Hanlon scoring tries, you had Barney Mullan scoring tries and Paddy Reid scoring tries.'

The 1948 squad have been wined and dined many a time since, and there's the old story of the two guys from the 1948 team coming out of Lansdowne Road after Ireland were going for another Grand Slam. One says to the other, 'That was a close shave – Ireland nearly won!' But Ireland's 2009 Grand Slam win has put that story to bed, and Kyle, for one, was delighted to see the current generation fulfil their potential with a stirring victory over Wales in Cardiff. Kyle travelled to the Welsh capital that day, and even made it down to the sidelines afterwards to shake Brian O'Driscoll's hand. A famous photo even captures that moment.

Kyle again inspired Ireland to a Triple Crown in 1949. There were no coaches in those days and teams often played without any clear strategy. 'Except once, against Wales in 1949 (we won that game 5–0 at Swansea), when we were going for another Triple Crown and I remember Karl Mullen saying to me, "Look, we're fitter than the Welsh guys and we don't want to be getting ourselves involved in mauls and battling it out. I want you to put the ball in the left side of the field and in the right side of the field." And we ran these guys all over the park and they were unable to get any ball. And that was where Karl was a very good captain – he was cute enough to see that things like that would work. I think that was the only time I remember us executing any kind of a game-plan in a test. Nobody ever said that I want you to do this or I want you to do that. Except when I heard Des O'Brien saying to me before a game at Lansdowne, "God Jackie, you haven't done very much recently – you better do something today!"'

As for the Lansdowne crowd, nothing stirred Kyle more then running out to be greeted by that famous roar. And he even admits to taking great pride in lining up for 'Amhrán na bhFiann'. 'When we lined up for national anthems, we turned to face the flag. There was never any problem doing that. We felt like guests of the country, if you like, though we were playing for Ireland. There was never the slightest bit of trouble – it was just an acknowledgement that here we were in Dublin. There was nothing mentioned about the politics of the time at all. I think it has been a great thing for Irish rugby, and we in Ulster were – and still are – very fortunate to play on an Irish side. It was a thrill to play for your whole country rather than, say, Northern Ireland – it would have been hard to get a side together if we'd had to.'

Ireland won another championship in 1951 and, two years later, Kyle took over as Ireland captain, a position he admits with which he was never comfortable. 'It should never have been me – I wasn't a captain at all. There are certain players who shouldn't be made captain, but I think I got it because of my length of service to the team.'

Kyle had been star of the British and Irish Lions tour of

New Zealand in 1950, and reacquainted himself with the touring All Blacks at Lansdowne in January 1954. In hindsight, he says, his decision to play against the wind in the first half impinged on a historic result against the visitors. 'When we played New Zealand that year, there was a wind blowing – which there nearly always is in Lansdowne Road. Anyway, I won the toss and I thought if we could hold these guys in the first half against the wind, maybe then with the wind we could do something in the second half. We'd be fresher too. But it didn't work out – we lost 14–3.

'It's very easy to be wise after the event. Nobody today would play against the wind if they won the toss, they'd probably say, "Take your advantage – you don't know what the wind is going to do for a start." Maybe it wasn't a good decision, but at the time, I thought it was the right one. I liked playing with disadvantage in the first half and maybe an advantage in the second. But I suppose captaincy didn't rest easy with me. I think it would have been far better to leave me alone and not have me thinking for the rest of the side!'

While All Black Bob Scott was effusive in his praise of Kyle during the Lions tour four years earlier, Kyle was equally impressed with the New Zealand full-back. Poetry in motion is an oft-used phrase to describe a wonderful athlete, but, Kyle says Scott had the full package. 'When I was in Auckland in 2005 for the Lions tour, I phoned him up and spoke to him. As we were reminiscing, I remember saying, "In our last game in Auckland (which we lost 11–8), you kicked a penalty, you dropped a goal and converted a New Zealand try. If it hadn't been for you, we would have probably won!"

'We drew the first Lions test and lost the other two fairly narrowly. Even in Lansdowne Road that day, Bob showed wonderful balance. You'd be running towards him and, suddenly, he'd move to the side. He was a very good kicker, too. Would you believe he used to practise kicking in his bare feet. I don't how he did it with the old leather ball, but he was one of the great full-backs of all time. He always had plenty of time to do things no matter what kind of pressure was on him, and you always felt he was going to get out of this. He had wonderful hands and was a terrific kicker. Ollie [Campbell] is in touch with him still and says he was very influenced by Bob Scott.'

A player Kyle remembers with great affection is Marney Cunningham, a blindside flanker who made his debut against France in 1955, but played his last game the following season against Wales at Lansdowne Road. 'They were going for the Triple Crown – Marney, our wing-forward, scored a try that day and, the next day, the paper said he was entering the priesthood much to everybody's surprise. Marney was the sort of guy you wouldn't have thought would have entered the priesthood – the real life is what goes on in here [pointing to head] rather than what you show off to the outside world. It turned out to be his farewell to international rugby.'

Much was written at the time about the fact that, in over forty internationals, Kyle hadn't scored a drop goal for his country. 'The only drop goal I ever dropped in international rugby was at Lansdowne Road and that was against Wales in 1956 when Wales were going for the Triple Crown. Marney got the try and Cecil Pedlow kicked a penalty. I see Cecil and he reminds me of that game occasionally. And the last time I was sitting beside George Hook at a function, he told me that he was out in Barbados and there was a fellow out there who says he was responsible for my dropping that goal at

Lansdowne! The Welsh full-back kicked the ball towards the East Stand and gathered it on the ten-metre line. I looked about frustrated and didn't know what to do. Apparently, this fellow said, "Have a wee shot, Jack?" Why not indeed, so I gave it a shot.'

Kyle remembers it sailing high from forty-five yards, bisecting the posts and the crowd going crazy. He had now done just about everything he could in a green jersey – but not quite. More glory was to follow with a win over Australia in January 1958.

'It was hard old game. The Aussies were expected to beat us and it was their first defeat at Lansdowne Road. Nick Shehadie hit Noel Murphy with a clout on Noel's debut. Afterwards, I heard Nick became Lord Mayor of Sydney. I remember Noel Henderson's try too. The ball came out along the backline, I think David Hewitt got it, gave it to Noel and Noel set off. Tony O'Reilly was outside him but Noel turned in.'

Everywhere he goes, Kyle is treated with unwavering reverence. He was perhaps Ireland's first superstar. Today, he gets his two international tickets for the Upper West Stand and usually goes with his son, Caleb – he has to pay for the tickets of course.

He is proud of today's generation. He looks at today's incumbents at Number 10, Ronan O'Gara and Jonathan Sexton, and sees players blessed with all the out-half's skills. 'You could play brilliantly at out-half and still lose a game. In the long run, that's the thing that counts. O'Gara, for example, has been very successful and that counts for a tremendous lot. Because, in many ways, the out-half has to direct the play. They used to say to us in the old days, "There's nothing a centre wants less than the ball at the same time the opposite centre hits him." Also an out-half has got to see where he should kick and what he should do with his own kicking abilities, drop goals and so on.'

Kyle did it all with poetic class – definitely deserving of the name genius.

Donal Lenihan

Lock

1981–1992

He was fourteen when he and a few school friends first travelled by train to Lansdowne Road to watch Ireland play an Overseas XV in September 1974. Donal Lenihan was giddy with the prospect of watching Irish players – Willie John McBride, Fergus Slattery, Mike Gibson and Tom Grace – who had morphed into legends after the most successful Lions tours ever in 1971 and 1974. These were the names that fascinated him most as a schoolboy while training at Lansdowne, Christian Brothers College's aptly named training ground in Cork city. Little did the teenage Donal realise that he would one day line out alongside some of these luminaries.

The South Terrace was his vantage point that afternoon

when Ireland drew 18–18, but the day is locked forever in his treasure chest of Lansdowne memories. And, in an era when pitch invasions were the norm, Lenihan couldn't resist the opportunity of squeezing his way through the throng and onto the hallowed turf. The young Lenihan was developing into a second-row of some renown at CBC, so he could really only identify with and be drawn to one man. 'I remember Willie John going off the field and I managed to run over and give him a tap on the back. That was the first time I ever got on the pitch at Lansdowne Road.'

Lenihan worked his way through the Ireland system and was capped at schools, under-23 and B levels before going on to earn his first cap at senior level against Australia in the autumn of 1981. He had become good friends with Trevor Ringland, who also won his first cap that day, through their University Colours games; Lenihan lining out for UCC and Ringland for Queen's.

He wasn't without other friends on the team that faced Australia when Brendan Foley stepped in for the injured Moss Keane to partner him in the second-row. It was a partnership that had helped beat Australia five days earlier when the duo lined out for Munster. 'It's funny but, in those days, it was almost sacrosanct that you didn't play the Saturday before your first cap,' says Lenihan. 'I played for Munster against Australia on the Tuesday before my first cap [against Australia]. We beat Australia in Musgrave Park and a few days after I was playing the same opposition. So, in some ways, it was nearly an anti-climax that you played Australia in a midweek match, before playing them again in your first international game on a Saturday. But in those days – and again it's telling how things have changed – it was felt that Australia was a good game to get a taste of international rugby before the Five Nations came around in January.' Instead, it turned out to be a good game for the Wallabies who won 16–12.

Lenihan's second cap came the following January against Wales in the Five Nations at Lansdowne Road. Moss Finn was also making his debut at a time when few Corkmen got on the Irish team. 'Moss got concussed that afternoon but still scored two tries in the game. David Irwin broke his leg and Michael Kiernan, another Cork man, came on for his first cap. The three of us would have been great buddies, so for all that to happen in the one game – apart from the concussion to Moss – was phenomenal. Ringland also scored that day, so it was a memorable game from that point of view.' It was an extraordinary day for the Irish who beat a much-vaunted Wales team, 20–12, but Lenihan's memories of the crowd's contribution to the occasion lived with him long afterwards. As a columnist with the *Irish Examiner*, he wrote after the Munster–Leinster European Cup semi-final at Lansdowne Road in 2006 that, while Leinster fans came to be entertained, Munster fans came to participate. That's how it felt, he believes, in Lansdowne Road twenty-five years earlier. The large Wales following, blessed with so much success, waited for the fireworks; the Irish fans instead played the veritable sixteenth man and, allied with a mammoth input from the forwards, the occasion was momentous for someone like Lenihan new on the Irish scene. 'Try scoring wasn't as prevalent as it is now, so for Ireland to score three tries against Wales was special and the crowd really got behind the team.'

During his early days as an international, Lenihan roomed with Moss Keane and, before his first cap, he remembers waking up in the Shelbourne Hotel to the sight of Keane eating three raw eggs! He says their room was like an alternative medicine centre but Moss played a huge role in helping Lenihan through his first cap. 'I'd played with Moss for Munster for about a year beforehand, and we went on to play on the Irish team together for three years. We always seemed to end up rooming together. I've always said that if you survived the Thursday and Friday with Moss before a match, the game was a piece of cake! 'Moss would have around six eggs wrapped up in newspaper. He was definitely ahead of his time in terms of nutrition!

'After missing the Australia game, Moss came back for the championship and I held on to my place. He was coming to the end of his career so he allowed me to dictate the lineout on the premise that I would pick up their best man on their throw. So it worked in his favour as well! Moss would be thinking, "Leave the younger fellow [me] off", but we had a great relationship. He is eleven years older than me, and he used get great fun out of the pack being called "Dad's Army" because I had just turned twenty-two. He used tell everyone that the average age of the second-row was less than the average age of the half-backs.'

Away from the madding crowd and the buzz of match days, masochistic mornings were spent on the two pitches behind the East Stand at Lansdowne in preparation for the Five Nations. Looking back now, the memory of those sessions on the back pitch puts a shiver up Lenihan's spine, but he was thankful in the end for the thorough preparation. 'For those of us who trained there every Sunday morning before inter-nationals, we've horrific memories of being slaved to death on the back pitch. Half of the sessions were physical ones where you were run to death. While the glory part of the Five Nations is out on the main pitch, they say there are other parts of the Lansdowne complex where fellows would have a lot of shocking memories of endless training sessions!'

Normally, training didn't draw in big crowds, maybe a few curious observers, but the hype generated ahead of Triple Crown deciders in 1982 and 1985 swelled attendances on the Sunday mornings. 'You might have 1,000 people who'd turn up on a Sunday morning to watch you training. We trained in Merrion Road before we played Scotland for the Triple Crown in 1982 and Tommy Kiernan was running the legs off us the Sunday before Saturday's game. I always remember Willie Duggan going up to him saying, "Tommy, unless you want me to get sick in front of 1,000 people you better stop doing this training fairly quickly."'

Scrummaging in those days was 'live' and unmerciful, says Lenihan. The absence of scrumming machines meant facing the daunting prospect of eight against eight in full combat. To the players, it resembled the closest definition of sadism, with onlookers seemingly taking pleasure in the combatants' pain. Lenihan recalls a morning when 500 people gathered in a circle watching Ireland going backwards and forwards in the scrum. These sessions would be ultra-competitive, as players would do anything to get ahead of another for a place in the pack on match day.

'Players would be getting pent-up; they'd be playing for their places. I remember one famous incident in 1982 before Ireland won the Triple Crown. Ginger McLoughlin was the only forward who got dropped and Mick Fitzpatrick from Leinster came in at tight head. But we had one of those full-on scrummaging training sessions. Ginger was at loose head opposite Fitzpatrick; Brendan Foley was in the second-row behind Ginger and Colm Tucker was wing-forward. Fitzpatrick twisted in the scrum. The boys saw their opportunity and just drove right through it. Fitzpatrick destroyed his groin, Ginger got back into the team, held his place and we won the Triple Crown.'

Lenihan believes there is no stadium in the world where fans get closer to the players than at Lansdowne Road. As a youngster, he said he could literally smell the Wintergreen rub. He does, however, feel that the 'Lansdowne Roar' diminished into a squeal during the Celtic tiger era.

There was no better demonstration of this than Ireland's first Six Nations game against Italy in 2006. It was a one thirty kick-off and, when the players arrived out on the field seven minutes before kick-off, the East Stand was half empty and Lenihan, working for RTÉ Radio, empathised with the players who were greeted by the sound of hollow clapping and the sight of many, many empty bucket seats. 'As a player you're so pumped up before hand. Then you come out on the field and you're looking at an empty stand. That would never have happened in the old days – people would be in their seats forty-five minutes before the game started.

'I think the crowds have changed in the past twenty-five years, the corporate element has come into it. 'Cockles and Mussels' was the song most synonymous with Lansdowne Road. I'll always remember the 1982 game against Scotland. We were playing for the Triple Crown and there was so much hype because Ireland hadn't won it in thirty-two years. With ten to fifteen minutes to go it was obvious Ireland were going to win the game, and there was a constant strain of 'Cockles and Mussels' for ten minutes. I remember a twenty-two dropout for Ireland. The noise was so intense at that stage, an almost celebration that you were going to win something that hadn't been achieved for so long. Fergus Slattery had been on the team for twelve years at that stage and I remember just looking across – I was only a young fellow, my first year, my fifth cap – and catching Slattery's eye. He smiled as if to say, "Don't worry, lad, we have it won."'

There were many leaders in the Ireland dressing room, none more so than Willie Duggan, Slattery and Ciaran Fitzgerald whom Lenihan describes as 'real men'. He remembers going to the toilet ten minutes before kick off and seeing a trail of smoke snake over the top of one of the cubicles. It was Willie Duggan having the obligatory pre-match cigarette. 'That was sacrosanct, that was part of Willie's preparation.'

In 1985, Lenihan won his second Triple Crown and the build-up to Michael Kiernan's match-winning drop goal has gone down in folklore as a 'Cork' score. 'We were 10–10 with about four minutes to go. Michael Bradley, myself and Kiernan were involved. However Brian Spillane, a Kerryman, won the ball in the lineout but he was based in Cork at the time. I took it up the middle, Bradley fed Kiernan and Kiernan would have been shot if he didn't land the drop goal because we had a three to one overlap! I was in an unusual position under on the sticks on my back. And as the ball was going over the bar my hands were up in the air. It looked a bit embarrassing.'

The crowd invasions prevalent in the amateur era at Lansdowne, deprived the team a lap of honour. However, some players placed themselves some distance from the players' tunnel to allow themselves to indulge in a little glory on the final whistle.

'Hugo MacNeill was a great man to land himself in the far corner, so he always got shouldered off, whereas all the dopey fellows like myself ran off quickly! That's why he's pictured up on people's shoulders in some famous post-match photographs. I suppose he didn't have the pace like the rest of us to get out of there! At least players today have an opportunity to savour a victory.'

This was Mick Doyle's team, full of invention and running, and with Paul Dean, at out-half, the coach had someone who could execute a game-plan. Doyler's methods carried plenty scepticism and sometimes mockery from across the water, though. When Will Greenwood's father said that 'the nation would need a brain transplant for Ireland to play running rugby', the Irish players needed little more motivation for the England game, the first scheduled fixture in their Five Nations itinerary.

However, all that anger had to be in cold storage as the game was postponed because of a snowed-over Lansdowne, and pushed to the tail-end of the championship. But, following wins over Wales and Scotland, an intriguing Triple Crown face-off for the final game was set up. 'Certainly, in 1985 when we won the Triple Crown, we played superb rugby right up to that England game. I remember it lashed rain about an hour before kick-off and we had to change tactics in everything we did. In fairness to Doyle, that Irish backline was every bit as skilful as the backline that is there now. Dean was a gem at 10. Maybe he wasn't a great kicking out-half, but he had fantastic vision and superb hands.'

One of the Lenihan's proudest moments as captain came when Ireland beat the same opposition – 17–0 – in 1987. 'We destroyed them up front,' he says. 'It was another wet day, but the pack did the business. You don't often beat England 17–0.'

Lenihan continued to excel in his own position even if the

glory years of 1982 and 1985 were never replicated during the rest of his playing career. Before the 1991 Rugby World Cup, however, Lenihan accepted that the clock was ticking on his career ('There were bits and pieces falling off me at that stage!') and he was on a personal mission to help put Ireland back amongst the top nations of the world.

After qualifying from their pool, Ireland drew Australia in what became a memorable quarter-final at Lansdowne Road and, as Lenihan recalls, the noise level that afternoon was quite phenomenal. As the match wore on, Ireland's belief grew, and the Wallabies, pre-tournament favourites, were staring down the barrel of a shock defeat when Gordon Hamilton scored a try with only minutes left. The impossible seemed possible, but Lenihan says he'll never forget the silence around him when Michael Lynagh scored the winning try late in the game. 'My sister was at the game, and she said afterwards that she has never seen me so crestfallen after a match. Some of the younger guys were saying, "Didn't we play great?", whereas I knew we were within minutes of a home semi-final against the All Blacks, who it must be said weren't going great. Australia hammered them the following week.

'I nearly had to be held back in the dressing room because one of the new younger players wanted to swap his tracksuit with one of the Australians. I was at the other end of the experience spectrum to the younger fellows who had played Australia for the first time. I had played against them seven or eight times at that stage. Beat them in a Munster jersey, was close a few times with Ireland but never beat them in an Irish jersey. Australia were an outstanding side in 1991 and they went on to win the World Cup.

'On a lighter note, I remember a story about Nick Farr-

Jones' wife, who'd just arrived from Australia. They had a young baby and they were in before the game under the stand looking for the crèche facilities. I had to laugh. As players, we barely had showers!'

Following his playing career, Lenihan moved into management and later a successful media career where his opinions on the game are hugely respected. He wore the team manager's hat when a new era of Irish rugby beckoned following a demolition job on the Scots in Lansdowne Road in 2000. That game came hot on the heels of a thumping at Twickenham but, after ten minutes against the Scots, Ireland trailed their Celtic cousins 10–0. Then, almost in a twinkle of an eye, everything changed with new caps Peter Stringer, Ronan O'Gara, Shane Horgan, John Hayes and Simon Easterby, helping 'Young Ireland' to a 44–22 victory. 'Before the Scotland game, Warren [Gatland] had said that he was going to step down if we lost. Young fellows have no inhibitions, you see, and that's why if they're good enough, they have to be given the opportunity.'

Lenihan's one hope, following the demolition of the old Lansdowne, is that the new Aviva can retain the intimacy that made the old stadium so unique in world rugby. Having toured the new Aviva, he hasn't been left disappointed. 'When comparing the old Lansdowne Road to the new Lansdowne Road – there was an intimidatory factor there in the old one which you tend to lose in new stadia. Thankfully, that seems to have been retained in the new design.

'Because the old Lansdowne was different to everywhere else, even visiting teams liked it, but found the place intimidating when the crowd got behind the Irish. Yet, the one thing that put visitors off even more than Ireland was the wind conditions, particularly for kickers. In our time, our plan of action usually revolved around getting into teams, playing with heart and passion and soul, and the conditions probably suited us. In latter years, however, with the improved quality in Irish play, the conditions can be a hindrance to them.'

Michael Lynagh

Out-Half, Australia

1984–1995

In 1984, Michael Lynagh arrived in Ireland, twenty-one years old and poised to make his mark in this part of the world. Already earning rave reviews back home in Queensland, where since the age of eighteen he had occupied the Number 10 jersey, here was an aspiring star on a tour of Ireland and the UK and part of what is regarded as the greatest Wallaby side of all time. They were the Eighth Wallabies and became the first, and to date only, Australian side to win all four tests on a Grand Slam tour.

'Noddy' Lynagh, as his team-mates nicknamed him, went on to become one of the world's greatest out-halves, a self-appointed kicking machine (at one time he held the record as top points scorer in major internationals with 911), and on his first tour on these islands, Lynagh amassed ninety-eight points in eleven games.

He was proud to have played, however fleetingly, alongside the great Mark Ella, who, at the end of that 1984 season, stepped down from international rugby. The king may have retired prematurely but the rising prince was readying himself to take the throne of his idol.

Meanwhile, Australian management approached the 1984 test against Ireland annoyed and frustrated at developments off the field. Twenty-four hours before the third leg of their Grand Slam tour, a three-man disciplinary committee handed hooker, Mark McBain, a two-week suspension after an incident that arose in the England game. Coach Alan Jones discovered McBain in tears when news reached the team hotel. The three-man committee found McBain and Peter Wheeler guilty of fighting and, at the time, it evoked a strong reaction from Jones. 'Both players deny the charges and say they did not hit each other,' argued Jones at the time. 'Mark is in tears tonight and I must say I weep for him, too.'

The incident overshadowed the build-up to the game; this bombshell dropped so close to an international test only further ignited the Aussies' desire to put Ireland to the sword.

Ireland, meanwhile, had come out of a Five Nations white-wash with bruised reputations and were badly in need of a lift of some kind. Enter the Messiah, aka Mick Doyle. The arrival of Doyler and his promise of an exciting and brash style of attacking rugby philosophy reinvigorated Irish hopes. The Currow coach's mantra was simple: run the ball at every opportunity, though he also had a set of forwards capable of combating Australia up front.

And this is what Lynagh discovered in his first match at Lansdowne Road – an ultra-committed Irish side with Doyle's give-it-a-lash philosophy written all over their game. Lynagh saw a commitment in the tackle area, and remembers Donal Lenihan and Willie Anderson giving the three Steves of Australia – Williams, Cutler and Tuynman – a horrible time in the lineout.

Only in the scrummaging did Australia prove more powerful while, behind their front eight, they possessed a backline of all talents, which mesmerised the four home unions throughout the tour. And that proved the difference in their 9–16 win over the Irish.

Lynagh lined out at first centre; and inside him stood the mercurial Mark Ella, who directed play as any good out-half should, scoring a try and two sweet drop goals over the eighty minutes. It was an even first half and only a Lynagh drop goal separated the sides at the interval. Lynagh vividly remembers the only try of the game. 'Mark [Ella] had levelled matters with a marvellous drop goal and I think we upped our game after that and played with more confidence. I was able to break through the Irish cover, which had been fairly difficult to break down all afternoon. I laid off to Matt Burke, but Michael Kiernan came across to tackle him. Earlier Kiernan did brilliantly to deny Campese a certain try but Burkey, despite being dragged to the ground, did well to lay off to Mark who ran in for the try. We won 9–16 but, as we expected, we got a bit of a battle from the Irish. From memory, I didn't kick particularly well that day but we scored a nice try. Ireland were always really tough at Lansdowne Road. Still, I was disappointed with the kicking side of my game, which might have made the victory a little more comfortable than it was.'

Australia did create multiple try-scoring opportunities, but Ireland's fervour and brashness kept the final scoreline decent and their reputations intact. It also proved a baptism of fire for twenty-year-old Trinity student, Brendan Mullin, who lined up opposite Lynagh in his first full Ireland international.

Australia's next visit to Lansdowne Road was for a World Cup quarter-final on 20 October 1991 with Nick Farr-Jones' assertion that it would be 'a tragedy if Australia were to lose against Ireland' ringing in their ears. Coach Bob Dwyer added further pressure to the mix saying Australia hadn't reached their potential as a team even after successful summer victories over England, Wales and New Zealand.

If there was a growing sense of trepidation in the Aussie ranks, Ireland talked up their chances with captain Philip Matthews viewing the match as the perfect opportunity to do for Irish rugby what Jack Charlton's soccer team had done for soccer in Italia '90. He even went as far as to say Ireland would beat the Wallabies.

The heady old Irish ingredients of passion and pride were on full view that afternoon, the forwards giving it welly up front, while Ralph Keyes enjoyed arguably his best day in the Irish out-half shirt. But Australia's backline oozed class in a team that included top performers in David Campese, Lynagh, Farr-Jones and Tim Horan.

It might seem a little thing to spectators, but the playing of your country's national anthem is a great time to get the adrenalin moving. That day, the band forgot to play 'Advance Australia Fair' and the sight of the Wallabies looking around wondering what they had done to deserve such treatment must have left them thinking the gods had conspired against them. To them, it was the ultimate slight, and whether it was because of the early kick-off (one o'clock) or the seriousness of the occasion, the players tore into each other – literally – from the kick-off. Philip Matthews landed an uppercut on Willie Ofahengaue, then Neil Francis joined in before Ofahengaue smacked Nick Popplewell in the head. Lynagh maintains the anthem controversy and the sight of the Irish picking a fight only strengthened their own resolve. 'Phil Matthews set out to hit Ofahengaue from the kick off and that seemed to stir our boys up. As the game wore on, I don't think we were surprised by the Irish resistance at all. We knew a lot of their players and we knew the game would be fairly tough.'

The Wallabies had started in a fashion Ireland supporters had feared – a relentless phase of attacks and an early try courtesy of the dashing David Campese who scorched forty yards under the posts. You could sense then, by the silence of the crowd, that thoughts to the effect, "Oh no, not another trouncing", were running through their minds. It seemed Ireland would capitulate but that wasn't the case in a some-times bizarre but uplifting afternoon in Dublin 4. Ralph Keyes kept Ireland in touch but Campese struck another hammer blow when he notched his second try in the second half. Ireland refused to buckle and courageously – and then quite unbelievably – were within sight of a World Cup semi-final when Staples and Jack Clarke combined to put Gordon Hamilton through for a try in the West Stand/Havelock Square corner. Lansdowne erupted. Keyes followed up with an immaculately struck touchline conversion. It was dream stuff.

Ireland 18 Australia 15: it would have made some final score-line and, with four minutes left on the clock, all that was left for Ireland to do was hold on to the ball. Even Nick Farr-Jones' pre-match fears of an impending 'tragedy' were beginning to unfold. 'We got fairly comfortable with the way we were going in the game – made a lot of breaks, missed a few opportunities, scored some tries,' says Lynagh. 'It was Ralph Keyes who kept the Irish ticking over.'

Australia were three points down with four minutes left but, in typical southern hemisphere style, refused to panic. How often had Lansdowne Road witnessed the clinical side of southern hemisphere opposition in moments like these? The Wallabies worked their way down field and, created the try that crushed Irish hopes of a massive scalp. Rugby would have to wait another day to steal children's imagination, fused at that time to Jack Charlton's soccer team. 'You look up at the scoreboard and there was only a few points between the sides at any stage,' says Lynagh. 'It's a strange sort of thing to be saying, but we always felt that we were in control of the match. However, with four minutes to go, we weren't. Of course, we were particularly concerned at that stage. But if you start worrying about the game being over, you can't focus on what you need to be focusing on, and that's actually scoring points to win. We didn't really think of the negatives as such, but more, "How do we get out of this and win the game?" – and that's what we ended up doing.'

Lynagh, the acting captain after Farr-Jones departed through injury, calmly assembled the players and said, 'Guys, we will kick long, we will go for the field possession and we will win possession. If you get caught with possession, just keep on driving towards the Irish line, hang on to it, we'll get a scrum and we can win.'

Lynagh was at the beginning and at the end of what proved to be the match-winning try. Having initiated the move from a scrum outside the twenty-two, the ball was briskly moved to

Campese, who scampered for the corner. Brendan Mullin tackled him, but the mercurial winger managed to off load to Lynagh who had looped around the three-quarter line before diving for the corner. 'It was a particular play that we practised a lot at training, and we had done it a few games previously. We devised it around the star of the Irish defence, Mullin. We had practised it a lot, so under a stressful situation we decided to use it again and, thankfully, it paid off. It's a good example of showing that when you come up with a plan, you practise it and under pressure it seems to work.'

Lynagh thought about a drop goal but trusted his instincts and went for the try. 'I was unaware that had we kicked a drop goal it meant that we would win the game through try-count. I thought, "Let's go and win the game", and so I spurned the opportunity to kick for a drop goal and got the try instead. Who is to say I would have got the drop goal anyway? Those last four minutes were my best moments because I was captain and to be able to turn potential disaster into a win felt good in that role. And also, I think from that moment, we felt within the team that we were a unit that could do things, which we saw the following week against the All Blacks. I do feel that those four minutes against Ireland after Hamilton scored were a real crucial turning point for us in that particular tournament. That gave us a lot of confidence. Before that, we played OK in bits and pieces, but we hadn't really worked together – we were threatening to do it and, when we needed to, we went up that extra gear. I think that really defined that 1991 team as a successful unit. That was the moment that really defined us.'

Australia coach Bob Dwyer paid tribute to his backline afterwards, admitting it was their best performance all year but, sitting in the West Stand that afternoon, he said that he found it difficult to conceal his nerves as his legs turned to jelly, 'We talked all week about how tough it would be,' said Dwyer soon afterwards, 'but it was even worse. My knees have still not stopped shaking and I suspect only a shot of Irish whiskey will have the desired effect.'

The Aussies hired a PR company to handle their dealings with the media during the 1991 World Cup, a move that proved a wonderful success with plenty of access to their camp. Their openness and refreshing insights filled up many a journalist's jotter and, certainly, four days before their World Cup semi-final against the All Blacks, the Wallabies won over the assembled press corps with their amicable manner.

All that contrasted with the All Blacks' guarded responses in the lead up to one of the biggest matches ever played at Lansdowne Road – a Rugby World Cup semi-final.

If Dwyer's comment about needing Irish whiskey to steady the nerves was refreshing, consider the words of his flanker Simon Poidevin who, to that point in his career, had played Ireland on four occasions. He created a ripple of laughter when he described the Irish team as 'a collection of lunatics – very skilled lunatics – running around at speed' but, on a more serious note, placed Keyes' performance on a par with Ollie Campbell as a kicker.

As for the RWC semi-final, it wasn't every day Lansdowne Road got to host two of the southern hemisphere's heavyweights in a knockout competition, but seven days after Ireland caused more than a tremor in world rugby, the tournament's joint-favourites, New Zealand and Australia, descended on IRFU headquarters.

It turned out to be a great tie, with the likes of Lynagh and Campese, starring. The All Blacks, despite losing, still brought their own sense of mystique, vigour and style to the occasion and, as their captain Gary Whetton said afterwards, 'at least we bow out in style'.

'I think it was definitely our best game of the World Cup, particularly in the first half in terms of attacking opportunities,' says Lynagh of their 16–6 win, 'and, in terms of creating opportunities, it was outstanding.'

New Zealand's preparations were thrown into disarray when their Number 7, Michael 'Iceman' Jones, refused to play on a Sunday on religious grounds – the greatest flank-forward in the world missed the biggest game of his career. In his place, came Auckland flanker Mark Carter, though Jones' stance didn't provoke any hostility from fans mainly because of his legendary status. Hopes of a second successive final appearance for the All Blacks ebbed farther away, in the build-up when news that full-back Terry Wright was out through injury.

As for the game, Australia produced the tournament's most compelling display of attacking rugby in the opening half. It was simply brilliant stuff. Campese didn't take long to set Lansdowne alight once again – his hitch-kick had become part of an amazing repertoire of moves for beating defences. The hitch-kick saw him first jog and tease and then suddenly there was a one-and-a-half, then a two-and-a-half-step with one leg rising high in front of him and he was gone. His local Queanbeyan newspaper in New South Wales called it 'Campese's struggletown shuffle'. As he himself famously said, 'My mind doesn't know where my legs are taking me.' But Campese had more than one string to his mellifluous bow – a great runner and a devastating finisher as well, he gave Lansdowne more than his share of great moments. Michael Lynagh adds, 'One of the great joys of Campese's play is that he never knows what he's going to do next, so neither does the opposition!' Campese broke Irish, and subsequently All Black, hearts and went as far as saying during the tournament that he likes to play in the northern hemisphere away from the pressure and the criticism he came in for Down Under.

'I thought our first half was one of the best forty minutes that I have been involved in,' continues Lynagh. 'The second half showed that as a team we had a number of ways of winning games. We could score tries, we could kick, had a good forward pack and then we could also defend if we had to without the ball because New Zealand had most of the ball in the second half. Particularly in the first forty, every time we got ourselves into a position, we really did make it count. Look at the plays we scored from – Timmy Horan's try and David's try. They weren't planned moves. We were playing off the cuff, just reacting to one another and the opposition in front and, I think, that's what showed in what was a pretty special outfit.'

Campese's first try will never be forgotten. After Lynagh set up a ruck in midfield, Campese came off his right-wing position and took off on a diagonal line across field with a host of New Zealanders following him before squeezing in at the Lansdowne Road corner. Certainly, a try you couldn't teach. 'If anybody thought it was a pre-planned move for me to go up to the opposition and take on the All Black back-row, I wouldn't have agreed to do it to start with. That's where the ball came out, I saw a bit of space and off I went. Campo came back from the right wing and took the pass.'

Lynagh kicked a penalty after thirteen minutes and, six minutes before half-time, was central to Australia's second try. He chipped through for Campese who neatly gathered and then picked out Tim Horan with a deft pass.

New Zealand tried valiantly for a try of their own, but it never materialised. However, they did deliver on their reputation as a skilful, ball-carrying team capable of fifteen-man rugby. But the Australian defence survived a series of assaults on their lines. It was heroic stuff from the Wallabies proving they could mix the champagne rugby with a huge work ethic. The world champions never opened them and the All Blacks' only reward were two Grant Fox penalties.

'In the second half, we had to defend and we did. We probably knew – and no disrespect to the English – that this was the final. Both the Australians and the New Zealanders knew that, whoever won that game would go into the final as strong favourites, given that New Zealand had already beaten England in the first game of the tournament. I felt there was a lot of leadership out on the pitch that day – it wasn't just Nick and myself. There were a lot of guys out there that Bob actually picked to do a job and they delivered. I really think that was key; there was a bit of maturity within the team and some youthful enthusiasm as well. It was a very happy World Cup odyssey. I thought it was a particularly good time in Australian rugby. The team, the guys I played in that period were outstanding but I played in a period over fifteen years with a lot of guys and a lot of different oppositions.

'We knew how good the All Blacks were and how good they were back then. And a win against the All Blacks is a momentous occasion and we hadn't had a lot of wins over them in the previous few years. We did beat them in 1990 and then during the summer [1991], and that gave us confidence going into the World Cup semi-final. It definitely was a cause for celebration because they were such a good team. To beat them at Lansdowne and play so well was just terrific.'

Interestingly, New Zealand assistant coach John Hart went on record hoping Australia would go on and win the World Cup because of the style of play they employed. England were criticised in many quarters for their dour, conservative tactics. In the end, beauty won over the beast as Australia beat England in Twickenham.

When Australia returned to Lansdowne Road just over twelve months later, the hopes of Ireland replicating their World Cup heroics never manifested themselves. The Wallabies were simply irresistible though Lynagh, who captained the tourists on the 1992 tour, departed the game with an injury with twenty minutes left on the clock. He was on long enough, however, to mastermind the try of the match in the first half: another chip through and beautiful hands from Campese, Ofahengaue and Kearns to put Jason Little through.

The Wallabies proved they were real world champions coasting to 17–42 victory; Campese scoring again at his favourite ground to bring his tally to fifty-one international tries. 'I went off with a dislocated shoulder,' recalls Lynagh. 'I had tackled somebody on the ground, he passed the ball and whoever it was tried to jump over me, I put my arm up and grabbed his leg and he took my arm with him and took the shoulder out of its joint. So that was the end of my tour. It was the first time I went off in a test.'

Every time he returned to Lansdowne as either spectator or, latterly, as a Sky Sports pundit, he was consistently reminded of the day he broke Irish hearts with his match-winning try in 1991. 'Sometimes, if you are in a hurry home, it's a bit difficult. After the European Cup semi-final [Munster v. Leinster] in 2006, I was in a hurry to catch a plane. Unfortunately, I wasn't staying the evening but it was a bit hard to get out of the place. The Irish kept reminding me of 1991 and saying, "I'll never forgive you for that."'

Willie John McBride

Lock Forward

1962–1975

Few players embodied the spirit of Irish rugby more than Ulster's Willie John McBride. Raised by his mother on a little farm in County Antrim – his father died when he was four – McBride did not take up rugby until the age of seventeen, but his achievements for country and for the Lions have gone down in folklore. He won sixty-three caps for Ireland from his debut against England in 1962 to an emotional farewell test against Wales in 1975, and played a record seventeen tests for the Lions with whom he toured an incredible five times. Undoubtedly, the highlight of his career was captaining the Lions on their famous unbeaten tour of South Africa in 1974.

One of his earliest Lansdowne memories came against the

famed New Zealand All Blacks in 1963, a side he describes as probably the best in the world at the time, an unbelievably good series of teams filled with strong men, physically and mentally, who possessed tremendous skills. While McBride frankly admits that the Ireland of the 1960s didn't have fifteen players of international standard, it still wasn't a bad side peopled by the likes of captain Bill Mulcahy, Ray McLoughlin, Ronnie Dawson and Tom Kiernan, players McBride says 'wouldn't be cowed or frightened by the sight of the All Black jerseys lining up opposite the Haka'.

McBride, aged just twenty-two, came up opposite Colin Meads, aka 'Pinetree', New Zealand's celebrated (and no-nonsense) second-row forward. It was on this Lansdowne day, McBride admits, when he became a man on the rugby field – and he has the story to back up this assertion. 'I was the tallest forward in the Irish pack and was inevitably seen as the main source of lineout possession. The New Zealanders had obviously come to the same conclusion. And so the nonsense began! I went up for an early lineout ball and was pushed out of the line. We played on and came to another lineout and the same thing happened, so when I got to my feet, I had already decided I wasn't going to put up with this for eighty minutes. At the next lineout, I arranged for our lineout thrower to call for me and prepared as though the ball was coming straight for me. It did, but I didn't jump. Didn't move a foot off the ground, as a matter of fact, but what I did do as the New Zealander opposite me jumped for the ball was swing my whole body around to face him, leading the movement with my fist. It struck him deep in the solar plexus as he was in the air, catching the ball.

'There was a deep groan and the player sank to the ground.

He went down so fast that he made the *Titanic* look tardy by comparison. The next thing our captain, Bill Mulcahy, said to me, "Jaysus, McBride, d'you realise who you just hit?" "I don't know but I'm not having that treatment at every lineout," I said. Mulcahy replied, "Christ, you hit Meads – now there's going to be trouble."

'Anyway Meads was helped to his feet and he was groaning and holding his rib area. He wasn't very well. Mulcahy's advice was, "Just be careful for a minute or two." Within those couple of minutes there was a ruck, and to this day I don't know who or what hit me, but I got it, smack full in the face and I was dazed. I went down and I knew why I had got it. But I got up and I survived. When it came to the next lineout, no one pushed me out of the line and I won our ball.'

When Ireland went 5–0 up thanks to a Johnny Fortune try, converted by Tom Kiernan, McBride remembers the excitement inside the stadium growing volubly. Though Kel Tremain got a try for the All Blacks to make it 5–3, McBride believes the visitors were struggling to get a grip of the Irish. Was one of the biggest upsets in world rugby history about to take place in Dublin 4? McBride believes it was. 'We had reacted as Irish sides can: the dog in us had emerged, the sheer refusal to lie down and accept the inevitable was obvious.'

But midway through the second half, New Zealand were awarded a penalty from a long way out and Don Clarke, the All Blacks champion goal kicker, lined up a penalty attempt. 'Everyone sensed that if he kicked it, New Zealand would win,' says McBride, 'but if he missed, victory was ours. I was standing near to where he placed the ball and studied him very closely. Lansdowne went silent. Don was a big man, heavily built with large feet. He was no great player, but his kicking, out of hand or to goal, was phenomenal. He approached the ball for his kick at goal and the ball flew off his feet like an Exocet missile. When I saw it soar away, I sensed it would go over. Which it did, and New Zealand went on to win the game 6–5. One of the biggest upsets in world rugby history had been averted, but it was an injustice, because we had given everything.'

Though they had their jostles on the field that day in 1963, both McBride and Meads went on to forge a strong friendship that has remained to this day. 'From that day in Lansdowne, I never had another problem with him and we had some tremendous battles against each other. The All Blacks were hard, competitive but, above all, fair. Colin was one of those players whom I called an honest-to-God rugby man; no matter how hard you hit him, knocked him down or whatever, he was always back up and in your face again. I loved that sort of player. Give me eight of that type of person and my team would beat the world.'

Tough, gnarled, no-nonsense forwards also came in the guise of the French, and McBride has some tales to tell of his first meeting with *Les bleus* in Lansdowne. It was January 1963, and McBride was winning only his fifth cap. Even his tales from the sanctity of the dressing room merit a mention. 'I remember we trooped into this old wooden shack in a corner of Lansdowne Road where the teams used to change. That hour in an Irish dressing room was unbelievable. There were guys knocking their heads against the wall, while others were kicking at benches and doors and working themselves up into a right old frenzy. I'd never seen anything like it. Someone else was running around, saying to anyone who'd listen, "Has anyone got a spare lace?" It was all highly professional, seriously thought-out preparation for the main event!

'Those were the days when you provided everything yourself apart from the jersey that the Irish Rugby Football Union gave you for the game, so there were guys polishing their boots, putting studs in and smearing Vaseline across their faces to try and look as fit as possible. There was a wee little guy called Charlie McCorry and he was jack of all trades. If you needed a sponge, a wrench to change your studs, a new lace or whatever, he had everything. Well, the referee knocked on our door about ten minutes before kick-off, wanting to look at our studs. However, someone shouted, "Don't let the bastard in", so the ref banging on the door added to the racket and, quite honestly, I couldn't wait to get out of that hell hole. I reckoned the French would be a piece of cake after surviving in that lunatic asylum for the past hour!'

However, despite being well psyched up beforehand, the French met fire with fire. McBride remembers one of the first scrums from which all hell broke loose. 'We crashed into each other – French arms were grappling with Irish shoulders and vice versa. Then there was the explosion, as if someone had just tossed a can of petrol in the midst of this sweating collection of humanity and thrown a match in after it. The whole thing went up   Irish fists crashed into French chins; sometimes Irish fists crashed mistakenly into Irish chins. French fingers searched out Irish eyes to gouge … there was widespread shoeing … and then there was the verbal abuse. "Ah, yer a feckin' French pig," can just about be heard above a stream of Gallic invective, which I don't think is enquiring as to the health of our dear mothers back home!

'I remember after another scene of chaos, Bill Mulcahy was lifting two French forwards off Syd Millar. "What's the matter, Syd?" asks Mulcahy. "That bastard's bitten me on the arm," was the response. Bill's advice is a key point. "Now, Syd, when we go into the next scrum, get hold of yer man's ear and give it a bite." Millar looked shattered at this pearl of wisdom. Here he was, a proud rugby man of Ireland, and he's been humiliated by this Frenchman, biting his arm and pinning him on the ground at Lansdowne Road in front of 50,000 of his fellow countrymen. Millar then looked at his captain with anguished expression, and said, "Sure, I can't. Me feckin' teeth are in the dressing room!"

'We worked the French out all right that day, so much so they won 24–5, by four tries to one. It was their highest score and biggest ever winning points margin in matches against Ireland in Ireland up to that time.'

In the early 1970s, the Troubles were causing plenty headlines in Ireland and it was against this backdrop that Ireland's hopes of a first Grand Slam since 1948 were dashed. The Five Nations Championship of 1972 had started brilliantly for Ireland. They had done the hard work having gone to Stade Colombes and beaten the French 14–9 before recording a 16–12 win against England in Twickenham. 'What excited most of us in the Irish squad that night in London after the game with England was that we were two matches away from a Grand Slam. And both matches against Scotland and Wales were due to be played in Dublin. However, there would be no Grand Slam for us that year, not even a share of the championship. In fact, the championship was not won by anyone because Scotland and Wales both refused to travel to play us.

'There was no disputing the fact that the Troubles were causing plenty of headlines in Ireland at the time. In fact, when I was playing rugby football for Ireland and the Lions, I had quite a high profile in public relations terms and there was a 'list' that appeared somewhere, although I never saw it, with my name on it. I was told by the police it was a terrorist organisation's death-threat list. Now what that meant, I have no idea – I cannot even begin to get inside the minds of such people, nor would I ever want to – but the security people were sufficiently concerned to come to my house and put in lights and panic buttons and that sort of thing.'

McBride believes that rugby in Ireland had lived through an awful lot, that the game carried on whatever the background and however difficult it may have been. He expands upon this view, adding that rugby had proved itself bigger than any man of violence. 'That was something of which all of us involved in rugby in Ireland felt intensely proud. Imagine our feelings then when we were let down – and I mean those words – by the administrators. It was not the players from Wales and Scotland who were to blame but their governing bodies who claimed that violence in the North might have repercussions in the South. But by whom? Against whom? Those gentlemen who took the decision to abandon their matches with us that year failed Ireland, failed their own countries and failed the game of rugby football. In my view, they should have been ashamed of their actions.'

In contrast, what happened in 1973 in Lansdowne Road will never be forgotten by McBride. England were due to come to Dublin for a Five Nations fixture, but whether they would come or not would be endlessly debated in the media. 'In the end England travelled,' says McBride. 'When they ran out in Lansdowne Road that February afternoon, I for one had never heard a roar like it, on any rugby ground anywhere in the world. I was winning my forty-second cap that day and I'd played the game all over the place, but the warmth of the welcome and the noise was unique in my experience.'

England supporters were also afforded a special welcome – they were also risking their lives coming to Ireland. Any Red Rose supporters walking down Lower Baggott Street in Dublin's city centre had a job getting a pint of the dark stuff himself in any pub. The Irish supporters demonstrated their good nature inviting them into the pubs and buying them pint after pint in stead.'

McBride played a part in bringing England and Lions luminary David Duckham to Dublin. Duckham's wife, Jean, feared for his safety but, after a phone conversation with McBride, England's most celebrated player of the time decided to travel. It was thought that if Duckham opted to remain behind it would probably have meant the entire England squad would remain behind. 'What David and Jean did at that time for the future of rugby football was incalculable,' he said.

That Pullin's men came to Dublin in ways demonstrated Churchillian valour in the face of threat and provocation. At the post-match dinner in the Shelbourne Hotel later that evening, Pullin uttered the immortal words during his captain's address, 'We may not be very good – but at least we turn up', which drew an impassioned applause from the black tie gathering.

In March 1975, Ireland trounced France 25–6 at Lansdowne Road. It turned out to be McBride's final home international on a day when he also scored his first and only try for his country. Remember, this was in the days before high security when pitch invasions were commonplace. Naturally enough, McBride's try was met with delirium, the crowd running onto the pitch and McBride was embraced by a young man. 'I was going through security at Heathrow Airport not too long ago. As I was sitting down tying my shoes this guy beside me was doing the same thing and asked how I was. I asked whether I knew him. "Well, not really," he said. "I haven't seen you for a long time. Do you remember you scored your try at Lansdowne Road?" He told me he was the schoolboy sitting on the touchline, who ran out and jumped on my back after I scored.'

Yet, McBride got one more chance to lead out a team at Lansdowne Road when the IRFU marked the centenary season of Irish rugby with a match between an Ireland–Scotland XV and an England–Wales combination in April 1975. After the game, events took a twist when McBride was 'hijacked' by the late Eamonn Andrews and whisked away to become a subject of an edition of *This is Your Life*.

'I always liked playing in Lansdowne Road. I always liked the terracing, the closeness of the crowd. It was nearly like a family scene, that whole thing, but now it's all gone. It was the atmosphere, one I didn't get anywhere else. Maybe everybody feels that about their own home ground. There were just huge lumps of concrete all over the place, but Lansdowne Road was a family ground. There was something about it that was unique. You could nearly reach out and shake hands with the crowd. We had a very good record in Lansdowne and beat most teams there – and almost beat the All Blacks in 1963 (5–6) and 1973 (10–10).'

Probably the only regrets he's had during a remarkable playing career.

Colin Meads

Lock-Forward, New Zealand

1957–1971

One team and one player dominated world rugby throughout the 1960s and Lansdowne Road shared their company on a mild December's afternoon in 1963. New Zealand came to town, but the thousands who came to the match came to see Colin Meads, a champion of the game's old values. He was part of an All Blacks team peopled with special players, but no one carried an aura or a reputation as great as Meads. Already a legend, his fame grew even more in retirement and, such is his standing amongst the New Zealand populace that the *New Zealand Rugby* monthly magazine voted Meads New Zealand Player of the Century and the NZRFU chose the farmer from King Country as the greatest All Black of all time. In a country laden with so many greats, there was no dispute and no tribunal – Meads was simply the greatest, an icon. In the New Year Honours list of 2001, he was made a New Zealand Companion of Merit, the equivalent of the by-then scrapped knighthoods.

To his team-mates, Meads was known as 'Pinetree', but to commentators he was euphemistically known as 'the enforcer' because of his involvement in many controversial moments. Opposition players regarded the lock-forward, who won fifty-five caps and dominated the game from 1957 until 1971, as a teak-tough player, an uncompromising performer feared by many but respected by all. Bill McLaren tells a good story of Edinburgh University's Earle Mitchell who, on his debut, was down to mark Meads in the 1967 test against Scotland (a game in which Meads became only the second All Black ordered off in a test when Irish referee Kevin Kelleher dispatched him for dangerous play). After the game, friends of Earle enquired how Meads had fared and Earle replied, 'I just looked him straight in the eye and told him I would not tolerate any nonsense from him during the game. But,' he added, 'I whispered it.'

Meads, along with a star-studded All Black XV, came to Dublin in 1963 brimming with confidence, having clocked up seventy-five points in their previous two games, albeit against provincial competition – Midland Counties and South Western Counties.

Lansdowne Road was an enchanted place at the best of times, but there was always an extra buzz when the All Blacks came to town. But, after eighty stirring minutes against a Tom Kiernan-inspired Ireland, Meads and his colleagues ended up extolling the virtues of Ireland's play – the best team performance they came across on their tour. In Alex Veysey's biography, *Colin Meads: All Black*, Meads refers to the 1963–1964 tour of Britain, Ireland and France and criticises the northern hemisphere teams' defensive outlook and their inability to score tries in open play. However, it's difficult to believe he had Ireland in mind. 'From the first match against Oxford University, when we might have expected some sign of intent from the British teams to meet us halfway, the Oxford backs stood as flat as last year's beer not only on our ball but on their own,' Veysey wrote.

In the book, Meads emphasises the benefits of second-phase rugby which, inevitably, leads to more attack-minded rugby and, as a consequence, more tries. On the 1963–1964 tour, he discovered that the teams he came up against were boring conservatives, who preferred to play simply off set-pieces. 'Ours was winning rugby but, more than that, it was try-scoring rugby. We scored sixty-four tries through our centres and wings. The British public are strongly inclined to demand attacking rugby miracles from touring teams while setting themselves up to negate any such possibility.'

Mead's criticism of the British attitude to rugby may have been understandable, but Ireland served up the rugby of their lives to nearly pull off the shock of the century against the – almost – all-conquering All Blacks. 'It was a great tour,' remembers Meads. 'We got beaten early in the third game against Newport and I think that was, in many ways, a blessing because we didn't have to carry that mantle of being unbeaten or invincible. The Irish game was a real cracker. I enjoyed it, naturally, but the greatest disappointment of my rugby career was when we didn't get back to Ireland in 1967 because of the foot-and-mouth outbreak.'

He liked the Irish climate and the hospitality, and likened

Lansdowne to Athletic Park, Wellington, but, most of all, he loved Ireland's rugby. He played opposite Willie John McBride and, today, the two still share stories about the game. 'A lot of stories revolve around what went on between Willie John and I. Willie tells it differently, but I got flattened in one lineout, and it was Willie John because Wilson Whineray saw it. Willie tells it that he went back amongst their forwards to sort someone out and Bill Mulcahy says, "What the hell did you do that for?" And Willie said, "Well I had to do something, he [Colin] was all over me pushing and shoving." Then Bill Mulcahy said, "That's all right for you, now we're all in for it!" I think in the next lineout, Willie got a little tickle up front from some of our players and he thought it was me for a long time afterwards. I had to tell him it wasn't - our skipper did it to him.'

Visiting teams were never sure what kind of Ireland they would meet in Lansdowne Road but you could hardly say the All Blacks were insecure in their own ability. The odds were certainly stacked against the Irish, especially up front where they conceded nearly a stone a man against the New Zealand pack. But Ireland came desperately close to causing the greatest upset of the time. New Zealand were on guard, according to Meads, and they could sense from the off that the Irish were up for the game. 'We were always aware of it at the time. Rugby in those countries in those days was a lot stronger in comparison to today, but I always remember that Ireland game as one of the great games. We didn't know what Ireland had; we hadn't played against any of them before, it was a new experience for both sides. Apart from Bill Mulcahy, Ronnie Dawson and one or two others, who had been with the 1959 Lions, we didn't know many of them at all.'

The great irony of the day was that the men in green conjured up all the magic, not the fabled All Blacks. The wizardry came from the Irish backs, scoring a try fashioned from a blend of good hands, speed of thought and great finishing. Johnny Fortune's try and Tom Kiernan's nonchalant conversion had Ireland in the lead until the sixty-second minute and, even then, Lansdowne dared to dream of celebrating its finest hour.

The story of the game is stirring and the try is worth retelling again and again. Meads was in the scrum near his own line and saw that Ronnie Dawson got a quick heel. 'Initially, Tom Kiernan had sent a sixty-yard kick down field to find position well inside our twenty-five – Tommy was doing that all day. He had an amazing ability to find touch from long range from slender angles.' Indeed, throughout the game, Kiernan outshone his opposite number, the revered Don Clarke, and got three fifty-yard touches from slender angles. Clarke was a legend in New Zealand but, that day, it was Kiernan who had his reputation enhanced by a thoroughly rousing display. Debutant Alan Duggan had come off his wing to bolster numbers in the open and take a pass from Jimmy Kelly, 'Dixie' Duggan cut through a chink of space between two All Black shirts. The winger was snared and swallowed up but still managed to get the ball away to the outstretched arms of centre Jerry Walsh. Displaying adroitness and speed of thought, the second centre lobbed the ball over Pat Casey's head into the waiting arms of the unmarked Fortune and the winger scored. Some All Blacks complained that the pass was forward, but Lansdowne rejoiced at another golden moment.

The All Blacks were stung but, through their awesome set of forwards, struck back with a Kel Tremain try in the thirty-fourth minute. It is worth naming the All Blacks pack because New Zealand will never see their likes again: Wilson Whineray, Denis Young, Ken Gray, Allan Stewart, Colin Meads, Kelvin Tremain, John Graham and Stan Meads (Colin's brother). Still, one New Zealand writer wrote after that game that the Irish pack was 'the toughest and best pack seen in the tour so far'. Meads agrees, 'They took the game to us and we had a hell of a hard tussle. As regards Kel's try, we were pretty close to the line; there was this scrum formed and Kel was a great flanker and would be at the end of anything close to the line; he was a very strong loose forward. Wilson Whineray was our captain and he was a very mobile prop, and had great ball skills, and loved running with it. By world standards, he wouldn't have been one of the strongest props, but he always held his end up and was a great support player in the lineouts and around the field.'

Ireland might well have felt unfortunate that they got on the wrong side of a referee's decision thirteen minutes from time. Scrum-half, captain and man of the match Jimmy Kelly initiated the move sending a beautiful pass to centre Pat Casey. Casey running from well inside his own half was faced by two All Black defenders but chipped the most delicious of cross kicks under the New Zealand posts. In one split second, a dozen things happened. An All Black defender was hit hard by an avalanche of green shirts, the ball spilled over the line and in came flanker, Eamon Maguire to touch down the ball. The referee was slow to arrive at the point of scoring and adjudged that Maguire had knocked it over the line and, instead, awarded New Zealand a scrum. Ireland protested that they got a hand to the ball. 'That's always the case until after the game!' jokes Meads. 'There was probably some reason we protested, we should have got more penalties, I don't know, but that's the way it went.

'I always remembered the great time we had in Dublin, we had a great after-match function, and dinner. The Irish were good sportsmen, good to play against. It was one of the hardest games of our tour; it was a real cliff hanger and one of those games that could have gone either way.'

As for his impressions of Lansdowne, Meads was charmed by the venue. 'It was one of the great stadiums in those days, a good rugby stadium, the crowd were right beside you, right on top of you, that sort of thing. It had a good atmosphere and, obviously, was very good for the home team. It was little bit like Carisbrook in Dunedin but I tell you it was more like the old Athletic Park in Wellington [which was pulled down to make way for a rest home] but it had a huge open stand on one side.'

In the end, Meads left an incredible mark on his first and only game at Lansdowne. And agrees he was just glad to get the win.

Syd Millar

Prop

1958–1970

Twenty-four hours before the arrival of a glittering France team to Lansdowne Road in 1959, Syd Millar remembers the final Irish training session. He and the Irish pack were planning something special for *Les bleus*. For thirty relentless minutes, Syd Millar, the Ballymena tight-head prop, and his forwards executed moves similar to those that had given the French all their success to date.

At this time, the French were a delight to watch, and had earned a reputation throughout the 1950s as the most exciting team in world rugby. Quite simply, they just loved to run the ball, with sleight of hand and adventurism the key components in their attacking armoury. They brought a flamboyance and romance to the game when most teams seemed happy to just kick to the corners and work off set pieces. They invented what became known as the Lucien Mias peel (or as the French called it *percussion*). This move involved throwing a ball to the back of a lineout and flicking it down to a forward before driving at an opposing defender. It worked best off a lineout five yards from the opposition tryline.

For that half hour at Anglesea Road, Ireland felt they could do the same. Ronnie Dawson, the Ireland captain, directed a series of drills and tactical manoeuvres including the so-called Lucien Mias peel that he hoped would catch the French cold at Lansdowne Road.

Dawson's manoeuvres were indeed forward-thinking, and the team felt they could topple the reigning champions that season. 'There was a spring in our step going into that; after Ronnie drilled us in the finer arts of French forward play, some of us thought we were bloody invincible. But it was good to see so much confidence in the squad.'

On Saturday, 18 April 1959, Ireland was at its best for some years, devising a fearless victory based upon the brilliance of a pack superbly led by Ronnie Dawson and Number 8 Tony O'Sullivan.

There was no stopping Ireland in this famous 9–5 win over a French team that could not get to grips with the pace and power of the Irish. France, aiming for the Grand Slam, bottomed out and, though showing signs of a recovery late in the second half, had to give second best on a memorable day for the Irish at Lansdowne.

'1959 was an exceptional year,' says Millar, 'because France were playing football differently. They had creative forwards where they could roll around the back of a lineout, and where they used their back-row effectively in scrums. We didn't play that way – nobody in fact played that way. Everybody said that was the game of the year and it probably was. We just shaded it. Our forwards were good; we got on top that day because we had a quick pack of forwards. We proved we were the team people said we were.'

Millar praises the half-backs who controlled matters against the French. He recalls Mick English playing 'hide-and-seek' with the French flankers and the amazing sight of the Limerick out-half slaloming by a few tackles and coming within inches of scoring a try. But the decisive score came after an inspired cameo from a young Wanderers centre named Kevin Flynn who set up Noel Brophy with a delightful pass for Ireland's only try.

In the other games of the 1959 championship, Ireland lost narrowly to England (0–3), beat Scotland 8–3, before going under 8–6 to Wales at a muddy Arms Park. Against England at Lansdowne, Millar remembers Ireland wasting numerous opportunities to put points on the board having dominated the English for long periods. It was incessant, relentless stuff as Ireland stormed the English line from kick-off but could find no breakthrough. England survived and managed to conjure up the only score during this period of Ireland dominance, a Beverly Risman penalty. 'He was only twenty-one at the time, but Risman [England fly-half] was exceptional.' says Millar. 'We were hammering away at their line for the first twenty minutes but could not get a try or win a penalty. They were very disciplined under all that pressure. Still, I found they had a tough, abrasive pack. We were always accused of falling asleep in the last twenty minutes – that wasn't necessarily so. Teams would think, "Ireland teams always go hammer and tongs for the first twenty minutes – if we hold out for that, they'll tire and make it easier for us." But our team wasn't like that at all; it was a very good side, especially Ronnie Dawson at hooker.

'I remember Ronnie took about 50 per cent of their ball against the head. And I remember Mick English, who I think got better as the tournament progressed, struck what we thought was a nice drop goal late in the first half. Most of the crowd thought it went over but the referee adjudged it to have gone wide.'

When South Africa came to Dublin in December 1960, Millar knew he was in a game – the battle up front was the ultimate battle of brawn. But Springbok teams of the 1960s were exciting and adventurous, too, and those amongst the 40,000 at Lansdowne Road got the perfect opportunity to see some South African rugby greats. One of the most celebrated at the time was their centre, John Gainsford, the Western Province player who won thirty-three caps for his country. 'He brought physical presence to midfield, a trait which modern Springbok teams possess to this day,' says Millar. 'He also was a first-class crash tackler, and Dave Hewitt was faced with the task of marking him that day.'

Captain for the Springboks was Avril Malan, the lock-forward regarded as one of the great leaders of South African rugby, but Millar's focus was on their feared props – loose-head Fanie Kuhn and tight-head Piet 'Spiere' du Toit. 'South Africa came and beat us, but only just, and that team was only beaten once on their tour – by the Barbarians at Cardiff Arms Park. Gordon [Wood], Ronnie and myself were in the front-row for the Baa-baas, but throughout that tour they out-muscled almost everyone in the scrum.

'As for the Ireland match, we held them and took four against the head. But we thought very carefully about our scrum. They had a certain way of scrummaging – they went in very low and that could be troublesome. In those days, the tight-head could catch your jersey turn in and drive you down. Piet du Toit, for example, a very strong guy, would take people down that way. We could have won that game. I remember they scored a pushover try at the end.

'I still have a tape recording of that game. Samuel Walker did the commentary and he was saying at the end, "How are these packs still running?" It was a five-yard scrum and we got down a bit late. They managed to move and made it a two to three-yard scrum before shoving us across the line. I walked back into the dressing room exhausted – we all were, especially the front-row. The scrummaging then was brutal. The difference between scrummaging against South Africa or New Zealand was the greater body contact exerted by the South Africans.'

Ireland's 1961 Five Nations started positively with a home win over England, a match that owed more to Ireland's defence than attack. It grew increasingly tense in the second half as a talented England side launched a series of furious attacks on the Irish line and, though the visitors' rugby was open and attractive and they brought the margin down to three points, they were foiled by stoic Irish defence.

Millar remembers England's out-half, Richard Sharp, as the real danger. In possession, he knew the Number 10, who alongside Dickie Jeeps, was capable of conjuring up the unexpected. England probed and asked questions of the Irish defence but the home side had all the answers. Five minutes after the break, Ronnie Kavanagh's try and Jonathan Moffett's conversion made it 11–0, though Sharp and Rogers got tries to bring the margin down to three. The *Cork Examiner* pointed out that Millar 'with even more than his usual power did a towering job in the scrums and rucks'. Millar praised the Irish defence but he pointed to the coolness of scrum-half, Jonathan Moffett, who scored eight of his side's points – two penalties and conversion into a difficult breeze, so strong that Ronnie Dawson had to hold the ball down for all three kicks.

'I had told Ronnie before the game that this guy can knock them over from well out the field. I remember a cup final in Ravenhill when the kick was ten yards inside our half and Jonny hit it over. Now in those days we played with a heavy ball. So when we got our first penalty, Ronnie turned to me and asked, "What do you think?" "Give it to the lad," I said and Jonny just whacked it over. The two touchline kicks he got were far out as well. Jonny went to New Zealand subsequently and still is there (a very big fruit farmer). But he was a hard man, who got just two caps.'

Millar remembers the role Tommy Kiernan played in setting up Kavanagh for a try early in the second half. Kiernan came into the Irish team against England at full-back in Twickenham the previous year. 'Tommy was a very skilled footballer,' says Millar, 'and in later years got a reputation as a classic full-back. He was a guy who could run and who changed the course of a game. Tommy always blamed me for dropping him when I was coach and I used to joke, "No, Kiernan – I kept you on too long!"

'England was the one game we wanted to win more than any other. Lansdowne Road was our home and you could see people in the crowd that you knew. It held over 50,000 then, so you always felt you'd a responsibility to these people, like you owed them something, something like what Munster have today. To win in Lansdowne Road in front of your own supporters was huge because you were doing something for them, never mind yourself. And beating England was special. I used to say, as coach even when we played in Twickenham, "When you win here, every Paddy in England is standing tall for a year."'

Syd Millar learned that he was surplus to requirements at the end of the 1964 season when the Irish selectors dropped him. Even Ulster dispensed with his services. The selectors considered him too old to continue propping their scrums, but Millar didn't curl up and fade away and knew props in the northern hemisphere often reached their peak in their thirties.

A dedicated player, the Ballymena tight-head aimed to become even stronger and fitter by undergoing a strict training and dieting regime. And he did. In 1968 at the age of thirty-three, Millar returned to the Ireland team, this time on the other side of the scrum. The game was played at the Stade Colombes, the very same venue where he won his first cap.

The result also went along similar lines – a 6–16 defeat – but the season picked up with a draw in Twickenham and wins at home to Scotland and a star-studded Welsh side.

Later that year Ireland beat Australia for the third time in three seasons. This wasn't a bad Wallaby XV – earlier in the year they 'beat the French and lost by just a point to New Zealand – so to see Ireland again triumphing (10–8) brought into sharp focus the depth of talent on this Ireland side. In many people's eyes, this Ireland side was potentially on the cusp of greatness.

Against the Wallabies, Ireland dominated the forward exchanges but displayed little imagination in the three-quarters. The game was won up front where Millar and his Ulster colleague Willie John McBride were immense. Other notable contributors included Mick Molloy, Mick Hipwell and Ken Goodall. 'That quartet was masterful in every aspect of their game. We won an enormous amount of ball and perhaps should have scored more than ten points that day.'

Australia said fatigue contributed to this defeat, but this didn't cut any ice with the Irish – the Aussies had been out-muscled up front and, besides, only for the industry of their half-backs, John Ballesty and John Hipwell, and the tireless foraging of flanker Greg Davis, they could have lost by more than a mere two points.

The crowd had little to get excited about, and even Millar and McBride were reminded of their "duty to entertain" coming back out for the second half. 'I remember walking out with Willie John after half-time and one or two of our committee members weren't too happy with way we were playing, that it was a bit dull. But Willie being Willie turned around and snapped, "Do you want us to win our not?"

The match narrative should revolve around the best moments, which were the three tries. Ireland's first arrived after only seven minutes. Gibson's chip in behind the Australian defence was inch perfect, new cap Jimmy Tydings kicked it towards the line, Barry Bresnihan followed up and touched down, and Kiernan added the extras.

Australia got on the score sheet close to the half-hour mark. A garryowen was sent into the Irish twenty-two and Taylor combined with Ballesty for the out-half to score. The conversion was missed. Ireland completely dominated affairs in the second half, but their only reward was a try on sixty-five minutes.

'Willie John's strength and quick thinking saw him break from the lineout, cut through the Wallaby defence and put Mick Doyle into space to run for the line. Doyle was halted but Goodall was in support, took the pass and scored.' Moroney, who was handed the kicking duties after Kiernan discovered it wasn't his day when he missed a few chances, converted to hand Ireland their third successive victory over the Wallabies.

Though the performance wasn't perfect, the confidence within the side was rising as they headed into their 1969 Five Nations campaign. Another great Lansdowne memory was created against the reigning Grand Slam champions France in the opening game, while England fell in the next home game. Their win in Murrayfield put Ireland on course for a Grand Slam showdown in Cardiff but the bubble burst, the dream died and their chance of immortality was gone as the Welsh ran out comprehensive winners.

Millar was part of the Irish team that played South Africa at Lansdowne Road in January 1970. 'We drew 8–8 and they didn't like it. They didn't play as well as we did and they blamed the referee for playing extra minutes.'

Massive anti-apartheid protests surrounded this fixture. A rally and march to Lansdowne was organised the day of the game, and Millar remembers the scale of the anger when he and the team left the Shelbourne Hotel for the short bus trip to the ground. 'As we walked down the street, they threw fruit at us but rugby players want to be apolitical – they're just interested in playing. We're better playing than trying to shift things along, I think. When we went to South Africa, we said we wanted to play against mixed teams, which we did, and we wanted a mixed crowd, which we didn't quite get. The Dublin match in 1970, whether it was right or whether it was wrong, I'll never know. We were getting loads of stick but, once a game like that starts, you try to put it to the back of your mind.'

Being an Ulster Protestant lining out for Ireland, Millar never had any issues coming to play in Lansdowne or facing the Tricolour for the national anthem. 'I took great pride in playing in Dublin. As far as we're concerned, when it comes to rugby football we're one country. To wear the green jersey, well, that's a source of great pride. I'd never any trouble facing the Irish flag. I felt comfortable with that. In later years, some of the Paisley faction would make comments about us playing in Dublin, but it doesn't matter what a man's religion or politics are – that's his own business.'

Millar has the unique distinction of playing for his county in three different decades and, in 1970, played his last game for Irleand against Wales in Lansdowne Road. Ireland triumphed 14–0, a revenge result of sorts from the previous season when their Grand Slam ambitions were thwarted in Cardiff.

Four years after retirement, Millar was the coach and architect behind Ireland's 1974 Five Nations championship triumph. Ireland probably should have had a few Grand Slams by then; in 1972 Wales and Scotland refused to travel to Lansdowne after receiving death threats from the IRA, but the following season John Pullin's England side travelled and received an emotional welcome and standing ovation at Lansdowne. 'Ronnie [Dawson] had already developed a very good side as coach. Maybe I tweaked it a bit more. I just felt sorry for Ronnie – he didn't get what he deserved and that was a Grand Slam-winning team.'

When Millar took over as coach in 1974, he oversaw one of the greatest ever Irish teams, peopled by such legends as Mike

Gibson and Willie John McBride. It was a monumental achievement by Millar – coaching wasn't really in vogue then, with Dawson having been Ireland's first de facto coach in 1969. Millar's emergence as a top-class coach, however, drew praise later from Dawson who described him as one 'who had a fine rugby brain, was a good communicator and tactician'.

'We won the championship in 1974, Ireland's first success since 1951. That year also signalled the arrival of Moss Keane against France,' says Millar. 'We lost in France and beat England in Twickenham, Mike [Gibson] scored two tries that day. Then we beat Scotland in Lansdowne to take the championship. As coach, I always emphasised the need for a good attitude and the need for pride in a performance. We were proud to be Irishmen that day.

'As coach, I used to do quite a bit of analysis on a white board, and show it to the boys. I would ask them to analyse, say, a red team and another group analyse a blue team. They do these swat tests now, squad analysis etc. We looked at some key factors like using quality possession or giving quick ruck ball to the backs. The forwards know that the best ruck and mauls are the ones that keep the ball alive, which the French were very good at. We carried that philosophy through to South Africa in 1974 [where Millar coached the Lions and won twenty-two games from twenty-two including the three tests]. We wanted to keep the ball and change the target of attack.'

That they did and more, and Lansdowne Road witnessed one of its greatest ever occasions when Scotland were defeated 9–6.

At long last, after twenty-three, Ireland could celebrate a Five Nations title.

Munster Supreme

The European Cup, 2006

Paul O'Connell &
Declan Kidney

Who'll ever forget Lansdowne Road's transformation into a riotous sea of red colour for Munster on two glorious spring days in April 2006, the year of the province's first European triumph?

On 1 April 2006, Munster's travelling horde helped in no small way to transform the old stadium into a most compelling European Cup theatre. The sound created inside by the red multitude resonated like Thomond Park on its best days, and the estimated 47,500 Munster fans in attendance were going to give their boys the perfect backing track against French giants, Perpignan.

As for the game, there were plenty mind games in the build up, and there's no one better at this than then Munster head coach, Declan Kidney, who spent the week talking up Perpignan's strengths. Kidney's ability to play down Munster's chances and play up the opposition's is part cute Corkonian, part psychology, and he arrived at a press conference in Thomond in midweek armed with a book of stats on Perpignan, going on to praise the French side's mean defence, and the way in which they could handle some of the most intimidating atmospheres in French rugby. Kidney wasn't telling white lies; in fact Perpignan's record in the qualifying pool stages made for impressive reading and Kidney was quick to accentuate this point: they'd conceded a measly fifty-two points and five tries in six matches.

Yet Munster boasted the second-best record from the pool stages conceding just eighty-seven points and six tries in six games. One bookmaker had Munster five to one on to win and, when the information was relayed to the top table, Kidney, typically, just deflected the attention away from his side. One felt that the province rested more easily that night with this man in charge. 'Thankfully, we didn't pay any attention to them [the bookies],' Kidney reflects, 'because they [Perpignan] had the best defensive record in the European Cup and we hadn't played together for over two months. Anyway, a lot of guys were trying to cope with things happening off the pitch too.'

Indeed, the weeks around the tie had become difficult ones for the Munster players, still coming to terms with the tragic death of their friend, Conrad O'Sullivan, the Cork Constitution player who had worn the Munster jersey with distinction at various levels. A minute's silence was respectfully kept when both teams lined up in front of the West Stand, but the poignancy of the moment, wrapped into the biggest game in world club rugby that weekend, was too much to bear for some players. Especially for Conrad's good friend and Munster out-half, Ronan O'Gara, whose tears bore all the signs of someone deeply affected by Conrad's passing.

Emotions, naturally, were running high, but the moment spurred some players to greater performances. Earlier that week, they'd spoken about Conrad and vowed to give a performance that would do their former team-mate proud. Paul O'Connell's friendship with Conrad went all the way back to their school days. 'A lot of guys played with him, a lot of guys knew him growing up,' O'Connell says. 'It was very emotional. We were discussing all week what things we could do to remember him. It became a big motivating factor for us that week. He was a great guy. His career was destined towards Munster and maybe it had taken a turn in the last few years. I think, though, he would have come back into the fold. If you look at the minute's silence, a lot of guys did get very emotional. The funeral was huge – so many guys from UCC, from Cork and from the greater rugby scene in Cork Con were present. From that you could tell how popular he was. I was on the same Munster schools team as him.

'I remember they played a video of him at half-time on the big screen, and, though we were in the dressing room, we were all aware of that happening. It was mentioned several times, and I thought it did his memory proud.'

With a home venue and backed by their huge volume of support, the odds were stacked heavily in Munster's favour, but there were mitigating factors going into this tie, their eighth consecutive European Cup quarter-final. The last time they had lined out with a full team was against Sale Sharks in Thomond Park on 21 January. Mind, nine of the side that defeated Sale had just come off a successful Six Nations, where they helped Ireland capture a second Triple Crown in three years, but naturally there was a fear that the lack of playing time together might impinge upon their latest European assault.

Things took a turn for the worse seven days before facing Perpignan: their Celtic League game against Llanelli Scarlets was cancelled because of a flooded Stradey Park, while Perpignan, on the other hand, looked in fine fettle, scoring an amazing three-point victory away to Bourgoin in the French championship. Over the previous six weeks, they had played each of the other French Heineken Cup contenders, Biarritz and Toulouse, as well as other French heavyweights, Stade Français and Clermont Auvergne. The French, arguably, could not have been in better shape coming into this tie. 'We came off the Six Nations and had no game as a team for three months. That was a big issue,' says O'Connell. 'No matter how good a team you are, if you don't play together week in, week out, you don't get the consistency you need, not to mention not playing together for three or four months. So that was a big thing for us.

'But, essentially, we were at home, we were in a very focused frame of mind, and I think guys were in very good shape after the Six Nations. Sure, we didn't play well against Perpignan but I don't think we were ever going to lose to them.'

Kidney hadn't been in charge the last time Munster played a knockout tie in the European Cup at Lansdowne Road. In 2004, on a balmy afternoon, Warren Gatland's Wasps came and spoiled the Munster party. Kidney, as a spectator then, saw battle-hardened men like Lawrence Dallaglio and Joe Worsley unfazed by the red tsunami on the stands and terraces and knew, deep down, that Perpignan were of the same ilk. And he knew, too, that Perpignan had the added advantage of having won a semi-final against Leinster in Lansdowne in 2004. 'There's a little bit of a belief that if you get a home quarter-final against a French team you're OK but that's very far from the truth – that's like saying we can't win in France. The last time Munster had played a European Cup match in Lansdowne Road, we'd lost and the last time Perpignan played a European Cup match in Lansdowne Road, they'd won – so thankfully we didn't feed into that. The game was exactly as we thought. There were a lot of things going on leading into the 2006 quarter-final. For example on match day, the television was on in the hotel, and we watched the first half of the Leinster match. They were flying. The semi-final draw had also been made and it was quite apparent that the winners of our game would be playing Leinster.'

Insider knowledge is always a help in sport. Munster had utility forward, Mick O'Driscoll, in their ranks who'd spent two years with Perpignan and understood the Catalans' psyche. He knew the French club possessed one of the most abrasive packs in European rugby. Not that Munster were shrinking violets in the forward exchanges; they're reputation, after all, had been forged on their forwards, but this would be a different kind of battle, and preparation was key. O'Driscoll and skipper, Anthony Foley, came up with a brilliant training drill that ultimately benefited Munster. 'Micko came in on the Tuesday,' says O'Connell, 'and said, "They'll hit us hard, really hard, boys. They're going to be offside in a ruck, so they're going to be offside in a maul and you have to deal with it. You'll have to hit them hard in rucks, you'll have to protect your rucks, get numbers to the rucks." We kind of trained like that during the week, struggled with it at the start until we realised what level we had to get to, to defend the way they play. That training was excellent.'

'It was a real squad effort to win this match,' says Kidney. 'Because the players were without any match practice, we had a ten-to-fifteen-minute training session on the Tuesday and the lads flaked into one another. The fellows who took the pitch on the Saturday were well used to what was going to come against them, which was just as well.'

The game against Perpignan fell on Saturday, 1 April, and a story hit the front page of the *Irish Examiner* that Ronan O'Gara might miss the game because of a hamstring injury picked up at training the previous day. Despite rumblings from supporters that this story was written in bad taste – it was April Fool's day after all – O'Gara's injury was no hoax. 'Yes, he was struggling badly with a hamstring injury,' says O'Connell, 'and he said that day was the closest he ever came to pulling out of a game. We didn't know ourselves up until the last minute whether ROG was going to be playing or not, but thankfully he made the field.'

Kidney adds, 'It was touch and go as to whether he would be comfortable enough to take the pitch and to be able to take it under those circumstances with everything that was going on. Then there is that case where you're 10 goes out. You get the best medical care, you weigh up the situations, but you don't put the player out unless he's comfortable – that's putting a huge onus on the player. You don't put anyone out who is unnecessarily in danger. When you have an injury like that and you're the place-kicker, you're a pivot for the team, it takes a lot of courage to go out and do what he did that day.'

As predicted, the Catalans came out in bullish form. After the friendly fire posted by both camps in the pre-match build-up, it was down to an old-fashioned shootout in the oldest stadium in the world. From the off, the game took on the spectre of a war of attrition and the Mick O'Driscoll-inspired boot camp worked. 'I remember the start of the game,' says Paul O'Connell, 'where we took the ball into contact once or twice, literally in the first few seconds, and got blown off it. It was a real wake-up call for us.'

'There are many, many ways in playing the game of rugby – some are more television-friendly than others, but I respect all the types of rugby games,' says Kidney. 'They were playing to their strengths; they were incredibly quick on the counter-attack but, thankfully, we didn't give them the space to show that. We managed to close them down and not give them too many loose balls to come at us – I mean that's where they got their try in the first half.'

For the opening fifteen minutes, Munster engaged in an all-out attack, but the Perpignan defence remained unyielding and steadfast. If nails were being whittled to the quick amongst the red hordes, Kidney revealed afterwards it was a game of patience, even when it seemed a stalemate was ensuing. 'We were on the attack for the first ten or fifteen minutes. We didn't score, but kept the ball in hand. We were against the breeze, so you can lose games in the first fifteen minutes, but you don't actually win them either. It was a bit like the final in Cardiff. After twenty-one minutes in Cardiff the score was 10–10. After fifteen minutes against Perpignan, 0–0 wasn't the worst place to be, and we were against the wind, remember.

'It was a tough, tough game. If you asked any of the players, they'd tell you if it wasn't the most physical match that they played in 2006, it was right up there with it. We won a couple of penalties but opted to kick to touch instead of taking a pot at goal. Against the breeze, they weren't kickable options and they were around the halfway line anyhow. If we took the shots at goal and they fell short, that would have given them easy ball. It was better to kick to touch, retain the ball and play the game like that. At that level, you need to play two or three different types of game in an eighty-minute period.'

Eventually, the breakthrough came via O'Connell on nineteen minutes. That season the lock's form had reached extraordinarily high levels. Even comparisons with Superman began doing the rounds on internet chatrooms. He crashed over the low tackle of Christophe Manas to score in the very same corner of his first Ireland try (which came against Wales in 2002). Recalls O'Connell: 'Very often when you're hammering at a team's line, you may not score. But you're sapping them and you're taking the energy out of their legs. We were just working so hard to get over, we had a few pick-and-gos, a few one-off runners like Flanns [Jerry Flannery] running at their backs, and then Strings popped it out to me on the blind side. I probably could have passed it to Axel [Anthony Foley], but I think I flopped over the winger. We were on our way then.'

Because Munster were playing against the wind, they needed to keep ball in hand, with no place for the type of champagne rugby the backline served up away to Castres and at home to Sale earlier in the campaign. In the end, winning was all that mattered. 'It really was a case of just battering away,' explains Kidney. 'We just stayed at it and stayed at it. It might be unattractive but to be able to do that against a team of their record is commendable. It was tough, tough rugby.

The men out there on both sides have to be respected and I think you see it when the final whistle goes. They all shake hands. That's sometimes forgotten.'

On twenty-eight minutes, twenty-one-year-old Mathieu Bourret scampered through a hole in the Munster defence to dot down and Lansdowne fell silent. Some say Bourret eyed up the inexperienced Tomás O'Leary – nominally a scrum-half – and took advantage. That week the Cork man was asked to fill a position vacated by the injured Barry Murphy. 'We left a loose ball and they picked it up and counter-attacked,' says Kidney, 'and, if you like, we had a system error that wasn't actually Tomás' fault. Tomás was the easiest fellow to pick on because he was new to the position. We'd never name names; there was a system error between us, and it wasn't his error in any shape or form.'

'It was a half mistake,' recalls O'Connell, 'but give credit to Perpignan as well. It did us no harm, I suppose; it put guys on their toes. Because when we played Leinster in the semi-final, we defended outstandingly well against one of the best backlines in club rugby.'

Murphy's absence from the centre (he picked up a long-term ankle injury against Ulster in the Celtic League on 3 March), left Kidney with the task of rebuilding his backline. 'Any time a team plays, you try and play to your strengths. I've had many discussions with a good friend of mine, Tim Crowe in St Clements, as to whether you pick the best players or the best team. It's just different approaches to games. It was really a case of horses for courses on the day given everything that was happening in the lead-up to it – like not having played as a full squad for two months; the Llanelli game being called off the week before; O'Gara getting a hamstring strain, and, most important of all, Conrad's death – we all knew him. It was a real-life event.'

The collisions at the breakdown were colossal and fiercely competitive but, ultimately, Perpignan's indiscipline in this area proved costly and they suffered two sinbinnings. And, just on half-time, they got a little tetchy by the touchline under the West Stand. Coming to pick a fight in what was Munster's backyard for an afternoon was not the brightest move by Perpignan. 'They were full of aggression,' says O'Connell, 'and you have to meet that aggression every time and let guys know you won't be going backwards. They'd a few tough guys in their pack like [Marius] Tincu and [Rimas] Alvarez and there were a few schmozzles. You try not to throw a punch or whatever, but you let them know that we're not to be messed with. What they tried was an old-fashioned French thing that doesn't really work anymore against Irish teams. You just have to make sure they know that.'

Perpignan's indiscipline allowed Munster to turn a 10–7 half-time deficit into a 13–10 lead by the forty-eighth minute. Munster, sensing the finishing line, defended Perpignan's mauls expertly with O'Connell at the centre of them driving the French left and right, forbidding to allow them to build up any forward momentum. The French team's frustrations multiplied and, by the sixty-ninth minute, O'Gara had scored three more penalties making it 19–10. For his last kick, he grimaced. There was pain etched across the out-half's face. 'Obviously, his leg would've been tight,' says Kidney. 'When you kick, you extend your body to a limit, knowing that you have to go through that to get to the point where you can't hold back from the kick. But that's the nature of the game; it's the nature of all top-class sport that you push your-self to the limit.'

Still, Perpignan came hunting and carved open some opportunities, but Bourret missed three eminently kickable penalties in the last fifteen minutes while their attempted drop goals, a feature of their game in the French Top 14, all failed to hit the target. 'They took a drop goal from the ten-metre line, I remember, and it went wide,' recalls Kidney. 'Then we took a long twenty-two before Bourret tried another one from his own ten-metre line. He wasn't too far off it that time, but we knew drop goals were in their game-plan.'

'We needed to close the game off,' says O'Connell, 'and we just kind of squeezed the life out of them. We weren't as fluid as we would've liked to have been. We hadn't played in three or four months, remember. It became a game of patience; it was about winning the game, and that's what we did.'

It wasn't until the seventy-seventh minute that 'The Fields of Athenry' once again began to reverberate around Lansdowne and the Munster fans could rest a little easier. 'Anytime the Perpignan fans starting shouting, that's when the Munster fans dug in,' remembers Kidney. 'They weren't found wanting. At half-time, everybody would have been getting a bit nervous, but you have to play through that – the Munster fans are knowledgeable. And they know when you're trying. The only time they'd crib is when we're not.'

Afterwards, Perpignan felt they should have won the game. 'I wouldn't argue with that,' continues Kidney. 'That game could have gone either way. And that's why it was such a great win because, if you can come through days like that, they're good wins, like winning a pool game against Dragons earlier on in the year.'

A few hours before Munster toppled Perpignan, Leinster had travelled to southern France to take on Toulouse, the reigning European champions, in front of 37,000 in Le Stadium. On an extraordinary day for Leinster rugby, they produced one of *the* greatest performances in the European club competition. And with Munster winning later that afternoon, the stage was set for the mother of all meetings – a derby to capture the imagination of everyone in Ireland.

The media began describing it as an All-Ireland final, the culchies against the city slickers, a clash of rugby cultures or, as Matt Williams, former coach of Leinster, wrote in *The Irish Times*, 'Munster reminds me of an anaconda. They attack in a vicious and brutal way, pin you down and then squeeze the life out of you. You suffocate under the pressure. Leinster reminds me of a cheetah, so quick to strike you almost don't see it coming.'

The subplots, the head to heads, the strengths and weaknesses were dissected and trisected in the build-up to the Battle of Ireland: Ronan O'Gara versus Felipe Contepomi; Paul O'Connell versus Malcolm O'Kelly; David Wallace and Keith Gleeson – and was Declan Kidney about to mastermind the downfall of a Leinster side he managed the previous season?

How this derby had changed over the years is quite startling.

Eight years earlier, just 1,000 attended a Munster–Leinster inter-provincial match, ties which historically always had their fair share of needle and niggle and battle for local bragging rights. 'In 1998, we played a cracking match that finished 9–6,' says Kidney, tongue firmly in cheek. 'I think there might have been 1,000 to 1,500 at the game. The following year we were in Dooradoyle – we'd a big crowd that day – 2,000! And we managed to lose that one and then, around 2001, we managed to half fill Lansdowne Road for the Celtic League final.'

But, ever since their defeat to Northampton in the 2000 final, the European Cup had turned into a kind of crusade for Munster, as it was for their supporters. Each new season brought new hope, incredible highs and, too often, the pain of defeat in the latter stages of the competition. Many Munster fans, it seemed, were living their lives through this Munster team.

Twenty-two thousand tickets were made available to both provinces for the 2006 semi-final, but, as expected, there weren't enough to satisfy the red hordes. On match day inside the stadium, Munster's resourcefulness was yet again evident as they outnumbered the Leinster support by three to one. On the team bus from their base at the Radisson Hotel, the players passed through Ballsbridge and Shelbourne Road. All they saw was a tide of red shirts. If ever a team had found the formula for province-hood, it was Munster. 'There's a huge honour to try to represent the people who come along to these matches,' says Kidney. 'Whether people actually get tickets or not, it's all the one to us. Munster are a representative side and accept the responsibility that goes with that but also the honour that goes with being able to perform for them.'

The hysteria surrounding 'Seismic Sunday' reached epidemic levels but these were golden days for Irish rugby. Even the streets of Limerick and Cork were becoming battlegrounds for players brave enough to walk down either O'Connell Street in Limerick or Patrick Street, Cork. 'There was a massive build-up to it, but that's part and parcel of it,' says O'Connell. 'You can't hide away – you have to deal with it and get on with it. We've all played in big games, big games in Ireland and in Munster and, sure, this was maybe a little bit higher again but you just get on with it and deal with it. That's what we did – we dealt with it quite well. You don't try and pretend it's nothing. It is big and you acknowledge it and say, "God this is massive", but you just try and get on with your job. The money supporters spend is incredible. That's something we always try to get across to the supporters. It's not cheap to go to the south of France; it's not easy to go to Wales, England all the time. They've just been remarkable – the money they spend and the emotion they invest in supporting us is incredible and it has been brilliant for us.'

O'Connell says the red tsunami in the South Terrace and on the East Stand proved a huge motivating spur during the pre-match warm-up, and the bond between team and supporters seemed stronger than ever. 'You use any bit of motivation you get for every game, and the supporters are something we feed off all the time.' Clichés regarding the importance of the sixteenth man had never become more pertinent, not that Leinster's supporters – who proudly chanted 'Allez les Bleus' – shirked their responsibilities in cheering their men in the blue end of Lansdowne.

In one sense, it was strange and surreal watching best friends warm up in different corners in different colours, friends who'd spent so much time in Ireland camp, in hotels from Auckland to Sydney to Cape Town, who often in some downtime played boules on the manicured lawns of their hotel in Paris in the springtime. Only on the last St Patrick's weekend had they being celebrating a Triple Crown victory into the late hours in central London and suddenly … they were opposites for eighty minutes.

'Strange? It is – but it's actually just a game,' says O'Connell. 'There's no real mouthing going on in the game; there was no bitching at each other – just two teams going at it as hard as they could. And that's all it was.'

Injuries to key players deprived Munster of certain victories in previous European campaigns and, this time, Peter Stringer's participation was in doubt right up to kick off. He reported to be in good form that morning, the scrum-half looked waspish during practice in the gardens around the Radisson and, six hours later, looked fine in the warm-up. Kidney, his mentor since their days in PBC, gave Stringer every chance to prove his fitness. He remembered the moment Strings received a lash in the back at training four days before the semi-final. 'He got an awful clatter in the back which was reverberating right down through his leg like sciatic pain. But the power of positive thinking is amazing. Peter said, "No, I'll be fine." I had brought in two extra scrum-halves and that probably made him get better even faster! He was taking all the treatment, getting acupuncture and so on. From his point of view, they couldn't put enough needles into him! He took all that, got himself ready and played the match and, through experience, managed his way through the game.' Even O'Connell paid tribute to the big heart of the little fellow. 'He's a born winner. He has a refusal-to-lose attitude in every game he plays – it was a brilliant sight to see him take the jersey and say, "I'll play."'

Munster returned to the 'home' dressing room, the one they'd chosen after a coin toss. 'This was no different to when we tossed for the dressing room in Bordeaux in 2000,' says Kidney, 'or for a warm-up down in front of the South Terrace where the Munster fans were in situ. All of that is decided before the game.'

The dressing room was a special place before kick off. Former Munster full-back, Dominic Crotty, dropped in to say a few words while John Kelly emphasised the importance of playing for Munster. Messages from former players were also read out. 'All that helps,' says O'Connell. 'You use everything and anything you get your hands on. You could say the whole Munster fraternity came together that week.'

Kidney has been in these big matches in the past, and sensed the team needed to be left alone before kick-off. He left them to their own devices in the six minutes before they took the field again. Kelly spoke passionately, as did Foley, who'd seen and experienced it all. 'The six minutes before they leave the dressing room again, well, that's their time. They don't really want a whole lot more time in there,' says Kidney. 'It's about the players' ownership of what they're doing and Munster are very lucky that they have men to do that. The idea of the warm-up is that they're all but ready to go. You don't want to be cooling down too much. It's an interesting thing but the English [Rugby] Premiership has a fifteen minute half-time now. I'd say some of the players might not be too keen on that. If Claw was around, I could imagine him not being overly happy with having fifteen. It's bad enough having ten minutes sitting around the place – after fifteen you start getting stiff and the bones have to get warmed up again.'

Both teams walked out side by side to a deafening din, although Munster did keep Leinster waiting under the West Stand for a few minutes. Few players from either side made eye contact although, later, Rob Henderson said he winked at Emmett Byrne. When they walked up the steps and onto the field, the decibel levels rose higher.

Munster got the best possible start from the kick-off. Malcolm O'Kelly dropped a high hanging ball, Donncha O'Callaghan gathered and not long after, O'Gara banged over a penalty. But Kidney looks sympathetically on the O'Kelly error, pointing to the Lansdowne Road wind factor. 'You're playing in Lansdowne Road, remember. It's very easy to be critical from the stands. All of a sudden you got that little whip of wind, you're under the ball one minute, then a little breeze comes in off Sandymount and the ball has gone two yards away from you. That was the nature of Lansdowne. You don't have to worry about that in your indoor stadia; you don't have to worry about that in a lot of other stadia, mind. But if you got the nature of stands the way they were built there – two open-end terraces, not too far from Sandymount Strand – you never knew which way the breeze was going to go.

'Everybody would talk about the likes of Girvan Dempsey, Hugo MacNeill or Tommy Kiernan – that they were all safe pairs of hands. You'd want to be one hell of a full-back to be safe in Lansdowne Road. Nobody had any idea how good those players were and how able they were to cope with that side of Lansdowne. There's a lot of credit due to any full-back who could manage Lansdowne.'

O'Connell was a force of energy from start to finish and, on eight minutes, his lineout steal earned Munster a penalty forty-five metres from goal. Foley and O'Gara had a quick chat, and decided to go for touch. It seemed in that moment they were intent in making a statement to Leinster. O'Gara, in the form of his life, placed it beautifully in the corner and, from the lineout, O'Connell brought the ball down one-handed. Then an ensuing wedge to the line saw Denis Leamy power over. 'The maul was a bit of a messy one,' remembers O'Connell. 'I think good players have a very good nose for the line; you saw that with Axel [Anthony Foley] in his days. There was a lot of work to create that gap for Leamy, but he got the job done and got over the line.'

On thirteen minutes, John Kelly took a 'stinger' to his left shoulder and walked off disconsolately. In his place came Henderson. 'Rob hadn't a lot of time to warm up,' says Kidney, 'and he hadn't a lot of game time that season either because of different injures and bangs and knocks. Ronan, I thought, showed his experience from a lineout off the top, moving the ball to Hendo so as to give him a quick first touch. That's experience for you. I think Paul said that he didn't know who the backline was by the end of the game, but he didn't care because he knew that whoever came in would do a job.'

The fury of Munster's challenge had caught Leinster cold and inside the Leinster half, Munster pounded the blue line. But to the Leinster forwards' credit, they didn't wilt or leak another try until the eightieth minute. The greatest tribute that could be paid to Munster was their ability to deny the Leinster three-quarters possession for almost the entire first half. Felipe Contepomi, who did so much to bring Leinster to this stage of the competition, couldn't settle and looked ruffled and cranky for long stages. Only once in the first half did Michael Cheika's side manage to give legs to their backline. Keith Gleeson – Leinster's best player – turned over Munster ball, Contepomi swept wide to Shane Horgan who found Denis Hickie and the winger switched into fifth gear.

From these positions, Leinster had the capacity to carve open any opposition. Horgan's pass sent Hickie winging down the touchline and before O'Connell flung himself cross-field to put the flying winger off kilter. 'I may have pushed him a bit wider,' says O'Connell, 'but Shaun Payne was the one who essentially got across and made the tackle and got him into touch. It was outstanding work by Shauny – he was one of these guys who did his job week-in, week-out at the highest level without us having to worry about him at all. He was an outstanding athlete, a great pro and has been brilliant for Munster.'

Kidney, who had coached the so-called Leinster galacticos the previous season, knew their abilities intimately. Stopping Hickie was a huge turning point in the game, he says. 'Denis didn't really get past Paul – Paul pushed him enough to the touchline, then Shaun was coming across. The pitch in Lansdowne is four inches narrower than the pitch in Toulouse because Denis did the exact same thing against Toulouse – he wasn't pushed as much to the touchline. I think it was the way Paul pushed him that extra six inches closer to the line, and, when Shaun came across, all of a sudden there's a toe in touch. So, instead of the score being 10–7, Munster were 13–0 up. That's a huge advantage. That moment was pivotal.'

You could say Munster monopolised possession in that half; they'd a vice-like grip of the ball and wouldn't share it. It sucked the life out of the Leinster attack. In the upper tier of the West Stand, where former Leinster backs coach David Knox liked to sit, he urged his team to run with the ball. But with the little ball they had, they were swallowed up by a tide of red shirts. Leinster, in need of oxygen, flatlined. 'I think Leinster won the toss and went against the breeze, so we had to try to play as much rugby in their half as possible,' says Kidney. 'Leinster are the sort of side you don't give up the ball to too easily. They are capable of running in a lot of points in minutes. For example, look at their game against Bath, the previous season: they looked dead and buried, but, three minutes later, they won the match because they scored fourteen points in three minutes. It wasn't down to me. That was purely the players doing.'

Munster led 13–6 at half-time and continued to bombard the Leinster line after the interval. Leinster impressively withstood three quick tap penalty attempts by Munster close to the line, and then started playing a bit of rugby themselves, generating quick ruck ball and moving it wide. In the midst of all this counter-attacking stood O'Connell, putting in hit after big hit. Munster had lost the full-time services of their defence coach, Graham Steadman in January. In his place came Tony McGahan, a quality Australian coach who took over from Kidney in 2008. The changing of the guard was smooth and the results told, according to O'Connell. 'Defence is all about working hard and communicating and doing all the basic little things well. Graham leaving was a big loss to us but Tony came in with new ideas and refreshed us a bit, which was great. It kicked us on and, essentially, a lot of the newer stuff we were doing was very helpful in defending a team like Leinster. They love to off load so much; they look for one-on-ones and switches, and with Tony it was defending the individual a lot. We were under pressure in the game but that happens in every game.

'Every team has its purple patch and I think if you can react and defend well when a team has its purple patch, keep your head, not give away penalties just trust your defence which we did, you go a long way to winning a game. We came out of our line three times in the whole game but we managed to close up the gaps.'

'Thankfully we didn't panic,' recalls Kidney of that period when blue kept red from scoring a try time after time. 'Because we didn't get over at that stage, it was a case of fair play to them, they stopped us – we're in a hole but there's no need for us to dig further by forcing it too much. Then Felipe had a penalty in the second half that seemed to be going quite central, but Lansdowne Road and all its mysteries took over, and it hit the left-hand post. That would have brought it to 13–9. So with Denis' chance in the first half and that penalty in the second half, all of a sudden the game is turned on its head.'

Seven minutes from time, Freddie Pucciariello got sin-binned. The game still hung in the balance – 16–6 – and the thought of Leinster running in two tries in five minutes must have crossed Kidney's mind. The sinbinning was something Munster needed like a hole in the head. 'Freddie got sinbinned which was a bit of a worry,' says O'Connell. 'But, essentially, we stayed very patient, trusted our defence and kept going at them, weathered the storm and finished the game attacking.'

At the next scrum, Kidney withdrew his skipper and spiritual leader, Anthony Foley. Foley, who later became an assistant coach with the province, admitted afterwards that if he was in Kidney's position, he'd have made the same decision.

'The sinbinning was something we could have done without,' says Kidney. 'There were ten points in the game and they were worrying moments. Because you had put in a huge effort for seventy-odd minutes, you're hoping something like that won't cost you the game. But the other fourteen certainly dug in at that stage. You have to pick somebody to come off; there's nobody going to volunteer. Anthony is such a professional he will do that just like he did in the final in Cardiff. Whatever it takes, you know? That's the epitome of the man, that's why he'd been vital for us in the whole year with his leadership. Munster have been blessed with good leaders over the years – Mick Galwey, Pat Murray, Tom

Kiernan – you look down through it and there have been good men there.'

When O'Gara capped off his best-ever performance in a Munster jersey or in any colour – whether with Ireland or the Lions – with a smartly taken try, the game was up for Leinster. Flashing a smile as wide as Patrick Street, O'Gara jumped the hording behind the goal and embraced the few fans who spilled down to the field from the terraces to embrace the golden boy of Irish rugby. 'The eightieth minute wasn't it?' says Kidney. 'We had defended well for the previous six or seven minutes and we had got the ball, Ronan went for something and he got through. The nature of the game at that stage is you had fourteen against fifteen in defence so, anyone who made a line break was gone. The line break could just as easily have gone the other way but, fortunately, it went for Munster.'

O'Connell felt he couldn't afford to breathe a little easier, even after O'Gara's try. He couldn't say they had tamed the Leinster Lions yet. 'O'Gara's try was brilliant, but I don't think we had the game 100 per cent won at that stage. You never know with injury-time; you never know what's going to happen. Those guys are capable of pulling fourteen points out of anywhere, so I don't think the game was won. But, at the time, there was a sense that we might have it. We just regathered at the halfway line, put our heads back on and that is something that we did really well. You hear all sorts of horror stories of last minute tries to deny you, so we just wanted to make sure of victory.'

And they did make sure seconds later when Trevor Halstead intercepted a pass, running in under the posts from inside the halfway line. Kidney, though, admits the final score – 30–6 –

wasn't a fair reflection of the overall pattern of the game. 'I think the last score or two were maybe a reflection of how things went for us on the day. In the same way, maybe, as the Celtic League final the previous time [2001], a few things might have gone against Munster, but that's the nature of rugby.'

'It was probably not a true reflection of the day,' says O'Connell, 'that's the way it happens sometimes. It didn't matter whether it was twenty-four points or one point, it's all about who got the win – I think we deserved to win. Afterwards, O'Gara spoke of the stomach sickness during the week, the antibiotics he took and why he wore small boots to get a better 'feel' for the pitch.

O'Connell said there was no name written on the cup. 'You're never going to say, "This is our year." You might look back at little incidents throughout the year and say, "Yeah, it was our year, the bounce of the ball went our way, once or twice we got a few lucky breaks." At the time, you keep your feet on the ground and you keep working. Destiny had nothing to do with it – it's all about the preparation you put in, the players you have, the staff, the passion they have for it. After the game, we were just keeping our heads screwed on.'

For the record, Munster went on to win the European Cup, beating Biarritz 23–19 at the Millennium Stadium in Cardiff. Two years later, they captured their second European crown, this time beating Toulouse in the Welsh capital.

As for the Lansdowne experience against Leinster, O'Connell never felt so good in such a theatre. 'It was very loud but it was a great thing that the crowd was so close to you and you. I hope we won't lose that in the new ground. I know it was an old rickety ground, but it really was a fabulous place – the atmosphere for those two games was just incredible and couldn't really be replicated in grounds with that capacity. There was terracing on the sidelines which you don't see very often now. I think Newlands in Cape Town has it. It just added to a massive kind of atmosphere. Those few days in Lansdowne Road rank right up there as my happiest in the old ground – hopefully there's more to come in the new.'

Noel Murphy

Flanker

1957–1969

When Noel Murphy ran out for the first time in an Ireland shirt at Lansdowne Road against Australia in January 1958, he was following in the footsteps of his father, Noel Snr, who played for Ireland in the 1930s. While a student at CBC in Cork, Noel Jnr lined out at scrum-half, a position he temporarily filled for Ireland in 1958, when John O'Meara went down injured against Wales in the Five Nations. But he was a born flanker and showed his flexibility in the back-row, moving easily between both the open and blind side positions. Syd Millar, who played alongside him on countless occasions with both Ireland and the Lions, offered this frank assessment. 'Noel was very quick. He never flinched and never drew back.

He was very strong mentally, a huge tackler and a good footballer too.'

Murphy has mixed feelings about his debut. Nick Shehadie, a future Lord Mayor of Sydney, landed him with a haymaker in the second half of the match, but the Cork man survived to tell the tale of what turned out to be Ireland's first-ever win over a touring side. 'We were all delighted to see Jackie Kyle bookend a remarkable career with a win over a touring side,' says Noel, firstly. 'I played flanker but you would not like to be a flanker on a team facing Jackie – he was so quick, he'd dodge a bullet. There were six new caps that day and the selectors seemed to have got it right. Three of us would go on to captain Ireland – Bill Mulcahy, Ronnie Dawson and myself.' (The other three new caps were Dave Hewitt, J. Stevenson and J. Donaldson.) Murphy, Dawson and Hewitt then travelled with the Lions to New Zealand in 1959 – regarded as one of the greatest ever trips to the Land of the Long White Cloud.

Hewitt made a grand entrance onto the international stage against Australia in Lansdowne that day, creating the opening for Dawson's try.

The following year, Murphy was a member of the Ireland side that defeated then 'world champions' France at Lansdowne Road. It will be remembered as a match where Galway man, Tony O'Sullivan, gave his most complete performance in an Irish shirt. 'Covering, displaying great ball control and tackling almost everything in sight,' says Murphy of O'Sullivan's performance, and, today, still holds that France side, captained by the legendary Lucien Mias, in high regard.

That day, however, the French Number 8 was never afforded too much room to exert his influence on proceedings. Murphy depicts it now as one of those classy Irish performances where

Ireland mixed up their game very effectively: flick backs to fellow forwards, short passing, quick and solid blinding at ruck time, and a succession of neat heels to the scrum-half. It all came as quite a shock to the French, who were not used to this sort of Irish play.

'The French were as physical then as they are now, and I suppose at the time they were introducing a different type of game to what the other four nations were playing. They had beautiful hands, great pace, and they were the first side really to begin introducing back-row moves, like the peel-off a lineout. These were all the new things that they brought to the game of rugby.'

In some ways Ireland – led superbly by Ronnie Dawson – and aided by fine performances from O'Sullivan, and the brilliant half-back pairing of Andy Mulligan and Mick English – did their best to imitate their Gallic counterparts, at least for an afternoon. Murphy points especially to the contribution of a young Wanderers three-quarter, Kevin Flynn, who turned the game in Ireland's favour. 'Kevin was the star of that victory, a wonderful footballer and should have got more caps for the Lions. That game, for me, belonged to Kevin.'

In order for Flynn to get his hands on the ball, Ireland needed to force turnovers and there was no one better at scavenging than Noel Murphy, a foil to any semblance of continuity the French tried to bring to their play. The try started with Murphy getting stuck into the French. From a scrum, the Ireland flanker eyed up their out-half, Montoulan, grabbed him and when the ball spilled, Flynn scooped up the ball and initiated the move to put Ireland 6–0 up. Mick English had already landed a fourth-minute penalty before Flynn again took centre-stage, engineering Niall Brophy's try, picking up a loose ball, darting away from the opposing forwards and then drawing the French defence. Then, he dispatched a clinical overhead pass to Brophy.

Despite a late comeback by France, Ireland proved worthy 9–5 winners. Even French newspaper *Le Journal du Dimanche* applauded Ireland's heroics the following morning, attributing their success to a superb all-round game. 'Ireland, unlucky in its other matches of the five-nation tournament, was intent in avoiding last place in the final classification,' said *Le Journal*. 'The Irish forwards were stronger than the French. Mulligan and English dominated the French backs. O'Reilly, Brophy, Hewitt and Flynn were faster than their French counterparts.'

Murphy adds, 'It was a great victory because they came as champions and came with the reputation of being fast, highly skilled and difficult to defend against. How did we manage to contain such a team? Well, we spent a lot of time at the practice on the Friday dealing with how we were going to stop their back-row movement, their peeling, their counter-attacking, their fluent passing and the running off the ball. Physically, it was a hard game – it was probably the hardest game of all championship. And mentally you had to be strong as well. You were always thinking, thinking. It was a great victory because it surprised a lot of people, came out of the blue. It was one of the great wins but, then again, Kevin Flynn's try that day was talked about for years and years after. He was so unlucky because had the Lions team being picked after that match Kevin Flynn, then only nineteen, would have made it.'

The win also marked Noel Henderson's final game in an Ireland jersey. 'He was one of these wonderful characters who played for Ireland and graced Lansdowne Road. He was an unbelievable captain, a very enthusiastic player. He was very good to me when I came on the scene. He looked after the younger members.'

After suffering a whitewash in the 1960 Five Nations and a narrow loss to the Springboks that December, little was expected of the Irish when the 1961 championship campaign opened against England at Lansdowne Road. When the final whistle blew and the home side won 11–8, there was a tangible sense of relief around the old ground. It was Ireland's first international win in nearly two years and first over the 'old enemy' in ten. Regarded by many as the best international Ireland featured in since the win over France in 1959, it saw the emergence of a new exciting scrum-half in Jonathan Moffett, who notched two penalties and a conversion into a capricious Lansdowne wind.

Still, no one stood taller than Murphy's cousin, Tom Kiernan, playing in only his second full season at senior level and still a student at UCC. 'Ronnie Kavanagh got the try but it was brilliantly set up by Tom,' recalls Murphy. Indeed, Kiernan's run bore all the hallmarks of what great full-back play is all about. Firstly, he gathered a kick ahead by Dickie Jeeps, the England scrum-half and captain, on the halfway line, hit fifth gear to bypass the English pack, then dropped a shoulder to glide by England out-half Ricky Sharp, and swerved left to draw John Wilcox to send Kavanagh over untouched.

Jeeps, considered England's greatest attacking threat, was snuffed out by the Ireland back-row with Murphy again prominent, repeatedly taking him in possession. And despite picking up a facial injury late in the first half, Murphy proved an inspiring figure as England probed and searched for that all-important try near the finish. Ireland's defence stood firm, while the sight of white shirts bouncing off Murphy and company in those frantic closing moments brought everyone in Lansdowne to their feet and, at the end, a massive roar went up.

'All I remember is managing to throw back wave after wave of Englishmen. We put in tackle after tackle, and the crowd loved it. There was a pitch invasion and I remember being carried off. I suppose everybody liked to beat England. I always felt it was a compliment to beat England because they were the people everybody wanted to beat. I wouldn't say they were the enemy; a lot of us toured with English players on Lions trips and made great friends. But, to this day, you can see what a win over England – especially at Lansdowne Road – means to everybody. But, as I say, it's a huge compliment to beat them because they felt they were the country that invented the game.'

In 1962, Murphy broke his collarbone against England in Twickenham and that kept him sidelined until the visit of the All Blacks to Lansdowne Road in November 1963. 'We should have won that game. In fact, we scored a try that was disallowed for offside and I'm convinced to this day that it wasn't. Johnny Fortune, though, scored a try on his debut but the All Blacks were unbelievable. They were unbeatable at the time.

'Munster, though, should have beaten them as well, but I will always remember their forwards, players like Colin and Stan Meads, Wilson Whineray and Kelvin Tremain – Kel Tremain scored their try that day against Ireland. Sadly, he is no longer with us, he passed away in 1992, but I will always remember him as being a real leader who had a great ability to score tries. And, of course, I thought the contribution of Donald Clarke from full-back was truly stupendous. He is one of the greatest ever All Blacks.'

This heroic Irish performance seemed the perfect prelude to the 1964 Five Nations. Things started very promisingly in Twickenham where Murphy scored a try in a victory that should have propelled Ireland to greater things and a possible Triple Crown. But the Irish contrived to lose to both Wales and Scotland at home, failing to capitalise on their excellent showings against New Zealand and England.

The following season offered more in the way of victories with a draw against France and a win over England at Lansdowne Road. The win over Scotland in Murrayfield then set up the prospect of a Triple Crown against Wales in Cardiff. This upsurge in form and performance coincided with the appointment of Ray McLoughlin as captain, the prop who brought his own methods to training and who prepared his charges thoroughly for the campaign ahead. His preparations and scientific approach to the game won Murphy's admiration, though it was said that McLoughlin's methods were too inflexible in theory and not workable by the players at his disposal.

'Ray was technically as good a prop forward as there was during that period of time. He was also a deep thinker of the game. He is, basically, a very intelligent person, and spent a lot of time preparing for matches. We prepared well before Ray came along but he added a little bit more to it. He was probably stricter in the routine of preparing – he used tell us not to read the papers, or that we should get more rest and plenty of sleep before big matches. He was captain of sides that should have won Triple Crowns and didn't because we were beaten by Wales, who had world-class players then. It would be mischievous to say that players didn't like his methods.

'There's a responsibility coming with lining out for Ireland and it was his responsibility to prepare us as best as possible for the matches.'

McLoughlin's influence was written all over Ireland's victory over South Africa in April 1965 at Lansdowne, less than a month after the agony of losing in Cardiff. It proved to be Ireland's first victory over the Springboks. 'It was strange to have a game played in the middle of April, and the wet conditions weren't ideal. As usual, we had to contend with a wind and there were the odd rain bursts during the game which made handling difficult. Still, they came into the game as favourites and they'd world-class players. They'd beaten the All Blacks and beaten the Lions.

'I will remember it for different reasons. I broke a little bone in my back and spent five weeks in plaster down to my toe. The injury happened as I fell to the ground and somebody double-tackled me. I went to the hospital, got my back x-rayed and they put me in plaster.'

With the wind to their backs in the first half, South Africa conceded the opening try. Scrum-half Roger Young was the creator, chipping a ball over the line for winger Pat McGrath who managed to get the touchdown despite the efforts of the covering Springboks. South Africa piled on the pressure before the break but a stoical Ireland held them to 3–3 before half-time. It looked ominous for Ireland when W.J. Mans scored a try minutes after the restart but the sides were level soon after when Tom Kiernan notched a penalty. Mike Gibson had also gone over for a try, but it was disallowed because of an outfield infringement. The stadium then exploded into life when

Kiernan scored the winning penalty to give Ireland a wholly unlikely victory.

On 21 January 1967, Noel Murphy captained Ireland to another 15–8 victory over Australia at Lansdowne. 'We had a good record against Australia. Looking back we were very unlucky not to win a Triple Crown that season after beating Scotland and Wales, but lost to England because of a last-minute try in a game where we did everything but score. We were attacking on the twenty-two when a crash tackle by one of the English forwards, Danny Herm, ended the move and the ball was turned over.

'Danny had connections with Munster. In fact, he got a final trial with Munster two years previously but we didn't pick him and then he played for England. His tackle denied us a Triple Crown.'

Murphy missed the entire 1967–1968 season through injury, but returned in January 1969 for the win over France at Lansdowne. He scored a try against England in a 17–15 victory in Dublin, one that will stay with him for a long time. It came eighteen minutes into the second half and, with Tom Kiernan converting, it gave Ireland a 17–12 advantage. It proved to be the winning try. Mike Gibson broke but was bottled up, and from a loose ruck, Murphy emerged with the ball to saunter over the line. He could be seen smiling as he walked back after scoring the try because he'd realised how easy the English had made his run.

Murphy was seen as the experienced hand in the pack and never stopped working from the first whistle. 'We came from behind to equalise on four occasions. I thought everyone put their shoulder to the wheel in the last twenty minutes. Some papers wrote that it was Munster's win because all the points came from Munster players. Barry Bresnihan and myself got the tries, Tom got two penalties and conversion while Barry McGann scored a drop goal. We went on then to beat Scotland in Murrayfield scoring four tries but lost then in Cardiff. That one really hurt.' It hurt because it came on the day Noel Murphy played his last game for Ireland. A bad day got worse when, ten minutes in, Murphy received a punch from Brian Price.

Though he hung up his boots, Murphy remained involved in the game. He took up the position of Ireland coach from 1977 to 1980 in a period when Ollie Campbell and Tony Ward vied for the Ireland Number 10 shirt. Murphy handed Ward his first cap against Scotland in 1978 in Lansdowne Road but, on the two-test-winning tour of Australia in 1979, the coach opted to play Campbell at out-half.

Talking of his years as coach, Murphy says, 'Nothing compares to playing for your country. It's hard to explain. We were different coaches in the 1970s and the 1980s, more in the category of organisers and motivators, and worked very close to the captain. I was lucky I had Fergus Slattery, a great forward and a very good captain, and, in my view, a dedicated player. We had a certain amount of success. My years as coach will be remembered for the dropping of Tony Ward. Much is written about it and much is written wrongly about it. Ollie Campbell did the job we wanted done against Australia, and I think I was proved right.

'Ollie, as we know, was picked by several other Irish selectors and sometimes people forget that Ollie contributed hugely to the success in Australia. If it wasn't a success, it would probably have been the end of Noel Murphy. Tony did bring an excitement to Irish rugby and we remain very good friends today. We meet regularly and I find him a dedicated individual. He is well able to write and has got a lovely attitude when he's coaching the younger lads. Look, most internationals get dropped at some stage in their lives – I don't know how many times I was dropped.'

Lansdowne holds many dear memories for Murphy. Naturally, he was sad to see it go, but is impressed with the new Aviva. 'The old stadium still means an awful lot to people. Ex-players loved matches at Lansdowne Road, and no matter what people say about how rundown it was, a lot of people in world rugby have happy memories of it.'

Bertie O'Hanlon
& Jimmy McCarthy

Winger & Flanker

1947–1950 & 1948–1955

Scoring two tries on your debut in the home of Irish rugby is usually the stuff of fantasy. Bertie O'Hanlon lived that dream, his two tries helping Ireland to a then record 22–0 win over its closest rivals on a bitterly cold February afternoon in 1947.

Dolphin's Bertie O'Hanlon arrived up from Cork, a rebel with a cause and something of an unknown quantity, but, by full-time, the darting debutant was the name on everyone's lips. Lansdowne didn't unnerve the twenty-three-year-old three-quarter; instead, he says, the pulse of the ground inspired him, and the memories today are locked warmly inside his heart: the cacophony of unbroken cheering amongst an Irish support that had little time to draw breath; the roar when he twice crossed the whitewash; and the sorcery of his team-mate, the enchanting Jack Kyle.

O'Hanlon remembers wearing heavy-duty boots for the game, uncomfortable as they were on a hard surface, the great freeze that winter left many grounds around Great Britain and Ireland unplayable. O'Hanlon remembers straw scattered around the field and a scything diagonal wind, but would it matter to the Cork athlete who was known to run the 100 yards in 10.1 seconds? Not a jot – it's said the jet-heeled winger's feet never touched the ground that afternoon.

The first Five Nations campaign since 1939 had kicked off a fortnight earlier, and Ireland, with fourteen new caps in their first championship game since the end of the war, came agonisingly close to beating France at Lansdowne Road. It ended 12–8 in France's favour with Kyle marking his debut with a stylish performance. When England arrived in 1947, nobody expected Ireland to score such an emphatic victory, but the visitors' giant pack was pulverised by an inspired Irish effort up front. This was a young Irish side that would evolve as the championship progressed, and which a year later, completed a Grand Slam.

O'Hanlon's emergence as a finisher of real quality and a robust tackler may have been one of the main talking points, but the Dolphin man says the advent of a half-back pairing of Ernie Strathdee and Kyle signalled the start of something special in Irish rugby. 'There is something similar in their arrival on the scene in that time to that of Peter Stringer and Ronan O'Gara at the beginning of the new millennium,' says O'Hanlon. Jack and Ernie was a match made in rugby heaven;

they were almost telepathic. There was an easiness between the pair that is hard to describe, and Jack always seemed to receive the perfect pass.'

M.F. Landers, writing in the *Cork Examiner*, lavished praise on the two wingers in which Hanlon and Barney Mullan shared a try apiece. 'It is no exaggeration to say that O'Hanlon's wonderful pace saved the situation on several occasions,' wrote Landers. 'His crashing tackles on Swarbrick, the English wing-man, stopped all English hopes in that direction, while his two tries were the highlight of the game.'

O'Hanlon's skills were honed at Rockwell College in County Tipperary. The dribble was one skill practised by most rugby players in those days, he says, but O'Hanlon was coolness personified as he demonstrated his neat foot-work when rounding both Swarbrick and Gray for his first try. It came on twenty-nine minutes when the ball arrived at his feet after Barney Mullan's attempted drop goal backfired Swarbrick fumbled Mullan's effort before the Dolphin flyer utilised his soccer-like dribbling skills to stunning effect and punished an English mistake. 'In my day, you dribbled a lot. I learned that in Rockwell. Today, it's all handling. I dribbled the whole way to the line; there were two Englishmen there and, with the ball about a yard from the line, I managed to dive over with it. That was the first try.'

He delighted the packed ground when he once again crossed for his second in the sixty-fifth minute. He gathered possession inside his own half, then swerved and slalomed his way to the line past Swarbrick, Gray and finally White, who had come cross field to try to prevent the try. 'I gathered that ball on my own twenty-two. I slipped the winger, the full-back and the wing-forward and touched down behind the posts. Sheer pace, boy! Lym Hall was the English out-half, but when he kicked for the corner flag, I gathered it and put it under my arm. In those days, we learned how to side-step also. And when I was in Rockwell, I learned how to kick with both feet, learned how to swerve, and to side-step. You never see that at all now. We ran for the corner flag; now it's a case of blowing the guy in front of you out of the way. The game is rugby league now.'

It wasn't O'Hanlon's first game in Lansdowne; he had to cut a path to the Irish team via the obstacle courses that were the famous Irish trials. 'I was exactly twenty-three when I got a call-up to play for Ireland. The first trials were inter-pros, and then you had a Combined Universities versus a Rest of Ireland selection. I was on the Rest of Ireland because I was with Dolphin. Jack Kyle, for example, was with Combined Universities, which drew players from UCD, UCG, Trinity and Queen's. Then you had the final trial – Possibles versus Probables. I remember playing in the Possibles and got picked thereafter. The Ulster Branch carried huge weight when it came to selection. In those days, you had more Ulster men on the team than Leinster, Connacht and Munster combined. You had players from Instonians, North of Ireland, Malone, Queen's – which had very strong senior sides.'

With England taken care of, hopes of a first Triple Crown since 1899 were kept on track with a 3–0 win away in Murrayfield but the wheels then came off the wagon against Wales at St Helen's in Swansea. Even Kyle couldn't conjure up anything special as Ireland fell 6–0 to the principality. In December, Australia came as the Third touring Wallabies to Lansdowne Road. In fact, it was only the second fully representative side from Australia, as the Second Wallabies had come and gone in 1939 without playing a match. O'Hanlon

Lansdowne Road has seen many great visitors – one of the most popular
is the All Blacks. *(Above)* Irish captain Willie Anderson faces up to New
Zealand captain Wayne Shelford as the All Blacks perform the Haka,
1989. *(Below)* The greatest All Black, Colin Meads, who brought his
magic to Ireland in 1963.

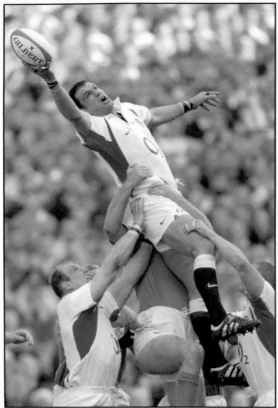

My ball: Martin Johnson claims a lineout during this Grand Slam clash between England and Ireland at Lansdowne Road in March 2003. Having being denied Grand Slams by each of the Celtic Nations in 1999 (Wales), Scotland (2000) and Ireland (2001), Johnson's men made no mistake on this warm day in Dublin 4, winning 6–42.

Under pressure: Scotland full-back, Gavin Hastings holds on to possession despite close attention from Keith Wood (left). Michael Bradley (centre) and Paddy Johns close in during this Five Nations clash in Lansdowne in 1995.

Michael Lynagh was a regular visitor to Lansdowne Road. The Australian broke Irish hearts when he crossed for a last-minute try in the 1991 Rugby World Cup quarter-final, but beating New Zealand in the semi-final, also at Lansdowne, remains one of his all-time favourite memories.

Gareth Edwards may not have won too many games at Lansdowne but the Welsh legend loved the stadium's unique setting. 'It had an electric atmosphere and was a wonderful arena in which to play rugby ... and the Irish crowd could make it an intimidating place for anyone, too.'

The old foe: Matches against England always hold something special. *(Above)* This 2003 clash will be remembered for different reasons. The teams line up in an unorthodox fashion after England captain, Martin Johnson, refused to move his men after being misinformed about Lansdowne protocol. *(Below)* Even though they had just won the 2001 Six Nations championship (despite losing 20–14 to Ireland), a dejected England still can't believe they let another chance of a Grand Slam slip through their fingers.

The crowd has always been part of the action at Lansdowne. *(Above)* Celebrations on the field after Ireland claimed the 1982 Triple Crown following a 21–12 victory over Scotland. *(Below)* Irish supporters mob Eric Elwood after Ireland fashioned a wholly unexpected 17–3 victory over Will Carling's England in the 1993 Five Nations.

Kings of Europe: *(l–r)* Gary Longwell, David Humphreys, Simon Mason and Andy Ward are shouldered high by their adoring fans after Ulster defeated Colomiers, 21–6, in the European Cup final at Lansdowne. Ulster became the first Irish province to win club rugby's most coveted prize.

Time to say goodbye: Leinster Rugby has played its part in some of Lansdowne's greatest days. After their final game on 31 December 2006 – a 20–14 victory over Ulster – the players say goodbye to their fans. In 1876, the first game at Lansdowne Road had involved these two sides in the old inter-provincial championship.

Red tsunami: Munster supporters played a huge part in Munster's quest for a first Heineken European crown. Here a section of its massive support celebrate in the East Stand corner moments after Munster defeated old foes, Leinster (30–6), in the never-to-be-forgotten 2006 semi-final at IRFU headquarters.

Farewell but not goodbye: (*Above*) Brian O'Driscoll, Leinster's and Ireland's greatest player of his era, waves goodbye to the old stadium as he heads to the tunnel. (*Below*) Despite the best efforts of Neil Best, Jamie Heaslip scores the last ever try at Lansdowne Road.

would have loved to have played southern hemisphere opposition but fate dealt him a cruel blow. 'I was injured for the Australia game. I sprained my ankle after an inter-pro match and had to cry off. Kevin O'Flanagan came into my place. He was a soccer international, a champion athlete and later a golfer and brother of Michael, who also played soccer and rugby for Ireland. That time, Australia beat us 14–6. In those days, you didn't get caps against touring sides; the caps were given against the home countries.'

Ireland hadn't won the Five Nations since 1935 and, on 1 January 1948, played France in Stade Colombes. O'Hanlon was joined on the team by his Dolphin team-mate Jimmy McCarthy to compete in the toughest and most volatile stage of all. France were viewed with a degree of suspicion, for in the eight seasons leading up to the Second World War, they had been excluded due to allegations of professionalism within their clubs. 'Jimmy had boundless energy,' says O'Hanlon, 'and he was tremendously fit. He trained and trained and trained. In terms of weight, there was only a pound or two between the two of us. Jim was about five-foot ten inches and I was only half an inch taller then him. I was twelve stone five pounds and he was twelve stone six – but he was playing wing-forward and was like a terrier in the pack. He timed his runs to perfection. He'd arrive with the ball and hit the opposing out-half at the same time; a great defensive player, a great man to handle the ball and a great dribbler.'

Alongside Bill McKay and, later, Des O'Brien, McCarthy completed, arguably, Ireland's greatest ever back-row. Bill McKay, known as 'the enforcer,' was an Ulster boxing champion and packed a heavyweight tackle as well, and also possessed great stamina as evidenced by his prowess as a 400-

yard runner. McCarthy was Kyle's real collaborator, who
caused enough fuss in the opposition cover to allow Kyle the
latitude to breach a defence. And, for the England game in
Twickenham – which Ireland won 11–10 – O'Brien completed
the great back-row line-up. O'Brien was an international
squash and hockey player but his greatest deeds lay on the
rugby field. O'Brien recalled in Peter O'Reilly's *The Full Bag of
Chips – Ireland and the Triple Crown*: 'In those years, when we
played for Ireland, none of us had a wife, let alone a motor car.
We either walked or cycled. It gave us a natural fitness which
players don't have today.'

In Munster in the late 1940s, Dolphin was regarded as the
best club side in the province accumulating silverware like the
Shannon side of today. In 1948, they did the clean sweep –
Munster Senior Cup, Munster Senior League and the Cork
Charity Cup, and both O'Hanlon and McCarthy were at the
centre of their success.

When they lined out together at Lansdowne on the third leg
of their successful Grand Slam journey in 1948, the duo
worked as much as possible in unison when the first whistle
blew. When not scavenging for possession, McCarthy was on
O'Hanlon's shoulder, a willing proxy to any opening that may
occur near the tryline. On one occasion in the first half, a
combination play between the Dolphin pair nearly produced a
try. 'It was hard and it was tough against Scotland but not
dirty,' says McCarthy. 'I remember reading afterwards that the
real heroes on the day were the sixteen forwards. There were
some ferocious battles around the fringes – these were as tough
as Munster club games – but I felt we had the edge. I think our
scrummaging was far superior. Karl [Mullen] won three out of
every five scrums against the head.'

'I didn't get over for a try but Jack Kyle was magnificent,' recalls O'Hanlon. 'Barney Mullan got the first try after a magnificent overhead pass from Des McKee but, in the last ten minutes, I remember we had to put in some last-ditch and desperate tackles. Then, with about five minutes to go, Jack Kyle cut through the Scottish defence and scored near the post. We had the championship wrapped up before attaining the Grand Slam against Wales. Against Scotland, I thought Kyle was absolutely outstanding, brilliant in my eyes, in all our eyes; he was the brains behind the Irish team. He had a superb swerve, and he was great to read a game. Often he'd knock a great ball over behind a defence onto the wing so I could run on to it.'

McCarthy adds, 'My job would be to protect Jack and he'd always slip the ball in to me. Jack was the best. A lot of people compare O'Gara with Humphreys but they don't compare him with Jack.'

Ireland went on to win the Grand Slam in Ravenhill on 13 March, beating Wales 6–3 with tries from Barney Mullan and Christopher Daly. O'Hanlon puts his try famine in Grand Slam year down to the presence of two Olympians on the England and Wales sides. 'The Olympic Games were in Wembley that year and Great Britain had two entrants, Ken Jones of Wales and Owens of England who were also on their national rugby teams. No way could I round those fellows – they were sprint champions.'

Ireland's hopes of retaining the Grand Slam went up in smoke in their first outing against France in the 1949 Five Nations, but their Triple Crown ambitions were kept alive in the next month with a resounding win over England. McCarthy and his back-row colleague McKay upped the ante from what McCarthy describes as a 'sluggish' forward display against the French. 'We were in England's faces from the beginning, breaking quicker than we did against France from rucks and scrums and making life hell for their half-backs Rimmer and Hall.'

Before the match, Hall would have been regarded as England's most lethal weapon, but McCarthy met fire with fire from the off, taking the out-half in possession at every available opportunity. Despite McCarthy's efficiency as flanker, he says the reasons for their success again lay at the dancing feet of Kyle. 'Kyle was again outstanding. There was a lot of messing the year before as to who should partner Kyle at half-back, but I thought Ernie was on his wavelength.'

O'Hanlon agrees, 'Kyle's running in attack that day was outstanding and, before the game, I discussed with him that he should use the kick ahead as often as possible and allow myself and Mick Lane run on to them. But he was great in other ways too – the way he'd be in the right place at the right time to gather a loose ball or when another Irish player got into difficulty there would be our Jackie.'

O'Hanlon was once again a thorn in the English defence for the second time in three years. The creator, again, was Kyle who feinted past Rimmer and Hall, laid off to McKee and the centre took a more direct line to goal crashing through a few English defenders and finally setting up O'Hanlon who scuttled up near the touchline and over in the corner. Before he went over, he has a sneaking suspicion that he might have put a foot in touch. 'Des McKee broke on the blindside and I was playing on the left. Bill flashed the ball to me, a couple of yards from the line. A Sunday Press photographer took a photo and it showed my foot on the line scoring for Ireland; but the touch judge was from Connacht! There was a picture I think of a dog getting in the way of the touch judge and I often thought afterwards – if only the dog could tell tales!'

The Triple Crown was attained at St Helen's with McCarthy getting the try in a 5–0 win. The following season was O'Hanlon's last for Ireland as a succession of injuries took its toll on a short but remarkable career. 'I played against France in Stades Colombes, then Louis Crowe took my place. Louis was better than me – and I was a travelling sub for all the remaining matches. If a guy cried off before a match commenced, a sub would get in, but if something happened during the match, no way. Once a team goes out onto the pitch and loses two or three players to injury, you just played on. You could be playing with twelve or thirteen for a while.'

'Bertie was around for about five years and he only got eleven caps, but if he was around today I'm sure he would have got double that,' says McCarthy. 'If you play for Ireland over one year now, you can earn sixteen caps.'

By 1950, O'Hanlon had departed the international stage and McCarthy missed all five games through injury (a burst knee). 'I cried off three times with an internal lateral ligament in an Irish trial at Lansdowne Road. It happened down in the Lansdowne End as I was going over to score a try beside the post. But Des McKibbin hit me. I never forgave him because it nearly cost me a place on the Lions tour, and certainly cost me three caps.'

McCarthy returned in 1951 when Ireland won the championship – a 3–3 draw in Swansea denying them a second Grand Slam – but that win brought an era of unprecedented success to a close. Between 1948 and 1951, Ireland played seventeen games, won eleven, drew two and lost just four – a respectable record in any era. It was a side that didn't know the meaning of the word failure, a special group with a winning mentality. 'Our best year, funnily enough, was 1951 when we won the championship,' says McCarthy. 'We threw away a game in Wales. We couldn't even manage three points from in front of the posts. That was an absolute tragedy. We were a winning team. The Munster team today seem to be the same. Losing? We didn't talk about losing, only about how we were going to win. That's the way New Zealand think and that's why they're winners.'

Jimmy McCarthy is regarded as one of the greatest flank-forwards ever to play for Ireland and he was one who lived and breathed down the opposition on the offside line. This was also the era of the foot-rush. Defending backlines weren't required to stand ten yards behind the lineout, while the offside line was in the middle of the scrum. Kyle's ability to evade the attention of opposition flankers was indeed an astounding feat, while McCarthy appeared to be in a perpetual state of offside.

'Bill McKay, Des O'Brien and myself played twenty times together as a back-row combination for Ireland: I played at Number 7 but McKay and I used play left and right. At that time, you were always training. I used go to seven o'clock mass every morning so Jesus would help me play well every Saturday. Your preparation would start on the Wednesday: you'd do a certain amount of running, then the next day some passing and sprinting. We always wore spikes and, when you do, you must always get up on your toes. When you put your boots on, you automatically got up on your toes. It made you faster. I always say to be fast, you've got to train fast.'

A special Lansdowne memory for McCarthy is when Ireland beat France 9–8 in 1951, an extra special day because of the arrival on the team of another Cork man, John O'Meara from UCC. 'There were four new caps that day but O'Meara had a spectacular outing. O'Meara was a marvellous passer of the ball and I'll always remember the heading on the *Sunday Independent* the morning after the match, it had 'O-O-O'Meara' right across the page.'

McCarthy captained Ireland in the middle of the 1954 Five Nations and played his last game – one he skippered – against England in 1955 – a 6–6 draw. Afterwards, the selectors never capped him again for his country. It ripped him up inside. 'This with two games to go in the championship – you'd think the selectors would leave me on,' he rages. 'I never, ever forgave them. It tore the heart out of me. When you have the guts and heart you want to keep going for ever. I was going to chuck it in that season because I was getting married and we were having a baby! The real reason behind me being dropped was age: I was thirty. In our time, they threw you off the team when you hit thirty or when you got married. It was a real anti-climax. I was at mass at Clarendon Street church the morning before the team announcement for the Scotland game and, halfway through the mass, I turned to my wife Pat and said, "I've just been dropped." The message came from above – I just knew that I was gone then!'

Still, both McCarthy and O'Hanlon look back fondly on those magical days during a golden age for Irish rugby, proud Cork men who starred at the Dublin 4 venue.

Nick Popplewell
Prop
1989–1998

The opening lines of his book *Time to Ruck and Roll* best capture Nick Popplewell's emotions on winning his first cap; a moment he'd looked forward to all his life. 'On a Saturday afternoon back in November 1989, I raced as fast as my short legs would take me onto the international rugby stage for the first time. The place was Lansdowne Road. The team at the opposite end of the ground, sharing the billing with Ireland, was the All Blacks.'

He'd arrived in his kind of rugby utopia; 50,000 spectators and a madding Lansdowne crowd and a couple of hundred thousand watching on television. Could life get any better for the twenty-five-year-old prop from Gorey, County Wexford?

'It appeared to be the perfect start,' he wrote. 'Lansdowne Road, the All Blacks, and yours truly in the green Number 1.'

He was so consumed in the moment and the enthusiasm to live every minute, that he remembers the exact moment he cracked two ribs in a scrum. 'Eighteen and half minutes later, my international rugby career came to a grinding halt. I was slowly led back to the sideline and into the Irish dressing room. It was a huge baptism of fire. It was unfortunate. I cracked three or four ribs and, when you're scrummaging, it's like standing on a nail – you can't walk after it, so off you go.'

Not many players get the opportunity to pull on the green against the All Blacks and run onto Lansdowne Road. It is the ultimate dream debut and, though Poppy's first cap ended with a whimper, it was still a moment to savour and to roar about loudly in the pubs afterwards. 'It was a great, fantastic, totally enjoyable eighteen and half minutes, and I can definitely understand how players who have only played for Ireland once still feel that they have experienced just about everything in their career,' he wrote later.

The prelude to the match was entertainment in itself. Willie Anderson's famous tête-à-tête with the New Zealand Haka set the Lansdowne crowd into a frenzy. Led by Anderson in the centre of the line-up, Ireland – linked arm to arm – crossed the halfway line shouting and roaring into the faces of the New Zealand players. Popplewell admits that Ireland's response to the Haka wasn't premeditated, but the new kid on the block ended up about three inches from Wayne Shelford's teeth. Scary stuff for a new fella, but confronting the Haka had the desired psychological effect as a pumped-up Ireland put up a good fight – though, ultimately, never came close to the then reigning world champions, losing 23–6. 'Was I intimidated by the Haka? No. I think if you are worried about it, all you have to do is look at the new cap – who is hopefully white – and follow him. And it's quite funny because he's totally out of sync. It's a bit like learning to dance. I think looking on at the Haka, you respect it for it is; it's part of the occasion, part of the folklore. It's just a sequence of events. You could say our action was disrespectful but it was also a spontaneous action.'

After a quick examination of his ribcage and a few painkillers, Poppy watched the remainder of the game from the sideline. 'I delayed going to the hospital until the Sunday afternoon. I didn't want to go on the Saturday night. I drank a few pints. To be honest, I drank more than a few pints before the night was over. Ribs or no ribs, I collapsed into bed in the end and slept my head off.'

Whether his was the perfect or imperfect start to an international career, Popplewell's injury cost him the best part of two years in the international wilderness. 'The first time I heard I was dropped was on the radio. Squad announcements then were quite casual. It's just as well I had a radio, I suppose!

'They dropped me for a year, then they brought me back to play Argentina, then they dropped me again for another game. And then they couldn't get rid of me for seven years after that!'

In the 1990s, Irish rugby entered its darkest period, and Poppy, though dropped for close to two years, suffered plenty of heartbreak when recalled from the international wilderness. 'Since I've retired, it seems they haven't lost a match and, when I was playing we hardly won one – so you kind of wonder what the common denominator is. It was a tough time. There was a huge amount of change. We were coming off the back of Fitzy's [Ciaran Fitgerald's] Triple Crown win, and that squad was held together for a long period of time. A huge feat was accomplished and then there was a huge transition. We went through so many coaches and players. Every f***ing year, it was a different coach. That was desperately unsettling.'

As he says himself, the whole country was pulling its hair out for three years – 1990, 1991 and 1992 – watching the Irish rugby team go from defeat to chaos to complete capitulation. 'A lot of people were mad as hell with what they saw,' he says now.

In October 1991, Popplewell played against Australia in that famous World Cup quarter-final – a peak amidst all the troughs in a transitional and forgettable period for Irish rugby. The Aussies won an epic clash, but only just. 'I got concussed from the start after a belt from Willie Ofahengaue. I was totally concussed for the rest of the game, and everyone says after it, "You made that tackle there, you got there, you got that man … geez, Popps is there again!" Maybe I should have got a few more slaps before other matches!

'We should have had it in the bag but experience cost us and they were bloody clinical.'

Fitzgerald, then Ireland head coach, did his best to try and lift players afterwards. 'He never stopped trying to build us up,' adds Popplewell, 'individually and collectively. He was brilliant in the dressing room and deserved better on the field.'

Popplewell made his debut in the Five Nations Championship in the middle of a ten-game losing sequence crossing Jimmy Davison's, Ciaran Fitzgerald's and Gerry Murphy's reigns as Irish coaches. The game was against what he considered an inept Welsh team at Lansdowne Road in January 1992. But Ireland still managed to lose 16–15. Cue more disillusionment among Irish supporters. 'The whole ground seemed to be quiet and depressed by the end of the afternoon, even though there was only one point in it, and even though the fantastic World Cup game against Australia was still in everybody's system. People expected so much that day ... that one-point defeat was like fifty points and it ruined the entire championship.'

The team went from heroes to zeroes within three months of the World Cup quarter-final. Some players got it worse than others, no one more than out-half Ralph Keyes. A darling of the 1991 World Cup, Keyes got jeered every time he kicked the ball during the 1992 Five Nations match against Scotland, for instance. Irish supporters expected more fireworks after the World Cup; expectations were high but the team couldn't deliver. 'The Irish public had had enough and the Irish players did not know which way to turn,' says Popplewell. 'We honestly didn't. There was not much fun left in playing for our country. Confidence was almost at nil.'

The mood in Lansdowne Road had altered considerably from that giddy October day when the Wallabies almost fell to Irish heart and passion; now the singing was replaced by jeering, booing and slow hand-clapping as Ireland lost to Scotland for the fifth successive time. 'When we played Scotland, they were without Finlay Calder and John Jeffrey who had both retired after the World Cup. We had them in Lansdowne Road, but lost 18–10 ... it was during that match that Molly Malone and all her friends left Lansdowne Road and all we could hear was booing every time the ball went near Ralph Keyes. It was a sad day for Irish rugby.'

If the players thought the season couldn't get any worse, next up were trips to Parc des Princes and a summer tour to New Zealand. Defeat followed defeat. And then Australia arrived for the autumn internationals, a day to rekindle old scores a year on from that epic World Cup quarter-final. Popplewell's good buddie John 'Spud' Murphy finally realised a life-long dream and won his first cap at hooker that afternoon.

'Nobody in the team was up for it,' Popplewell remembers. 'We were all wishy-washy, apart from Spud, of course. John was very talented and he would have been one of the most talented rugby players I ever played with – he could play wing-forward and hooker equally well. I felt very sorry for him. Johnny came in very late to play, and that was the Willie Anderson era where we had about 150 lineout calls, an absolute ridiculous number, and Spud had to learn those before his first match for his country. For your first test, you have enough things on your mind, but to have to learn these lineout calls and every one of them had different names. Years ago, you got to the halfway line and you knew what the lineout was going to be: either over the top or middle going backwards.

'And with the noise of the crowd as well, I felt sorry for Spud. He was made a scapegoat. It was unfortunate, but I think he had an extremely good game around the park that day; it was just the lineouts were a disaster, but through no fault of his own. Somebody should just have said, "Let's bring it down to basics with three lineout calls and revert to easier calls."'

Management looked for scapegoats in a further fall from grace for Irish rugby and they cast Spud Murphy aside forllowing this defeat to the world champions. Later, Popplewell wrote fondly of an old mate, who answered Ireland's call and more. 'At the end of his career, Spud has one Irish cap and that is one cap more than 99 per cent of the rugby players in this country. It's proper that he won that one cap at least. People talk about 'one-cap wonders' and try to feel sorry for those players, but why be sympathetic? Spud played for Ireland, and that's something.'

Ireland seemed to have turned some make of a corner in Cardiff Arms Park in the 1993 Five Nations. That 19–14 win over Wales will be remembered for Popplewell's tears as he borrowed a handkerchief from a cameraman and wept openly. Could anyone blame him? After playing seventeen times for Ireland, he had finally won a game in the championship.

Next up were England, who needed a good win to clinch the championship. Popplewell and Ireland, however, had other ideas. 'We had just beaten Wales in Cardiff and then we had England in Lansdowne. Everyone builds themselves up to play England. It's a major bloody scalp to get. Eric [Elwood] kicked the ball to start off the match but, before anybody got a touch on it, Paddy Johns took one of their lot completely out of it. Paddy could be an old briar at times. He'd surprise you. If you annoyed him long enough, he'd swing. He wouldn't go in with the fist but, if you're playing against him, there'd always be a knee and an elbow or something.'

Paddy's action triggered the rest of the team into berserk mode. '"Big Paddy is getting annoyed, Jesus Christ something must be up!" I said to one of the players. Paddy would lead by example and always got his ball in front of the lineout and make the hard yards. He'd be very honest.'

Ireland blazed to a wholly unexpected but deserved 17–3 win over Will Carling's England. Corner turned? Maybe. Monkey off the back? You bet. Not since Donal Lenihan led Ireland to a wholly unexpected 17–0 win in 1987 had Ireland scored a victory over the auld enemy. 'In the 1993 game, we didn't need a last-minute kick to win it. We knew we had the game won long before the end. The amazing and funny thing was that we won the game in the lineout more than anywhere else. On paper, that should not have been possible. They had Bayfield and Rodber. Galwey was at Number 4, and I was looking after them, shunting them up, as well as disrupting the opposition. There were quite a few digs going in from both sides, I have to admit.'

He remembers big hits and tackles and personal duels happening all over the ground. He says Pat O'Hara was phenomenal 'the hardest tackler I have ever witnessed up close', but it was Elwood and McBride, together, who totally creased Rory Underwood early on and, along with John's indiscretion, set the tone for the rest of the day.

He remembers Claw [Peter Clohessy], Terry Kingston and himself putting in the hard tackles too. The front five were producing the goods in the loose and Poppy had a good feeling about the outcome. Early on, Elwood put Ireland 3–0 up, converting beautifully into the wind from an angle. Then another bout of fisticuffs ensued after Stuart Barnes launched a garryowen and, after the ball returned from the heavens, a slap landed on an Englishman and Jonathan Webb added the resultant penalty.

It stood 3–3 at the break and, after the interval, Elwood's precision from placed kicks pushed Ireland 12–3 in front. Popplewell was at the other end of the field when Galwey scored the try that really clinched it. 'Near the end of the game, I suppose we were shouting our mouths off a fair bit, especially in the scrums. I never said anything to [Jeff] Probyn. I would respect him far too much to start down that road with him, but I enjoyed myself with Brian Moore, "Come on, Brian", that sort of stuff, "Good boy, Brian … No, Brian, that's no good." Claw and myself had several good chats in the scrum. "What do you think, Claw? Will we push them back a bit?" It's OK doing that in Moore's face, because he would be the very one who would be rabbiting on and laughing at us normally.

'It's not often we have England on the rack. They were in pain and we were dead right to smile at them. Things went very sweet that day. Certainly, a lot of the problems over the years have been that, although, yes, we're a fifteen-man team, you always seemed to be carrying four or five people. There were certain days where everything clicked like the Australia match [1991] or the English [1993] where everyone was on full cylinder and covering everyone else and you just seemed to be doing no wrong. If Dean Richards was playing, you were Donald Ducked because he was able to dictate the whole game and he wasn't playing that day with England. With Probyn, you'd never get much change out of him – he was always a difficult opponent, he was a light prop, only about fifteen-and-a-half stone, he had a huge work ethic around the pitch. We were able to psyche them out a little bit.'

Later on, in the early hours the morning after the England match, a Dublin taxi driver refused to take his fare from Poppy and his wife, Rachel. 'He told us we had paid enough having watched Ireland that afternoon. That night also, the Lions team to face New Zealand was picked – Clohessy and Probyn (England) were overlooked and they brought over Paul Burnell who didn't really cut it during the tour. Probyn should have been brought out there as well as Clohessy.'

Between 1994 and 1998, the heavy losses were sometimes tempered by an odd heroic win to lift spirits, but it always seemed a struggle playing for Ireland. Through it all, Poppy soldiered on despite the criticism and pessimism and jeering.

'There were loads of games where the supporters booed and slow hand-clapped. That's why we used wear bandages around our ears, you see!'

Even in the dark days, there was a support mechanism in Noel Murphy ('Noisy'), to lift players with bruised egos and shattered spirits. 'He helped the team enormously,' says Popplewell now. 'He was most human and good fun, and certainly kept me going in the latter years. He had a terrible job to do, and was asked to do in his spare time when the national team manager really should be a full-time position. He came into the job at a time when the Irish players were on the point of revolt, but Noisy was like a father to us from the word go. I toured New Zealand with Noel, and Eddie O'Sullivan was on it starting off on a long coaching career. When you tour a country, they pay your expenses but they only pay so much for thirty players and eight management. Eddie wasn't part of that eight, but Noel gave Eddie his own daily allowance – and these were times when every bloody pound was precious.'

Popplewell was also part of those Irish teams who like to forget those defeats to Italy at Lansdowne Road. Back then, losses to the likes of Italy only added fuel to the critics' fire. And the media didn't hold back. 'I think I lost to Italy twice in Lansdowne Road and once away. If you had a bad referee against Italy and you didn't sort it out yourselves, you were dined and ducked. They were offside all day long, the way we used to play. But they were always offside, pulling people's jerseys, and, if you weren't able to null that out and the referee wasn't doing anything either, what chance did you have? It was open season for them.'

Popplewell made his last full Lansdowne appearance against

Canada on 30 November 1997 (his last at the old ground was against Scotland on 7 February 1998 in a 16–17 loss, when he came on as a temporary replacement for Paul Wallace). He captained Ireland for only the second time against the Canadians and led them out under the newly installed floodlights. Poppy made way for an up-and-comer from Greystones named Reggie Corrigan. 'I was captain against Canada and Japan in the 1995 World Cup. We won both. I can proudly claim I have a 100 per cent record as captain! Reggie was coming through and it was time to vacate. I would have coached him in school and that depressed me even further and told you how old I was!

'I remember going to Lansdowne Road when I was nine or ten with my dad to watch internationals. We were very posh; up in the West Upper! My first taste of playing on the pitch was coming up against Des Fitzgerald of Lansdowne FC and I got throttled that day too, so it was a bit like the All Blacks one. Dessie was the main man at the time, and I wasn't going to get in his way. I learned a lot that day – I learned what not to do. Now I'm bringing my kids there. It has come full circle.'

Fergus Slattery

Flanker

1970-1984

The week Fergus Slattery received his first cap for Ireland (on 10 January 1970), should have been one to remember for the Dublin man, but, instead, the whole week and build-up was clouded in controversy. It centred on the visit of the South African Springboks, and the anti-apartheid movement in this country cranked its campaign up a few gears in those seven days.

Slattery, a business student at UCD, even ended up in debate on campus opposite the vice-chairman of the Ireland anti-apartheid movement, Kader Asmal – the motion simply being: Should the fixture go ahead or not? For Slattery, it was a week of mixed emotions, pitted first against Asmal on the intellectual front and then in a physical confrontation against the fiercesome Springbok openside, Jan Ellis.

'It would have been typical of a university debate. The actual venue was in the medical part of Belfield, but it wasn't a radical meeting by any means; in fact I found it to be a very tame affair. And it wasn't used as a demonstration by the anti-apartheid movement either. Kader Asmal called a motion against the game going ahead and there was myself as someone who was playing in favour of fulfilling the fixture. After debating a vote was taken, but I could not tell who actually won the head to head on the show of hands.

'But apart from this debate, I think the trade-union elements and the anti-apartheid movement were probably more demonstrative than anyone else. It was a controversial time, yes, but I don't believe it was as controversial as the time we went on the 1981 tour to South Africa. The one thing about the anti-apartheid movement was that they were very good at making up numbers. I remember they marched by the Shelbourne Hotel (team hotel), we counted the numbers and we also went out and asked the guards what their interpretation of the numbers were. And, of course, the numbers that appeared in the newspapers the next day were a complete exaggeration. That didn't bother me, though.'

A barbed-wire fence surrounding the pitch made it impossible for anyone to attack any of the players – as had been threatened – and the ring of steel was further reinforced by a large number of gardaí positioned around the perimeter of Lansdowne. While managing to preserve the peace inside the ground, the gardaí also had to keep a close eye on any possible attempts by protestors to climb the walls of the stadium. One photograph taken on an emotive day captures a demonstrator scaling a Lansdowne as two gardaí try to thwart his efforts.

However, despite tight security, the match didn't entirely pass without incident. Ireland hooker Ken Kennedy suffered an injury when a bottle was hurled from underneath the East Stand, hitting Kennedy on the back.

Just 30,000 (Lansdowne's capacity was 50,000) paid through the turnstiles that cold January afternoon, indicative of the split in opinion around the staging of this fixture. The terraces lay completely empty, and the weather had been so bad that week that straw was liberally spread on the pitch. According to Slattery, it felt like running into a barn.

As for the game, Ireland was lucky to escape with an 8–8 draw as the Springboks failed to convert a far greater proportion of possession into scores. Often cast as bad losers, the visitors didn't hold back afterwards, complaining that the Scottish referee played too much injury-time, which, they believed allowed Tom Kiernan snatch a draw with a penalty goal.

As for Slattery, he proved that he could survive the rough and tumble of international rugby. 'I think it was Paul McWeeney who wrote in *The Irish Times* afterwards that I wrecked their out-half Lawless' confidence. They had a massive pack, which could move a bit too. We gave away a bit in weight and, sometimes, it was unbearable for the forwards in there.'

And Slattery has fond memories of playing alongside Ronnie Lamont and Ken Goodall in that match. He recalls Goodall might have been frustrated in his efforts to attack the gain-line more, but the Number 8 saved Ireland's bacon in the sixty-seventh minute by running cross field and tackling Andy van der Watt into touch in goal when the Springboks' left wing seemed destined to score a try. 'When people mention the name Ken Goodall, I just have one word – brilliant. He was very, very quick, had great pace and was very, very athletic. He was such a huge loss to Irish rugby [At the start of the 1969–1970 season, Goodall switched codes to play league in the north of England.]

'That tackle was just one facet of his game. I was so, so upset when he left for league. I remember he came to me to shake my hand when I played for the Barbarians against Fiji at the back end of 1970. We played that match in Newcastle, and Ken came across from Lancashire to see the game. I was struck that he went out of his way to meet me – I was moved by that. We really missed him and it was a shame to lose him. He was a big loss to Ireland; a serious loss.'

There were still plenty of characters left in the squad to inspire Slattery. 'Syd Millar came in to the side in 1958, Willie John [McBride] in 1962 and [Ken] Kennedy in 1965, Mick Molloy a year after that, Goodall and Lamont were both Lions in 1966 and 1968 – it was just really a fantastic pack. Then you'd players like Gibson, Kiernan, Roger Young, Alan Duggan around for five, six or seven years. It was a cracking Irish side.'

The genius of Gibson didn't pass him by that January afternoon either. He just watched with awe as Gibson picked up a bouncing ball on halfway, skipped through the Springbok line and laid off to Alan Duggan who sprinted under the posts from forty-five yards for Ireland's one and only try. Ireland led at the break but a converted try by South Africa in the second half put them in the driving seat as the game entered injury-time. Seven more minutes were played, much to the Springboks' annoyance, before Ireland were awarded a penalty. Duggan intercepted a Tonie Rous pass to van der Watt, the Irish winger then ran and chipped over the full-back's head and forced the South Africans to concede a penalty which Tom Kiernan converted. Ireland had their draw.

Slattery is loath to make comparisons with other 'momentous' victories at Lansdowne but beating Triple Crown-chasing Wales in 1970 – the team of 'All Stars' – is not easily forgotten. 'Beating Wales was a huge win. People look back now and when they see 14–0, it just doesn't sound like a great game; it sounds simply like two tries by today's standards, but 14–0 was a hiding in those days. We scored two tries [three points for a try], a penalty, drop goal and a conversion. They were hammered. We just got in amongst them, broke up their rhythm and the Barry John–Gareth Edwards half-back axis. And Goodall had a great game. One of the tries was a kick and run by him. He chipped the Wales defence, ran through from thirty yards out and scored what was very much an individual try. I thought it was a super try. It just showed his whole array of talents. And Alan [Duggan], at the time, was one of the most prolific try scorers. That was his talent – give him the ball, anywhere near the line and he'd score. Don't know how he managed it, but he just had an instinct, total confidence. The closer he was to the line, the closer he was to scoring.'

By 1972, Slattery was part of a team capable of achieving something really big. Slattery says because of the political situation in the North, and because Wales and Scotland would not travel to Lansdowne that year, a Grand Slam eluded that Ireland side. The circumstances surrounding that campaign hurt Slattery and the team to the core.

'It was the biggest tragedy of my career. I always thought I had loads of time. I was just so young but I felt really, really sorry for the likes Tom Kiernan and Mike Gibson and Willie John. Those chances weren't going to come around too often. You go to Twickenham, you go to Paris and you win your two hard games – today they're still regarded as the two hard games. And we hammered Scotland and Wales two years earlier. We'd have hammered them if we got them that year, there's no doubt about it. They would have had no chance and I can say that openly now, but we couldn't prove it. I just knew it as much as I knew we'd beat Scotland in 1982 for the Triple Crown, that they'd absolutely no chance.'

France did travel to Dublin in 1972 to fulfil an extra fixture on the rugby calendar, but by then, the season was dead. 'We played them twice. The poor old French came over and we kicked the bejaysus out of them! They didn't deserve it but I think they got it from us. However, the whole championship was a bloody nonsense but it happened and there's nothing we could do about it.'

Slattery thought the team could have at least achieved immortality if they had defeated the visiting All Blacks in January 1973. Ireland managed a 10–10 draw and denied Ian Kirkpatrick and his All Blacks the accolade of becoming the first team from New Zealand to beat all four home countries on a single tour since the Originals in 1905. 'In a lot of ways, we mightn't have deserved to win. I think that would have been fair comment. Based on one or two other matches we had against them, we might have been unlucky.'

All that afternoon, he tried to keep his eye on New Zealand scrum-half 'Super Sid' Going, whom he describes as one of the best in his position at the time. While Slattery was regarded as decisive and aggressive in his play, Going was a plucky character with a penchant for doing the unorthodox. Slattery, who had made mincemeat of Gareth Edwards two years earlier, had met his match in Super Sid, once described as 'a bundle of barbed wire, cast iron and rubber, [he] runs like a slippery eel making for the water'. Indeed, Slattery found Going fast and elusive and difficult to tackle.

The enduring memory of that game for many people is Slattery's intervention in the build-up to the Irish try that levelled matters. Newspapers reported that the ground shook a tad after Slattery brought their Number 8, Alan Sutherland, to the ground with a thunderous tackle after a lineout. Scrum-half J.J. Moloney gathered possession, stole away from the ruck and delivered a sweet pass inside to Tom Grace. 'Grace did brilliantly,' says Slattery, 'the old chip over the top, chase and follow. The ball ran over the tryline and Grace took off in a race with their out-half, Bob Burgess. The ball was crawling over the dead-ball line but Tom got there and beat Burgess. Still there are about twenty people on the Irish team who claim they got a hand on the ball that led to that try!'

Barry McGann stepped up to take the difficult conversion, but the phantom Lansdowne wind again cast its malevolent spell over the ground, taking the ball wide of the posts. 'I got to know a lot of the All Blacks during 1971 Lions tour. And they still had the nucleus of that New Zealand side. They were really hurt after that Lions tour and they wanted victory at any price. But that Irish side was good enough to play anybody, and they were capable of beating anybody. And that's why I say we were just robbed in the 1972 Five Nations. That was a Grand Slam on a plate. We don't win many Grand Slams and that year we had it on a plate.'

While regarded as one of the finest open-sides to have ever played for Ireland, Slattery was gaining notoriety on the airwaves as well. He was playing for Leinster against the touring Fijians in 1974 when a radio show he had recorded in London was broadcast at the same time as the match. Those who brought radios to the game were getting a little confused, but given that Slattery had the capacity to cover all areas of the field on any given day, they thought he'd mastered the art of bi-location as well!

'I did a BBC radio programme called *Man of Action*. The sort of people they had on were lords of the realm, prime ministers, stately types. The producer got this idea that they wanted a sports person on so they first asked Cliff Morgan of Wales. But Cliff suggested me. I went over to the BBC and did this programme which was one hell of a challenge because I wasn't up with serious music, classical music and the like. I think it was a two-and-a-half-hour programme. But it was broadcast at the same time Leinster played Fiji in Lansdowne – and, when I came off the pitch, this rather grand-looking member of the old empire came over to me, completely bemused by the fact that I was playing on the pitch while he was listening to me on the radio. I just didn't realise the show was broadcast at the same time as our game.'

By 1975, he began to notice that the end was nigh for this Irish side. 'The old brigade like McBride and Kennedy were starting to burn a bit of diesel in the pack. I think someone termed us "Grandad's Army". Later, of course, the 1982 side were christened "Dad's Army".'

By 1982, he and the 'Dad's Army' annexed a Triple Crown at Lansdowne Road. 'The Dad's Army label didn't annoy me,' he says. 'This was second time round now with labels for I had heard all that in 1975 with [Ray] McLoughlin, Kennedy and Molloy being labelled "Grandad's Army". I was used to it. The

1982 side was mature – that's the word I would use. That 1982 side sprung from the 1979 tour to Australia, a tour that proved hugely beneficial in our development. Then the tour to South Africa in 1981 produced players like Paul Dean, Michael Kiernan and Keith Crossan. Players, like that, just popped out of the woodwork. I think we found five or six players and many of them made it into two Triple Crown sides.'

He acknowledges the contribution of Ollie Campbell to their 1982 Triple Crown win. 'We wouldn't have won anything if it wasn't for Ollie. It's a bit like talking about Martin Johnson: how important was Johnson for England in winning the 2003 Rugby World Cup? Ollie was our man. It might be unfair on others to say it but that's the reality of it. He was just such a massive player for us. And the great thing about the pack was it was 'earthy' – there was good representation from all four provinces. You could say we'd a bit of people from everywhere in that side.'

He regards the 1982 Triple Crown win over Scotland as the most important game in his career. But most of all, he believes, it gave an Irish people and an Irish society – in the midst of an economic depression – a massive lift. 'It was like Jack Charlton's two World Cups. It was so important to the dignity of Irish people. We've seen how Gaelic Games and how Munster and Leinster winning the European Cup have had an enormous effect on people. But winning that Triple Crown in Lansdowne Road was so important for Irish rugby. It was a bit like the 1971 Lions tour to New Zealand, it was just so important to everybody. It broke the duck and it made the next thing possible and we won another Triple Crown three years later.'

However, Slattery wasn't about to bow out of Lansdowne

Road quietly – he notched a try against England in 1983, a year Ireland earned a share of the championship. In the game, Campbell was the architect of England's downfall, scoring twenty-one points, while for Slattery it was his sixtieth international and his third test try. In the immediate aftermath, an emotional Slattery quipped, 'I've been over the line more times than I care to remember. This time I managed to ground the ball!'

'I scored down in the Lansdowne Road corner, one of those messy old fumbles, a "pick-it up-and-drive-over-the-line" type of try' he adds. I actually drove through Clive Woodward. He was the man between me and destiny! I think it was Moss [Keane] who gave me a pass for you wouldn't get a pass from a back, I'll tell you that! You'd have to have been playing for Ireland for ten years before you'd get a pass from a back!'

Peter Stringer

Scrum-Half
2000–present

The great Bill McLaren once said that the ideal scrum-half has to be very brave; brave because he's in the frontline, brave because he has to deal with a big opponent coming around the corner. Peter Stringer, a Lilliputian in a forest of Gullivers, is someone who you would describe as having earned the tag as Munster and Ireland's Braveheart and, figuratively speaking, we have seen him knock down a few biguns over the years. Sometimes, we close our eyes and fear that he might never get up again, but he always rises, dusts himself down and moves on to the next play.

But, to focus merely on his five-foot-seven-inch frame diminishes the other facets of his game. The pass is his weapon, his forté – matched with that telepathic half-back relationship that has evolved with his long time out-half partner, Ronan O'Gara, since their schooldays at PBC in Cork, and subsequently with Munster and Ireland. And when O'Gara gave one of those utopian Lansdowne Road displays – cue v. Australia 2002, v. South Africa 2004 and against Leinster 2006 – the service from his Number 9 can sometimes be forgotten amidst the good work of the 10.

While there has been a changing of the guard at 9 and 10 for Ireland – Tomás O'Leary and Jonathan Sexton look odds-on to be the long-term half-back partners – O'Gara and Stringer have provided Lansdowne with some memorable moments. In the late 1990s, they were thrust initially into the limelight with Munster in the Heineken Cup. After two heroic victories over money-rich Saracens in December 1999 and January 2000, they were then cast onto centre-stage against Scotland for the 2000 Six Nations.

It was a changing time in Ireland both socially and economically. The turn of the millennium and the Celtic Tiger brought with it an optimism that swept the country. The arrival of Stringer and O'Gara came bang on cue to supplement this flighty excitement that Ireland was capable of achieving beyond the mediocre.

The new caps, young and holding few inhibitions, held no fear. Three more made their debuts alongside Stringer and O'Gara that day against Scotland in Lansdowne Road – John Hayes, Shane Horgan and Simon Easterby – and all five all brought vibrancy to a team one newspaper christened 'Young Ireland'.

After the bitter defeat to Argentina in the World Cup the previous November and the subsequent humiliation meted out by England in Twickenham in the first game of the 2000 Six

Nations, change was needed and Ireland coach Warren Gatland opted for youth and a daring game-plan in his next match. Gone was the plodding and the turgid rugby, the slow ruck-ball and staid three-quarter play. In its place came adventure and all-singing, all-dancing rugby and the Lansdowne Road audience lapped it up.

'We hadn't beaten Scotland since 1988,' says Stringer. 'For the build-up, I remember we were staying in the Glenview at the time. Out of the blue, Warren came up to me before the team was announced publicly and said simply, "We're going to go with you." Obviously, it was a shock, and I'm there thinking in the foyer of the Glenview, "Am I really good enough for this?" At that moment, all the doubts come creeping into your head. You're delighted on the one hand, but it's daunting enough to play with the likes of the Claw [Peter Clohessy] the Claw and Gaillimh [Mick Glawey] who have been there for years. In the end, you just go with it. Thankfully, there were four other guys earning their first cap. When you're on your own starting out, there can be nerves. I remember the media stuff was shared between the five of us instead of all the pressure being on one fellow. That made it easier really in the build-up to the game.'

The Twickenham debacle needed to be exorcised fast from players' minds following a painful 50–18 defeat, and Gatland and new backs coach, Eddie O'Sullivan, drew up a bold game-plan. To the supporters who saw Ireland beat Scotland that day, it was fast and it was furious, and Ireland ran roughshod over the Scots in a 44–12 win. And, more importantly, the famous 'roar' returned to the old stadium. 'If you looked back at the English game, the ball was slow. Everything was pedantic. Warren and Eddie wanted to bring something new to it. Since that week, we've relied on always getting the pace of the game up. We mightn't be the biggest team, but with continuity we could bring it to a pace and a level where the other team can't cope, and then you're on a good way to winning the game.

'Our aim was to get the ball away from rucks as quickly as possible and give our backs the space because we had a good backline. Probably for the first time in Irish rugby there was real threat out wide. We came off the back of a hiding over in Twickenham, and the coaches gave us the licence to have a go. The daunting task of going out for your first cap brings its own pressure but, in a strange sort of way, there wasn't that much pressure on because people didn't really know what to expect from us. "Have a go. What was the worst thing that could happen? Express yourself." These were the words running through my mind.'

In the dressing room before kick-off, Stringer remembers Gaillimh putting the new lads at ease, Woodie winking and smiling, telling the new caps to enjoy themselves. Galwey wrapped his arms around both Stringer and O'Gara for 'Amhrán na bhFiann' and 'Ireland's Call'. 'Ah, Gaillimh. Yes. Special moment,' smiles Stringer, 'and do you know I remember we stood in the same positions for the Italy game, and the following morning one newspaper had a photo and the caption titled it 'Goodfellas'. I think just going up for the anthem, it's obviously hard not to be affected by it. It's your first time out on the field with the Irish team. But then the doubts came back to my head again, "Do I remember all the calls because I'm in a position to make decisions? Bloody, hell, I hope all this works out." There is a lot of pressure there. Then the first twenty minutes pass you by in a instant.'

Playing alongside O'Gara should have lightened the burden, but O'Gara was in Stringer's boat too. Would they be one-cap wonders? Would they sink or swim? 'In the first half, we didn't really click. I threw ROG a few shaky passes and put him under a bit of pressure. He let me know about it … and still does! To this day when we ever play together, he keeps me on my toes. We got into them in the second half, got a bit more confidence and seemed to click a bit better. I always like to think that it's a game of rugby for eighty minutes. I remember Declan Kidney saying to me when I was a student in Pres playing cup rugby to concentrate on what I was doing and not be affected by what was going on around me. Schools Cup matches can be big, boisterous occasions, they test your nerves as a young fellow but were good bloody preparation when I look back now.'

He says he wouldn't normally go back and watch video replays of matches but his earliest memory of beating England gets a few runs now and again. If he likes throwing himself recklessly into tackles, then Stringer serves as Ireland's most famous leg-tripper. His ankle-trip on Dan Luger in October 2001 ultimately denied Clive Woodward's side a Grand Slam. It was England's final 2001 Six Nations game, pushed back to October because of the outbreak of foot-and-mouth in the spring. Keith Wood vividly describes this pivotal moment in the game in the Inpho Photographic Agency book *Putting it on the Line*: 'We led 14–9 [in the second half] and the battle is raging just inside our half when Dan Luger finds a gap and goes haring towards our line. The gap is my fault. I am slow off the ground and in rushing to get into the defensive line more quickly, I leave a gap outside of me and Luger races through. We all chase back but he looks home and dry. If he scores, they will go on to win the game, of that there is no doubt … but cometh the hour, cometh the midget and Peter Stringer's incredible ankle tap saves the day. We arrive in support and turn the ball over …'

'The midget' remembers the moment vividly. In his home in Cork, his dad, John, has this moment framed in a photograph. 'Dan Luger had beaten a few guys, but he had beaten me easily when I fronted up to him first. He side-stepped me and rounded me. For whatever reason, I kept going. I normally wouldn't have a hope of catching them wingers. He had to beat Girvan Dempsey after that, and stepped fairly easily as he had done to me. But I think for a split second he had to check and got through without Girvan laying a hand on him. That split second gave me the momentum to catch up with him. Despairingly, I just threw myself out there. I found Humphs [David Humphreys] saying to me afterwards that he had given up the chance of trying to catch him. In the video when I hand trip him, you can see Luger falling and, just before he falls, Humphreys has conceded that he's obviously going to score because Luger's one of the quickest guys in world rugby. And then, as Luger is falling, you can see Humphreys' reaction. I got behind for the ruck and kicked left-footed to touch. It nearly didn't make touch. I was like, "Jesus get into touch, give the lads a bit of a rest." It made it to the ten-yard line. It was a great feeling. The photograph shows the crowd in the background as Luger is running away from me. Irish fans have their hands on their heads. Yeah, that was a special moment.'

Though England lost the Grand Slam, they lifted the Six Nations trophy as championship winners. No bad feat, but Clive Woodward, Martin Johnson, Lawrence Dallaglio et al judged themselves on Grand Slams – though Johnson and Dallaglio were injured for the Ireland game. To witness the celebrations afterwards, you'd think Ireland had won the World Cup as an understandably downbeat England team collected the championship trophy in front of the West Stand. For about an hour afterwards, Stringer felt his feet never touched the ground. 'There's a photo of Gaillimh, Woodie and myself in the lap of honour. There I am just walking around with these two legends. They never looked happier. They had been part of some low days for Ireland, and here I was, my first real experience of really connecting with the Lansdowne crowd. Seeing how much it meant to the supporters, I felt proud of what we had achieved. Watching England collect the trophy was weird, yes, but when you're disappointed like they were, it must be strange going up to receive a trophy and try to feel happy about it. On the day, we were the team who felt we played better and deserved it and we nearly felt like saying, "Give us the cup!"'

The dressing room was a mix of hugs, champagne spray, tears, weariness and renditions of 'From Clare to Here' led by Killaloe native, Keith Wood. 'Stand Up and Fight' – a Munster anthem – composed by manager Brian O'Brien also got an airing. Even then Taoiseach, Bertie Ahern, stepped into the inner sanctum to catch a taste of a famous day in Irish sport. 'I remember Ronan going absolutely mad. In fact, everyone was freaking out, and seeing the Taoiseach coming in and the lads trying to lift him up on their shoulders – we also did it to Marty Morrissey in Limerick for the Munster homecoming in 2006. It was quite surreal.'

He remembers England prop Jason Leonard popping in to offer his congratulations. Leonard had earlier sought out his friend and London Harlequins club-mate, Keith Wood, at the final whistle offering the Ireland hooker a warm embrace. Inside with the Irish lads, his presence and magnanimous gestures were a throwback to the great amateur days. 'I remember that,' says Stringer. 'Jason is a great fellow, real old-school. I remember Rala [Paddy O'Reilly] handed him a cup of tea, saying, "There, two sugars, Jase." Jason sat down with his cup of tea, and had a chat with a few of us. He's a real gentleman, a real genuine fellow.'

After England, the good days continued to happen at Lansdowne, that's if you're inclined to call coming close to beating the All Blacks a good day. As Munster fans discovered in the week of their seismic clash with Leinster in the 2006 Heineken Cup semi-final, the wee man has a knack of picking up big injuries before big clashes – and in Stringer's mind nothing came bigger than the All Blacks in Lansdowne. He certainly didn't want to miss this one. For instance, he grew up admiring New Zealand's David Kirk, even imitating him as a young lad with Cork Con in Temple Hill.

'I injured my ankle the Thursday before the All Blacks game. Imagine that, just two days before the biggest day of my life. I was a real doubt. I had a fitness test the morning of the game, played the game – how I don't know – and then had a scan on it the morning after. I literally couldn't walk. It turned out, I'd cracked my heel bones. I managed to live the dream against the All Blacks, though, but I was out for eight weeks after that. I spoke to the Claw while assessing my chances of playing. He never got a chance of playing New Zealand and I felt it might be my only ever chance of playing them.'

Those at Lansdowne remember one of those real, edge-of-the-seat days at the old ground. After England, we thought we had enough of the drama for one year. Then Ireland got away and led New Zealand 21–7 two minutes after the restart. It was fantasy rugby and Ireland were on the cusp of something really big. Eighteen minutes later, the score stood at 40–24 in New Zealand's favour. Stringer blames himself for one of the tries. 'There I was next to a ruck on my own line, the New Zealand second-row picked and basically dunked the ball over me and over the tryline. I found myself in a position about a foot from the line and it was a case of this six-foot seven-inch guy walking all over me. I was disappointed and blamed myself for that try. We could have taken them. But I remember there was some noise in the stadium that day, the lights were on and that created an even better atmosphere.'

As for the head coach, Gatland must have been on a high. Here he was on the cusp of creating a bit of history and many felt his future was secure despite what happened in Murrayfield earlier that September (Ireland were well beaten by the Scots, ending any hopes of a Grand Slam). Having beaten England and having pushed the All Blacks close, he must have been a dead cert for a new contract. But the IRFU committee took an alternate view and, on 28 November, the former All Black was summoned to the Berkeley Court, near Lansdowne Road, and told his services were no longer required. Gatland subsequently went to London Wasps, coaching the capital side to three Premiership titles and a European Cup in 2004 – beating Munster along the way in a seismic semi-final at Lansdowne Road.

Stringer, however, will remember Gatts for one token of kindness in particular. 'He wrote me a letter after he finished up just saying he wanted to congratulate me as a player, not after any specific occasion or anything, but to say he had doubts about my size initially and whether I would survive in international rugby. He wrote that, as soon as he plucked up the courage to pick me, every doubt just left him about my abilities as a person and as a player. The letter is something I hold dearly. It's a great thing to get from a man who wouldn't be renowned for expressing his emotions that often and to get that was certainly very nice. That's something I'll always remember about the man. I didn't know which way to approach him when I came into the set-up first. I found him a difficult guy to relate to – I think a lot of people would say the same. He was very influential at the same time – he would have a quiet word with you rather than make it publicly known.'

A southern hemisphere scalp came sooner rather than later when Ireland defeated Australia in the rain at Lansdowne the following autumn. Stringer was playing opposite one of the world's finest scrum-halves, George Gregan. He remembers Gregan as someone who just spent a lot of time just "talking" to the referee and complaining as matters on field ran against the Wallabies. 'It was an absolutely miserable day. There were puddles of water all over the ground, but sometimes when it's like that, you get into a game more. You're not spreading the ball from touchline to touchline, but instead you're keeping it in close, making more tackles in around the fringes. There, you can get a real sense of wanting more. We were sliding around and, when you're tackling, it's so much easier than dry ground. There was a real sense that day that we were not going to allow them to beat us in our backyard. The win just brought our game to a new level. We felt afterwards that we could compete against these teams.'

Brian O'Drsicoll captained Ireland for the first time that afternoon in the absence of the injured Keith Wood and produced one of his finest hours in a green jersey. 'Brian was really special that day. I think intelligence on the field is his greatest virtue – that ability he has to read a game is impressive. As backs, we talk a lot about technical play and everybody stands and listens when Drico has something to say.'

Winning a Triple Crown against Scotland in 2004 was a special day for Stringer, too, because he scored a try. He can't remember exactly where he was when Ireland lifted their last Triple Crown in 1985 but he knows the 2004 win was special to Irish supporters. 'It was quite close at times. Matt Williams had Scotland well fired-up because of his former association with Leinster. He knew a lot of our players. There were a few nerves at the start of the game but I think when David Wallace scored, it gave us breathing space. Then I nipped in for a nice one! I felt very proud to score in that Triple Crown win. Normally, I wouldn't be the most flamboyant celebrators of tries, but I was on my knees, and threw the ball into the air. Scoring tries can sometimes bring out strange things in people.'

The big names in world rugby kept falling at Lansdowne. In the 2004 autumn internationals, South Africa learned that you should never underestimate the Irish. Off the field, the build-up got interesting when Springbok coach Jake White, who had masterminded two test victories over Ireland in South Africa a few months earlier, rather carelessly let slip at a press conference saying only three Irish players would make it into his match-day twenty-two. Many saw his remarks as a slur on Irish rugby, even if White tried to row back later in the week, going on the charm offensive. 'I've huge respect for Irish rugby,' he later said, trying to keep a straight face. 'The Willie John McBrides, the Syd Millars, the Noel Murphys, Ollie

Campbells and Fergus Slatterys are great players, and great people have come out of this country. So if it was seen as disrespectful then that is not the way it was intended.'

However, Eddie O'Sullivan – like many who had given their lives to Irish rugby – held an altogether different view. 'Jake's remarks were pretty much an attack on Irish rugby as a sport,' he said, 'We're as proud a rugby nation as anybody else. We mightn't be as good as South Africa, according to the record books, but we're proud of our rugby. What he said had nothing to do with the game. I just felt unhappy about what he said. I felt it was totally unnecessary.'

Going into the test match, he omens looked good for Ireland. Since their Triple Crown win over Scotland the previous March at Lansdowne, Ireland had won thirteen of their previous fourteen games at the ground.

On the day, O'Gara put in a quite magnificent performance scoring all of Ireland's points – including a try – in a 17–12 victory.

'Performance-wise, that was one of our best in a green jersey,' says Stringer today. 'In 2000, we were quite close to beating them but we didn't really have that self-belief to really go and win it. But to beat Australia and then South Africa in successive seasons saw a growing maturity in the team. We really clicked as a team and completely outplayed South Africa. I remember ROG sneaked in for a try in the corner, but he had a great day all the same. For Irish rugby and for Lansdowne Road that was another unforgettable afternoon.'

In the one calendar year, a Triple Crown and a win over one of the southern hemisphere Big Three had been achieved, but, in April 2004, Stringer was part of a Munster side that lost to Wasps in the European Cup semi-final. It was one of those hugely colourful days at Lansdowne Road, a packed house brimful with fanatical Munster fans. 'I remember Lawrence Dallaglio recounting the day afterwards that, when he walked out before kick off, he said, "What the f*** is this?" They only had a few hundred supporters over at it. They didn't realise what hit them, but the match itself was a horrible one to lose. I remember Trevor Leota got in the corner for a try. Myself and John Kelly tried to stop him, but I'm adamant to this day that I held up that ball in the corner where Leota dived.

'But when you lose like we did that day, you feel like you let people down. That was the worst part of it. It just felt like the day deserved a victory, but it didn't happen. It was so emotional. I remember there being a lot of tries in it. The lead changed hands so many times and for the supporters it was very emotional. I met Warren afterwards. Obviously, he shook hands and said hard luck but was delighted for his own team coming back. He was delighted that he had done it against Munster at Lansdowne Road. It was a sweet victory for him.'

For Stringer though, little will surpass Munster's victory over Leinster in the 'Seismic Sunday' clash in the European Cup semi-final at Lansdowne Road in 2006. 'The inter-pro games are always the toughest you're going to play in,' he says. 'The fact we know each other so well makes it that bit more difficult to break down defences. Sure, it was difficult going out to play some of your Ireland team-mates, but, for eighty minutes, there were no friends that day. Everyone fully realised that there was an opposition there standing in our way of becoming European champions. You hear of boxers who are good friends going into the ring and then belting the living daylights out of each other. It's just when you get into that arena it's not about friends, it's just about being selfish and wanting to win the game.'

Other great days followed for Stringer at Lansdowne. In the 2006 autumn internationals – the last Ireland matches played at the old Lansdowne Road – Ireland posted exciting victories over South Africa and Australia, the Cork man at the centre of those victories. Ireland completed a hat-trick of November test wins that month, demolishing a Pacific Islands combination before taking a lap of honour on Lansdowne's last big international day. Stringer remembers those days fondly but he hopes to be part of bigger ones when Ireland return to the new Aviva in November 2010.

Twenty-three years ago, Stringer made his first trip to Lansdowne Road, travelling with his father, John, for the Ireland–England Five Nations game in February 1987. Sitting on the Upper West Stand, he watched his fellow Cork Con men, Michael Bradley, Michael Kiernan and Donal Lenihan, fashion a thrilling 17–0 win, and the magic of the place took hold of him that day. 'It was tremendous, the whole thing about going up to Dublin, seeing the match – I wouldn't have experienced anything like it. I'd never seen that number of people before in my life.'

Ulster's Triumph

The European Cup, 1999

Simon Mason
& Gary Longwell

When Ulster lifted the European Cup on 31 January 1999 in Lansdowne Road, rugby in Ireland took off in ways no one could have foreseen. It was more than simply an Irish province making its claim as the High Kings of Europe, it was more than the sight of David Humphreys and Mark McCall becoming the first Irish players to jointly lift the European trophy. More than anything, Ulster's triumph acted as a catalyst for Irish rugby rejuvenation.

Twenty-four hours before the final against Colomiers, Ulster coach Harry Williams faced the press, saying an Ulster win would re-invigorate the sport in Ireland. 'Of course we want to win for Ulster,' he said at the time, 'but we also want to win for the whole of Ireland and make people proud of Irish rugby. I can promise we will do everything in our power to do that.'

Since that memorable afternoon in Lansdowne, Irish rugby has never experienced so many highs: Munster went on to contest four European Cup finals, winning in 2006 and 2008, Leinster also lifted European club rugby's greatest prize in 2009, Ireland, under Declan Kidney, secured a Grand Slam the same year, while Kidney's predecessor, Eddie O'Sullivan, guided Ireland to Triple Crowns in 2004, 2006 and 2007.

Ulster's triumph also opened the gates to greater funding for the provinces. Up to 1999, the provinces didn't have fully professional squads, but Ulster's win accelerated the move to full-time rugby across all four provinces. For instance at the beginning of the 1998–1999 season, Williams was dealing with a squad of full- and part-timers. How could he stitch together a cohesive outfit to take on the likes of Toulouse or Stade Français, he thought? Their first two pool games proved that it'd be a difficult path if they harboured ambitions of reaching a final in a season when the English clubs opted out of the competition.

In a 38–38 draw at home to Edinburgh, Williams' team leaked tries at a rate of knots even if they were scoring plenty at the other end. In their next match, away to Toulouse, Ulster conceded five tries, one more than against Edinburgh, in a 38–3 loss, and Williams felt drastic action was needed.

'Back then some of the players were semi-professional,' says Ulster's full-back of the time, Simon Mason. 'Harry made the decision that we were going to go full-time during the day. We ended the evening training sessions, and that made a big difference to the squad.'

Williams felt this was the only way of bringing any sort of tangible success to the province. 'In our third pool game, at home to Toulouse, we got off to a good start,' says Mason. 'The heads were more focused and there seemed to be more unity and more belief in the side. After beating Ebbw Vale comfortably, we then went to Edinburgh and won (23–12), effectively securing our place in the quarter-finals with a home draw. I think the aims in Europe today haven't changed: you try to get through your group and get a home draw in the quarters and that then gives you a hell of chance of progressing.'

Toulouse were in their crosshairs again in the quarter-final but, importantly, Ulster had them at home. The quarter-final was one of those typically fraught Ravenhill nights – the rain teeming down, the crowd in full voice and an underlying hope amongst home fans that the French might crumble, which they tended to do away from home. But Toulouse defied this French habit of falling to pieces away from home, and fought the good fight.

But Ulster took them on up front, and, in a cracking cup tie, beat the 1996 European champions, 16–13. The north-erners had made their biggest European statement to date; now all they needed was a favourable semi-final draw. Win that and a Lansdowne Road final beckoned.

Once again, Ulster got lucky in the draw. They may have clinched a home semi, but the opposition was of the Gallic variety once again. Parisian club side, Stade Français, arrived in all their pomp and majesty expecting Ulster to roll over, but the Irish province defied its underdog status with the performance of the season in a screamer of game that ended 33–27. Simon Mason kicked twenty points, the tries came from Humphreys and Stephen McKinty.

After the game, Williams walked into the dressing room and confidently told his team that the title was Ulster's. Whether that was a good or a bad thing, Williams made a statement some thought dangerous, others arrogant, while supporters felt they'd witnessed their team peak against Stade Français. 'I remember going into the dressing room in Ravenhill and Harry said, "Our name's on the cup,"' says lock Gary Longwell. 'Harry never said anything cheaply, and his words had a massive effect on us in a positive way.'

'It was turning out to be a very special year,' says Mason. 'We started in September by playing in front of relatively small crowds, but gradually the team got on a bit of a roller-coaster. The crowds built and built and we got to this memorable semi-final in Ravenhill when 20,000 turned up.'

As the final neared, the sense of expectation grew, and as predicted, the demand for tickets was huge. It wouldn't happen today, but in those early days of professionalism, the players often chipped in with some admin duty. 'I remember helping the staff at Ravenhill in sorting out the tickets – we could have comfortably filled Lansdowne three times. I was able to get ninety tickets for friends and family which would be unheard of nowadays but, as players, we got a massive ticket allocation.'

The grand relocation of Ravenhill to Dublin 4 began in midweek, and the Ulster squad and management booked into the Berkeley Court Hotel from the Thursday night, a location central enough so as not to feel too disconnected from the occasion. There were some supporters milling around the hotel lobby on the Thursday but the trickle became a flood by Saturday afternoon. Some teams might look upon the sight of hundreds of fans around their hotel as a distraction, but this Ulster team didn't mind. It only drove them on. They felt at one with the supporters and, as Mason thought, what would running away solve? 'I think Declan Kidney said something like they floated to Millennium Stadium for the last few miles of their bus journey for their European Cup final in 2006. We had that feeling too. After getting a tremendous send off from the hotel, we boarded our bus and I don't think the wheels touched the tarmac from there to the ground. All we saw was white and red; it was as if we were being shouldered to the stadium!'

That season, and despite his heroics on Ulster's European odyssey, Mason's international career had stalled. It was close to three years since his last cap, and, returning to Lansdowne and staying at the Berkeley, brought back memories of his first Ireland cap in March 1996 and a 20–17 win over Wales. He knew the routine on international weekends once, but the memory now had begun to fade. 'In my first cap, we beat Wales at Lansdowne Road, but then I dropped out of favour with the Irish selectors. However, a few years on, I felt more rounded as a player. I remember on the Saturday of my first cap, I went down to Lansdowne to practise my kicking – everything went right. We stayed in the Berkeley as well before my first cap; I roomed with Simon Geoghegan, and, against Wales Simon scored a try and I scored fourteen points. For me, the European Cup final was nearly a second coming.'

Late on Friday afternoon, he and his room-mate Stephen

Bell (reserve scrum-half against Colomiers) went down to Lansdowne, bounded a few fences and sat in the South Terrace. No talk, just imagining what it'd be like the following day. 'It was absolute dusk at the time, four o'clock on a January afternoon,' says Mason. 'We went down and bumped in over the gate, walked into the South Terrace. We were overlooking a very surreal situation, and thinking about the difference it would be in twelve hours time when it'd be jam-packed with 50,000 people. I remember sitting there thinking back to earlier eras of Ciaran Fitzgerald, Trevor Ringland and Triple Crowns and the first international I ever went to. I travelled to the game with Brian McDermott when Ireland played Scotland in 1988 to watch the likes of Trevor [Ringland] and Philip Danaher at full-back. All these memories came flooding back.'

They knew the whole of Ulster was behind them, but the messages of goodwill that poured in from every walk of life were, says Mason, overwhelming. There were messages from the likes of the British Prime Minister, the Irish President, GAA teams, the other three Irish provinces, Ireland internationals, Limerick rugby folk, and Dublin 4 clubs. Everyone in Ireland just wanted Ulster to win.

It stunned Harry Williams, says Mason, and the Ulster coach decided to turn all these gestures into something even more positive. Williams posted all the messages in the team meeting room in the hotel, and on match day, he asked that a selection of them be posted on the dressing room in Lansdowne. 'Harry hung up all letters of goodwill, faxes and cards. Our team room was awash with good luck messages from Tony Blair to Mary McAleese,' remembers Longwell. 'Everyone from both sides of the community in the North sent their wishes. All the Gaelic teams sent faxes to us as well. I think every player spent hours walking the room reading them all. It was those things that got us going. The weight of the support that was behind us was incredible and moving.'

The positive atmosphere Williams had created rubbed off on the team. 'On paper, we were not a great team,' says Longwell. 'There were certainly teams that seemed a lot stronger than us. I think from the amount of belief we had in ourselves, and the fact that we all got on so well as a group, I felt it was going to take a special team to beat us.'

Williams had wonderful people skills, says Mason, who cites times you might arrive in the morning to training, maybe despondent or unhappy with your game or down in the dumps. But after a meeting with the coach, your confidence levels would be back up again. 'He just had that ability to man-manage people. It was around that time when I was overlooked a few times by [Warren] Gatland and Harry was the first up to me, saying, "You are the first on my team-sheet. You're really important to me." He really had a good way of dealing with people. When you get to that level, you need someone to be cool, calm and collected. The demeanour he showed in the stands was very similar to the demeanour of the Harry Williams we met every day. To be fair as well though, if someone needed a telling off, he wouldn't be slow to give it.'

The pre-match warm-up saw Ulster strike the first psychological blow to their opponents. The Ulster supporters had transformed Lansdowne into a rawer and wilder version of Fortress Ravenhill. Colomiers realised they had entered the bear pit of Irish rugby and, on days like that, it is intimidating for any visiting team. 'I felt Colomiers looked beaten during the warm-up,' recalls Longwell. 'They left the pitch early. We looked at their demeanour and they didn't look ready for battle. We knew something was wrong with them.'

Mason adds, 'It disrupted Colomiers players. They obviously hadn't got there on a fluke. They'd been away to Perpignan and won and got to Lansdowne on merit. But I think the day was just too big for them. I felt the crowd and the whole occasion drove us on, and that was one of the reasons why we got such a comfortable winning margin in the end.'

After Colomiers had left the field, the Ulster team contrived to pump up the volume even more inside the ground by exercising a pre-rehearsed warm-up routine. Colomiers were lucky not to have seen this as they might have just thrown their eyes to heaven, packed their bags and gone home! 'A couple of guys who had played in England remembered how Gloucester always do a lap of the pitch before the match to get the crowd going,' Longwell explains. 'We did that, and the noise was unbelievable. All our friends and family were sitting in the East Stand, so the whole team lined up facing the stand and did a big salute before the game. The noise hit us as hard as a French tackler but we felt good after it.'

It was then Mason felt that no team was going to beat them, and Williams' words after the semi-final returned to him. He felt, not in a cocky way, that Ulster's name was on the cup. 'I just felt it was going to be a day of destiny for us. We were all very nervous because it was just such a big occasion but there was definitely a feeling that no one was going to beat us and certainly not Colomiers.'

Mason adds: 'I think the whole Ulster thing that year was

a bit like how Munster and Leinster have done it over the past few years. Their wins have been very much based on team work. You obviously have your O'Garas and Stringers and O'Connells who stand out, but it has always been a team effort at Munster. I think Irish rugby is very much based on that anyway. We were always a good team as individuals – there were no outstanding players except maybe for Humphreys who did the kicking, and Andy Ward, but there were no real individuals who stood out. For me, personally, coming up to the final, I just felt confident in the team especially in the likes of Jonathan Bell in the centre. I could concentrate on my job and, when the opportunities arose, I was able to slot them over.'

Colomiers seemed to lack spirit. Stories even seeped from their camp that players who had helped the small French club to the final were jettisoned in favour of a few returning stars. Their coach, Philippe Ducousso, came in for some stinging criticism back home for some of his selections. Still, how many coaches could have afforded to leave out players of the calibre of Jean-Luc Sadourny and Fabien Galthié? But their names alone could not beat Ulster. Sadourny's and Galthié's fitness was called into question before the game. Sadourny came back for the semi-final after a seven-month injury and Galthié had been out for four months before their win over Perpignan. Galthié was the biggest doubt and the night before the match the scrum-half was even undergoing fitness tests. On the day, however, their impact was minimal.

Humphreys launched a litany of garryowens early on in the game into Sadourny's territory, and the French international full-back contrived to make a host of handling errors to a background of whistles and catcalls.

It was Ulster's pack that surprised most people and, in the loose, Longwell, Mark Blair and Stephen McKinty applied enormous pressure on their counterparts that, ultimately, created the penalty opportunities for Mason. Colomiers' opening ten-minute spell was their best, with Laurent Labit (who later coached Montauban against Munster in the Heineken Cup) giving the French an early score. But Ulster's pack was thriving and, though the French took exception to some of Welsh referee Clayton Thomas' decisions, the Irish side deserved to go in leading 12–3 at the break thanks to Mason's four penalties in the first half. However, the full-back had to contend with the mysterious Lansdowne wind blowing, as it were, in four different directions. 'Lansdowne Road – she was always a tough customer,' says Mason. 'With the breeze blowing around, you had to take an element of risk. In terms of my confidence, I had always been a confident kicker, and once I got off to a good start, I never thought anything was going to faze me.'

'I think, from about thirty minutes into the game, I honestly believed in my heart we were going to win – I couldn't see us losing,' Williams said after the game. 'The French seemed like rabbits trapped in a car's headlights.'

'A lot of credit must go to Harry,' says Longwell. 'We had a game-plan and we stuck to it. I think we went behind very early on and got a bit carried away but we had a chat before the game kicked off again. "Back to the game-plan; stick to the game-plan," Harry kept telling us. Looking around the dressing room, you should have seen the fire in people's eyes. Some sat and listened. Others, well, you had to take them down off the ceiling they were so pumped up and anxious to get back out on the field! I knew it was going to work for us.

There was just a supreme confidence about us that day and, in front of 50,000 Ulster fans, there was no way we were going to lose the match.'

Longwell will never forget the impact the injured Mark McCall had on the side in the days leading up to the match and isn't surprised that he is now a top professional coach. 'He didn't let on, but he must have been absolutely devastated not to be on the pitch. He went round having chats with players, and he just made you feel ten feet tall. He was just such a motivating character, just one of those guys who said the right things at the right time.'

Two minutes after the break, David Humphreys, master-minding the game from out-half, dropped a goal and, from there to the finish, Ulster squeezed the life out of their opponents, with Mason adding two more penalties. 'I got a lot of good press for kicking the goals, but the pack, including Allen Clarke, Justin Fitzpatrick through to the likes of Andy Ward, all stood up to be counted that day. Their contributions summed up our season. Every player just gave 100 per cent in every game.'

Longwell admits the game-plan involved a simple rugby equation: territory and pressure equals penalties. 'Our game-plan was simple really when you look back, but damn hard work. If we could get the territory, force the mistakes, Simon would punish them every time.'

And so they did, Mason applying the finishing touches after his forwards scavenged and hunted for possession. 'The conditions weren't too bad for kickers,' recalls Mason. 'It was a dry ball. It wasn't raining, although it was a little bit blustery. There was always a bit of wind moving around the old stadium. Lansdowne was a big open stadium, and these days you see the international kickers when they're playing at places like Twickenham or Stade de France, they've got an enclosed stadium, the grass is perfect, and there's very little wind. Ironically enough, Lansdowne Road was always a great test of any goal-kicker.

'Rather than make me nervous, the day lifted me. And I had no negative thoughts that day which is not normally like me because, as a goal-kicker, you're thinking of the worst. Maybe it was the fact there were so many Ulster supporters around, the cacophony of noise. It was just an incredible atmosphere.'

It wasn't the most entertaining of spectacles, but the occasion was magnificent enough to merit a place amongst the great European finals. As Mason says, 'The final itself wasn't a great rugby match but I thought we did enough on the day to outplay them and take our chances. For me, personally, I felt a lot more mature, getting to that European final. The first few international caps go by you in a split second, but it was great to come back more mature after those few years out of the Ireland scene.'

Mason was born just outside Liverpool and followed the Reds on many a Saturday from the Kop End at Anfield, standing amongst arguably the most loyal set of the supporters in English football. Like Liverpool fans, there was no doubt in his mind that the Ulster supporters acted as a sixteenth man at Lansdowne that day. 'I'd played on the Irish side and I'd played at Lansdowne Road, at Twickenham, but I'd never experienced anything as intense as what we experienced in the Heineken Cup final. Having stood on the Kop for many years, this was as close as you could get to a 'football atmosphere'. Munster have created the same atmosphere with the support they have at Thomond Park.'

The final whistle was greeted with an almighty roar, one which had been absent from Lansdowne Road ever since Gordon Hamilton's try nearly knocked Australia out of the World Cup quarter-finals in 1991. In more ways than one, the win signalled a sort of liberation day for Irish rugby. Ulster achieving the unexpected gave Irish rugby the belief that they should no longer be the bridesmaids of world rugby.

This was Ulster's day, the pitch invasion that followed more akin to September days in Croke Park. 'It would have been nice to parade around the stadium with the trophy and to have spotted your family,' remembers Mason. 'I was reminded of it the time I saw Tyrone lift the All-Ireland trophy for the first time in 2003 – that sea of red and white brought back memories of our European triumph. It also reminded me so much of the red of Liverpool on big Anfield nights ... it's just one of those things you never forget in life really. And what an experience.'

It was a bright day for Ulster and the people of Northern Ireland and, for once, they could celebrate in unison. Rugby had succeeded where so much else had failed. 'I wasn't born in Northern Ireland but I was aware of the history of the place. Living there was just a fabulous experience. The people up there are so warm and I get back as regularly as possible because I have so many friends there. Sport can sometimes transcend a society.

'As a sportsman, you try not to get too involved in politics but, when you're living in Northern Ireland, it's always there – it's part of the culture of the place you're living in. The win happened in a period when there were a lot of positives coming out of the province anyway. We always look on the negatives in life. That day there were so many positives and just reflected

Northern Irish society at the time. You just have to look at Belfast over the last number of years – the heart of the city is great. Around that time there was a real feel-good factor. We united a few people even if it was just for an afternoon.'

Longwell couldn't help but be moved by the whole day. 'It was one of those days that united the province. It had happened before with people like Barry McGuigan – everybody in the province got behind him. We felt like that – people wishing us well from all walks of life. We had a function in the Stormont Buildings after. All the politicians were there: Seamus Mallon from the SDLP and David Trimble and they knew each of us by name. I know Seamus was at the semi-final as well because we met him afterwards. I think everybody had a bit of common sense around the thing. Problems were forgotten, and everyone was behind the team. We felt we were playing for the whole province.'

Williams, perhaps, best sums up what this red-letter day in Lansdowne really meant. 'It was a very, very special day. For Ulster, that day was more than just winning the Heineken Cup – it was a coming together of communities. It didn't matter what church you went to, what game you played or anything, it was just a wonderful, wonderful day where everybody came together.'

Tony Ward

Out-Half

1978–1987

You always get the impression that Tony Ward would've thrived in these professional times. 'Wardy' was the main man of Irish rugby when he first burst on the scene, an exciting Number 10 who was never far from the public eye, someone capable of filling as much newspaper space as any international superstar, today.

However, it seems Irish rugby followers were left short-changed for they never saw enough of Ward's talents to fully appreciate his range of skills. Though that was a big disappointment, he can still look back fondly on his career and some many happy moments from Lansdowne Road. While a student at St Mary's College in Dublin, for example, he first got hooked on the colour and uniqueness of the Leinster Schools Senior Cup and a dream of one day of running out at the national stadium.

In 1966, he watched his idol, the late Shay Deering, lift the cup for Mary's at Lansdowne Road, and as a first year student at the Templeville Road college, Ward had dreams of one day leading his school onto Lansdowne Road on Leinster Schools Senior Cup final day. 'We were a tiny school in the suburbs and didn't win too many cups,' says Ward. 'I was at the 1966 final when Shay's team beat Newbridge – that's where the hero-worship for Deero began. This guy in my eyes was amazing. In 1966, Mary's were actually expected to win it. Tom Grace, who went on to play for Ireland, was on that Newbridge team at the time. But in 1969 when we won the cup again, I thought we had had no right to win. We beat Terenure in the final, 10–9. Conor Sparks was captain of Terenure – he was a big star in those days. I remember Johnny Caffrey blocking down an attempted drop goal that would have won the game for Terenure. But Mary's held on. Derek Jennings was the Mary's captain and seeing that win was a huge influence on my wanting to play rugby for the school.'

Attending St Mary's offered Ward the opportunity of watching Ireland play at Lansdowne Road on international weekends. Securing a ticket through his school, Ward, like hundreds of schoolboys from around Ireland, watched from the South Terrace.

'We used get schoolboy tickets for the Lansdowne Road end. When I was in first year, Shay's twin brothers – Kevin and David – came in and they made the schools team and Leinster schools as well. They were in my class so we used attend the Five Nations or any of the internationals in Lansdowne. After the match, the Deering family used always gather underneath the posts at the Wanderers end of the ground. Then we'd all go onto the pitch and gather there. Everyone did in those days. No steward would stop you at that time from getting onto the pitch, everyone just went onto the field and gathered in different areas and chatted for half an hour afterwards. It's just the way it was.

'As a youngster, my fondest memory was of me and Terry Kennedy (who would go on to play on the wing for Ireland and who was in my class at school) trying to meet the President of Ireland at Lansdowne. Eamon de Valera used to attend the rugby matches in a big black Rolls Royce or Bentley – it was the famous Dev car anyway. After the game, the car used to be driven in near the Wanderers Pavilion. Dev would be having a cup of tea and cakes afterwards and then he and Bean de Valera would come out of the VIP area and get into the back of the car. It almost became a ritual for Terry and I. We had the timing perfected. Half an hour after the game, we would always be outside the Wanderers Pavilion waiting for the black car to come in. We used to run up, as old schoolboys used to do, and we'd always be the first two at the doors of the car. There'd be a queue of people, but we'd be the two right at the door when the president and his wife got in. We convinced ourselves that he knew us so well. That was a big thrill.'

As a youngster, Tony admits going to more soccer than rugby games at Lansdowne Road, but he witnessed many great rugby moments at the ground. 'One of the famous games I will always remember is the Ken Goodall try in 1970. Ireland won 14–0. It was a big upset at the time against a great Welsh side and Alan Duggan got a try in the corner. But in 1973, there was a famous reaction to John Pullin's England team as they ran out in Lansdowne Road. It was a very special moment. The applause was spontaneous. Today it might be done by some DJ on a pitch orchestrating the whole thing but it was a genuinely felt feeling for what they had done [in travelling despite receiving death threats from the IRA].'

Ward says he owes a lot to his coaches at St Mary's, Fr D'Arcy and Fr 'Wally' Kennedy, who groomed him as an out-half, and when he was made senior captain in his final year, there were high hopes of attaining another cup. And he got to live the dream of one day leading Mary's onto Lansdowne Road. It was for the semi-final of the Senior Cup against High School. 'It was my first time running out at Lansdowne as a player. I was captain of the senior team in 1973 but we were beaten 10–9 by High School – they went on to win the final, the only year they ever won it. John Robbie and Ian Byrnes were their half-backs. We were unbeaten all season, hammering everyone in our way in friendlies, including High School. To this day that was the biggest disappointment in my rugby career, including being dropped in Australia [in 1979] or not being on a Triple Crown team.'

To compound his disappointment in a season that promised so much, Ward was overlooked for the Leinster schoolboys team that year. Ollie Campbell – a player with whom he later battled with for the Ireland Number 10 shirt – and Ian Burns were picked ahead of him.

At that time, Ward also made a name for himself in soccer circles, and after school, seemed destined to play League of Ireland football with Shamrock Rovers. 'I was hugely into soccer. I remember watching Waterford play Man Utd at Lansdowne, the year after they won the 1968 European Cup. That United team contained all the stars including Georgie

Best, Denis Law and Bobby Charlton. Then, in 1973, Louis Kilcoyne organised a team – North and South combined – under the name Shamrock Rovers to play against Brazil in rugby headquarters. It was one of those great occasions where even the crowd appreciated the enormity of it because of the historical political implications.'

Ward, however, stuck to the rugby, and made his Ireland debut against Scotland in January 1978. Ireland had failed to win a game for two seasons so naturally – as there is for any out half – a massive weight of expectation rested on Ward's shoulders.

He was not alone that day. Three others made their debuts beside him – Paul McNaughton (centre), John O'Driscoll (flanker) and second-row, Donal Spring. It was also the day Johnny Moloney captained his country for the first time. The pair chatted for hours before the game and Ward remembers receiving plenty of messages of goodwill, including a letter from former Ireland out-half, Barry McGann, who assured the debutant that everything would be fine playing in front of a home crowd.

One thing Ward will never forget was the crescendo of noise he felt the moment he ran onto the field, and to this day he does not know from where came the streak of confidence that attended his game that afternoon. But the famous Lansdowne roar played its part in helping raise his game. 'Once I kicked a nice garryowen early in the game, I felt fine,' he says, remembering one of his first few moments in an Ireland senior shirt. Ireland won the game 12–9, Ward kicking two penalties and converting Stewart McKinney's first-half try.

Grand Slam-winning out-half, Jackie Kyle, watched from the stands that winter afternoon and said afterwards that Ward made a fine debut at out-half, 'I would not be despondent about Irish rugby after that performance,' he told one newspaper after the match.

'Certainly, my first cap will stay with me for ever,' says Ward. 'One of my abiding memories is arriving in the car park. This was before the Wanderers dressing room was built underneath the stand. It was the last season we togged out in the old Lansdowne Pavilion which was down in the corner near the Havelock Square terrace. There was an uncovered stand in that corner and the changing room was underneath that. I remember when we got off the bus before the game, I was so scared, so nervous. The pipe band or army band was warming up but the sound the bagpipes made was so eerie. I will never forget the feeling – it went right through your system. I remember thinking you just want to be at home with your mummy! Ridiculous thoughts come through your mind at those moments because you're so uptight and so nervous. That was my abiding memory of arriving in Lansdowne. We won 12–9, and, in the last few minutes, Scotland got a penalty. Dougie Morgan was the captain, a scrum-half, but he declined to go for goal to make it 12–12. It was very kickable. Instead, they went for the win because their logic was they wanted to stay in the hunt for the Triple Crown. That's how big the Triple Crown was at the time. We defended and held out to win 12–9.'

The wind that blew through Lansdowne Road was difficult to negotiate and nearly always threw up the ultimate challenge to some of the world's most consistent kickers. Ward converted one brilliant kick against Scotland. It was hit so sweetly even the touch judges went running back to their positions on the touchline before the ball had completely gone over the bar. He often remembers goal-kickers grimacing as they attempted to convert into the most precarious and most difficult wind conditions at Lansdowne. 'When I do RTÉ commentaries, I talk about conditions before the game, and I make the same point over and over again – and anyone who has played there will tell you the same thing – you could not judge the wind at Lansdowne Road. If you looked at the flags on the Lansdowne Road/South Terrace end, you'd see them blowing one way and then you'd look across the far side and they'd be blowing differently but not quite as heavily. It was just the design of the ground. The fact that it was not fully encircled meant it blew in all around the place. It was a very, very hard ground to play in or in which to kick tactically, particularly for those who were not used to it.'

If Ward had to make do without a kicking coach in his playing career, then life on an international weekend was made more difficult by not having the opportunity to practise at Lansdowne on the days leading in to an important match. 'When you look now at the professional players, they have everything laid on for them. I remember, in our day, you weren't allowed near the pitch beforehand. I remember being down there once and seeing Ronnie Dawson running a team off the pitch when he happened to be going by on the Saturday morning and they were out doing some lineout practice. You had to get very, very special permission to go on the pitch to do any kicking. Occasionally, you did, but it was never a given. These days teams can go to Lansdowne on a Thursday or Friday and do their kicking. That's standard now. Another reason maybe why we weren't allowed on then was that we didn't have tees – you had to make your own divot on the ground.'

Ward was a central figure in the Ireland–Wales 1978 Five Nations game. 'That was the great era of Welsh rugby. That was when it was at its zenith. You had all the greats – J.P.R. Williams, Phil Bennett, Gareth Edwards – it was just a never-ending list of greats. You got to see Welsh rugby pretty regularly on the BBC and they were megastars at the time. When I arrived on the team in 1978, we all stayed in the one hotel. And you literally spent the two days beforehand trying to avoid each other! It was a ridiculous carry-on. One day, I had to get into the lift with the Welsh guys. There was about seven or eight of them – it was packed. Genuinely, I thought they didn't know who I was. I kept my head down and there was total silence until I pushed the button to get off. We were on the third floor and they were on the fourth and when I got out, Gareth said, "See you tomorrow, Tone." I remember being on a high that Gareth Edwards knew my name!'

Ward might have been on a high after Edwards recognised him, but he was disappointed by the quality of rugby on view in that test match. 'Against the Welsh in 1978 it was a very dirty game. They were seeking a third consecutive Triple Crown and they won 20–16. Sadly, it was really tempestuous. Gareth and J.P.R. retired after that game – they said that finished it for them. They just found that the game had become too physical, too dirty and they decided enough was enough.

'There was an incident during the game where Gibson was playing centre and he chipped a ball over J.P.R. down at the Lansdowne Road end of the pitch. As Gibson was running around him, J.P.R. took him out of it. It caused a furore at the time. It was a professional foul. They got a late try from J.J. Williams but we might have won that game had we got the six points for J.P.R.'s foul.'

In 1979, Ireland drew 9–9 with France. 'I have two main memories of that game. In those days, you were allowed tap the ball to yourself for a free-kick and then have a drop goal. Towards the end of the game, it was 9–9, we got an indirect penalty or free kick on the twenty-two in front of the posts, I tapped it to myself, and it was blocked down by one of the French back-row forwards. I also remember getting a knock on the head in the first half of that game from Jean-Pierre Rives. Early on, I tried to do a side-step but caught his stiff arm on the side of my head. I was concussed. At half-time, I had to go into the dressing room for some attention. I literally couldn't see. It was a migraine. What I saw was a desert and just heat shimmering. I just had to go in and get some tablets. In those days, the teams stayed on the field at half-time. On my way back onto the field, I ran to the French huddle without realising it I literally just came out and veered towards them. It was very embarrassing. But I don't know how I got through that game.'

During his playing days, Ward came under the influence of Ciaran Fitzgerald whom he describes as the greatest ever Ireland captain. To say that Ward was moved by one of Fitzy's team talks would be a complete understatement. Fitzgerald was, according to Ward, every inch the army captain in the dressing room and he remembers days when he could have run through the old dressing room walls at Lansdowne such was the almost manic delivery of the Fitzy speech. 'In those days, the coach wasn't allowed onto the pitch at half-time. Instead he had to send out a message with the man who brought us the oranges. It was the captain who did everything. Ciaran was the best Irish captain bar none. Don't let anyone tell you otherwise. He was so far ahead of everybody in terms of preparation and work for the match. Whether it was talking to individuals and putting it all together or pressing the right buttons individually and collectively, Fitzy was in a league of his own. He was just one of those guys, a motivator supreme. When he asked you do something, he looked you in the eye. You knew what he was asking you to do, he was going to do it himself, whereas others will bulls**t their way through it. You get to learn very quickly the captains who are all "We're going to go out there and get stuck into them all … etc." but, with Fitzy, it was never like that. He was just unbelievable. And, thankfully, he has two Triple Crowns to show for it because the guy was torn apart inside after his experience on the 1983 Lions tour. Then the captain just had to do so much, whereas now, with respect to Brian [O'Driscoll] and everybody else involved, everything is done for them. Now, even at half-time, the coach, the defensive coach, the kicking coach all have their few words in the dressing room. In fact, there's little time for the captain to speak.'

But it was the way Fitzy handled the captaincy that impressed Ward. 'You handle different people in different ways. Captaincy in our times was so important and, I believe, it's how you handle personalities. Ciaran would tell one guy, "You're the greatest in the world and I want you to go out and prove it today," and he would do it. That kind of delivery was for the likes of me. He would tell another guy, "If you don't do it today, you're f****king gone." There were guys who would need a kick up the arse and he would respond enormously. Different people respond in different ways. There's no overall way in doing it but the great captains were the ones who knew what worked and what made people tick.'

After all these years, Ward holds fond memories of the old

stadium. Nothing gave him a greater feeling than running out onto the national stadium in any game. 'Because I'm Irish, running out on the national stadium always meant so much more than watching on television or simply going there to watch a game. And, I must admit, even in latter days when I went out and play Leinster Cup games or inter-pros and when there were two men and a dog at it, it still gave me the thrill – you were still playing in Lansdowne Road, it was still special. I don't care what anyone says. The national ground is special and I think it will be again when it's rebuilt for the generations to come.'

Keith Wood

Hooker

1992–2003

Keith Wood sat on the bench against Australia at Lansdowne Road in 1992, and watched one of the unluckiest hookers of Irish rugby John 'Spud' Murphy earn his first and only cap before disappearing off the scene. Wood, also a hooker, intended to hang around a bit longer, be in selectors' faces a bit more, and little did people realise back then the enormous legacy the Munster man would leave on Irish rugby after eleven years wearing the green.

'I came out of nowhere,' he says in relation to his call-up to the Irish bench against Australia that afternoon. But if he feels he sprung from the abyss, Ireland could not have wished for a more dedicated player. Lansdowne Road always roared louder when 'Woodie' was on the ball. Once, Frank Keating, the doyen of rugby writers, described the fifty-one-times-capped hooker as 'a potato on speed', in reference to the most famous bald pate in rugby, whenever Woodie embarked on one of his trademark breaks up field. This image is everlasting – the face contorted, ice in the eyes as he'd face down his opponent with a sometimes madcap stare, the shoulders hunched as he made more yardage than most back-rowers on any given day. On a rugby field, he was as close as a forward can get to being a free spirit. Wood performed his functions as a hooker, but he was a non-conformist of sorts on the field – he refused to play to type.

He was very much the focus and talisman of every Irish team up to his retirement after the 2003 World Cup quarter-final loss to France in Australia. He could have hung around for another year and picked up a deserved Triple Crown in 2004 at Lansdowne Road, but his body had been put through the ringer once too often and he decided enough was enough. In a sense, he was the iconic figure behind Ireland's renaissance, a believer in our worth as a rugby country, a symbol of what could be achieved. Above all, he was a winner and a champion.

He suffered so many disappointments and setbacks and black days – and he was a survivor of fifteen operations – for Irish rugby, that we forget sometimes what drove this most driven of sportsmen to the top of his game. There was the highpoint of beating England in 2001, with his breathtaking try in a win that went a long way to erasing the endless stream of bad memories.

Keith Wood's late father, Gordon, won twenty-nine caps for Ireland as a prop forward between 1954 and 1961 and, in the late 1950s and 1960s, was part of famous triumvirate in the front-row that included Syd Millar and Ronnie Dawson.

It was in a test match against the Aussies, in 1994 in Ballymore, Brisbane, when Wallabies coach Bob Dwyer singled out the Killaloe native as a potential great. How right he was.

Woodie played his first full international against the USA that November in Lansdowne Road. The Eagles were plucky and organised, he remembers, but the confidence gained after an encouraging tour to Australia gave the Irish a feeling that they would overcome their opponents. They didn't feel invincible but were confident enough to put teams like the Eagles to the sword. And so they did on a 26–13 scoreline. 'We were fairly comfortable with the idea that we'd go in and beat the States but it was bloody tough. They were a capable group at that time.'

Wood's first Five Nations game came against England in 1995 in Lansdowne Road and, despite the loss, he has an everlasting memory of the day and the atmosphere. 'As a superstitious youth, I always came out last and, on the first Five Nations game I played, I was blown away by the noise as I slowly climbed the twelve steps up to ground level and then floated the remaining steps to the pitch. It was the worst weather I had played in. We were well beaten by Will Carling's side and I, personally, got the crap kicked out of me. But that was it; I was hooked. I had played in autumn matches but this was altogether different. I was addicted to the buzz, to the wearing of the green and to Lansdowne.'

The 1995 Five Nations was an unhappy one for Wood and Ireland. Throughout his career, Wood was the type – sometimes even recklessly – to put his body on the line. And, after losses to England and Scotland (he was injured in

Murrayfield), he missed the remainder of the Five Nations championship.

There was something to put a smile back on his face (and that of Irish rugby) when Nick Popplewell, Peter Clohessy and himself packed down together in the front-row of a Barbarians side that defeated South Africa 23–15 at Lansdowne in April 1995. It remains a highlight in his career. With Simon Geoghegan also on the side and recording a splendid try, it lifted Irish rugby and the mood of the country – if only for an afternoon and if only for a Barbarians side. 'I loved it. It was my one and only time playing for the Barbarians. I remember the English were not allowed to play – the only guys from England who were allowed to play were those not in the English squad. We didn't play in a particularly Baa-baas style. Instead, it was real, hard nitty-gritty stuff, but it was a great game, and a really great occasion for Lansdowne.'

The shoulder injury which had eaten away at Wood's season returned to haunt him during the World Cup campaign in South Africa in 1995. After only nine minutes against Japan, he had to retire with a dislocated shoulder. But when he returned for the autumn internationals in November 1996 and a test against Australia, his leadership qualities were rewarded with the Irish captaincy. Here was someone who could optimise mental focus in a team. 'I was only approached that week to take on the captaincy. I was slightly taken aback. It was very much a case of me being the only one who could be captain at that stage. We had a distinct dearth of leaders in the team. An awful lot of the guys had retired at that stage like [Philip] Danaher and Brendan Mullin, so I might have been the only obvious choice. I remember Gerry Murphy saying a couple of years before when he was making me pack leader, "He doesn't

shut up anyway so we might as well give him an official job."
So I got the job!'

The platitudes – 'glorious defeats' and 'valiant losers' – were
the words ringing in the ears of the Irish team after they came
close to doing the impossible against Australia in 1996. But
Wood saw this test match as a classic example of an opportunity lost. 'It finished 22–12 with a try in the last minute.
They were leading 15–12 and we were pushing the game, trying
to get there and we could and should have overturned them.
We lost in the last couple of minutes which was bloody
annoying because we had played very well in a difficult enough
kind of scenario. Leading out Ireland at Lansdowne was pretty
special, though I just wished I had led my country to victory.'

This was another one of those 'difficult periods' for Irish
rugby. The 1996 autumn internationals series began badly – a
loss to Western Samoa, the most damning indictment of their
performance being the ability to fashion only a single try while
the Pacific Island side crossed the Irish line five times. The
inevitable cull followed the week of the Samoa match and, when
glory was snatched from them against the Wallabies, there was
some talk of a corner being turned. More or less the same team
lined out against Italy in early January 1997. But there was no
corner turned, Ireland lost 29–37 at Lansdowne and it marked
another downer, a players' and coach's nadir.

Players may have found the weight of expectation
unbearable, but Ireland's first full-time coach during this period,
New Zealander Murray Kidd, was also under severe pressure to
deliver. While the Australia match represented progress and a
step forward, the loss to the Italians at home in front of Irish fans
in dire need of some New Year cheer, watched the team regress
even further. It was another nightmarish day at Lansdowne and,

while some players' reputations suffered, the end was in sight for Kidd. A few days after the Azzurri defeated Ireland, Kidd met with IRFU officials and a severance package was agreed.

Some said Kidd could not connect with that Irish side; others that he was ahead of his time but, ultimately, according to Wood, it was an uncomfortable time to be an Irish player. 'It's very hard to talk solely on those sort of terms,' admits Wood. 'A lot of those things can be taken quite comfortably out of context. We would have had five coaches in four years, and none of them were in for such a long period of time as to make a telling contribution. It was a time when we changed coaches at every available opportunity and that was at very little value to us. We needed to have a coach come in, have a level of control and balance within it, which, ultimately, didn't arrive until [Warren] Gatland came in. What we needed so badly was continuity in coaches and continuity in selection.'

Brian Ashton succeeded Kidd as head coach, but the injury woes continued for Wood. A shoulder injury in another loss against France fourteen days after the Italy game meant an early championship departure. All these injury setbacks were becoming the norm in his career and, from the Lansdowne stands, the latest appeared extremely painful. 'I was carrying the ball and I had a feeling I tripped over Thomas Castaignède. I landed on my elbow and I popped my collar bone. It was pretty painful, though not as painful as you think – once you do all the ligaments, once they all go, there's no real pain.'

On the field, the signposts towards improvement were encouraging, but it was dangerous to talk of an Irish revival. It nearly had to be whispered. Ashton, with the reputation as a bit of an eccentric but whose expertise lay in cultivating dashing backline moves now hoped for progression. The IRFU seemed chuffed with their man. A win over Wales at Cardiff Arms Park seemed to confirm their selection of Ashton as being the man to lead Irish rugby through a turbulent time and through the early years of professionalism.

Wood thought Ireland were on the up, too. If they weren't winning, at least they tried to find solace in a good performance. 'I thought we had turned a corner in a lot of cases; where once we had a situation where nothing had been going our way at all, now we started by stringing a couple of good performances together.' But heavy defeats at home to England and away to Scotland eroded their confidence. The margin of the defeats and below-par displays in those two games was hardest to digest. And Ashton, it must be rememebered, had been offered a six-year contract before the trip to Murrayfield. The calls for Ashton's contract to be terminated were gathering momentum.

In November 1997, Wood returned for an autumn international against the All Blacks, scoring two tries in typical Woodie fashion. He always cut a dashing figure for a forward, he loved to bound around the park, glide into backlines, felt comfortable ball in hand and, with his penchant for putting boot to ball. He was never shy either to attempt a drop goal if the opportunity arose. Most of all, he gave every last ounce of energy for the cause. He was combative, whole-hearted, rugged, battle-hardened – many wondered if he could ever play a bad game for club, province or country.

Before kick-off against the All Blacks, Wood remembers some kind of protest taking place at Lansdowne. It wasn't one calling for Ashton's head on a platter either. Instead, the travelling support displayed black-and-white posters of protest: 'No Hart – Bring back Josh.'

The Wednesday before the match, Josh Kronfeld, a legend

of All Black rugby, lost his Number 7 jersey to Andrew Blowers. The tremors of Kronfeld's demotion were felt back in New Zealand, particularly in South Island where Kronfeld was revered. News of his demotion made front-page headlines there. Apparently, coach John Hart replaced Kronfeld in order to shake things up a little and tried to justify his decision by arguing it was for the benefit of the squad. But his decision was odd, especially in an era when the All Blacks rarely rotated and always strived to put their best team on the field.

The posters calling for the reintroduction of Kronfeld flashed around Lansdowne Road, but darting around the park indefatigably was the figure of Keith Wood whose two first-half tries had put Ireland into an unexpected 16–15 lead. Wood's heroics – not for the first time – brought Lansdowne Road to its feet. His second try saw him out-sprint winger Jeff Wilson after Eric Miller hacked on.

Kronfeld's replacement also put an end to Wood's time on the field, with a tackle that aggravated his already dodgy ankle. Looking back, now, Wood says he doesn't buy in to hackneyed comments of 'being on top of the world' after scoring a few tries against the All Blacks. 'I don't go in for trite comments. Yes, it is fantastic, yes it is unbelievable when you get the buzz. The buzz when you're going over the line in Lansdowne is incredible and I often describe the noise in Lansdowne as being like the beat. It was like a heart beating between a high and a low sound. You couldn't hear and distinguish individual noises and voices and suddenly there was a beat to the place and that was fantastic. I scored a couple of tries, but I never went on that mad "look-at-me-I-scored-a-try" thing. I could honestly tell you that, if you looked at the tries I scored, it's rare that I jump up and down after scoring them. You're there to score them, you're there to try and get a score on the board.'

Part of Wood's legacy to Irish rugby were his fresh soundbites at press conferences, his ability to accentuate the positive and to truly believe in the players around him. 'I remember saying before the New Zealand game that we had a twenty-five to one shot of beating them, and I was getting roundly criticised in the press afterwards. I would say, "You asked me a question and I gave you an honest answer and if it's too honest for you, I'm not going to be offended by the fact that I'm being honest."'

Brian Ashton was often termed a maverick genius by English journalists and, as if to prove that he was capable of the unexpected, he announced a team packed with fresh faces for that All Blacks test. He brought in five new players, a bold move by the coach, but he felt the new caps deserved their chances and added that they would spice things up after the bitterly disappointing conclusion to the previous season's championship. But facing a seasoned All Blacks side was no place for so many new caps. Kevin Nowlan, John McWeeney, Conor McGuinness, Malcolm O'Kelly and Kieran Dawson were thrown into the lion's den and they, and the Irish team, were torn to pieces by the All Blacks.

Four players at least saw another day out in green; though for St Mary's winger, McWeeney, it was the beginning of the end of his Irish career. Wood felt for those new boys, particularly for those that never came back. 'We'd a distinctly unsettled team. We had five new caps, some who were never really seen again. And we had a coach who was living in England, who had a lot of talents, but selection wasn't one of them. He didn't know half the players, he may have seen them once and then picked them and to do that for the test against New Zealand was wrong.'

And this All Blacks team, still hurting from their World Cup final defeat to South Africa in 1995, were a formidable bunch and seemed to hit the field in every test match to prove a point that they were still the greatest. Ireland lost 63–15 and the level of the All Blacks dominance could be measured in one fifteen-minute spell in the second half when Ireland could only get a hand on the ball twice, such was the All Blacks control at ruck time, their recycling abilities and sheer physical strength in all areas of the field.

It was a defeat Irish rugby didn't need.

That All Blacks team consisted of the likes of Taine Randell, Frank Bunce and Buck Shelford – great names who under-achieved at World Cup level. To have them perform at Lansdowne Road was then a rare occurrence; many believed the All Black jersey had a mystical quality, that the sight of it could instil a sense of dread into the opposition. Wood doesn't agree. Even during the Haka, he admits he found it difficult to keep a straight face!

'Mystique? No, never bought in to that. I respected the players, yes. You respect the players you play against and you give them the respect they deserve, but I always looked at the Haka as being a pretty good promotional tool for the All Blacks. The history of it was something that was never major for me and, for anybody who thinks that's a chip-on-the-shoulder comment, all you have to do is look back to the infamous match in 1973 between the Baa-baas and the All Blacks and you see the poor old New Zealanders doing the Haka – it looks like a group of Morris dancers! For example, I always had huge admiration for the distinct lack of respect

[David] Campese showed by kicking a ball around on the twenty-two while this was going on. I used laugh at it and giggled, winked and smiled, just to see whether it would provoke any sort of reaction.'

Wood suffered an ankle ligament injury in that game and had to retire in the second half. Ireland wondered if he would have scored more, but for the creaking ankle. 'Hardly likely, they were kicking me up and down the field at that stage!'

After a loss away to Italy five days before Christmas Day 1997, a doomsday scenario had been painted for the upcoming 1998 championship, while Ashton's uneasy relationship with manager Pat Whelan was also brought into the media mix. But a loss to Scotland in a Five Nations match at Lansdowne Road signalled the end for Ashton. He wrote a letter of resignation to the IRFU explaining he got an attack of shingles but his disillusionment ran deeper. He later hinted that he should not have taken the Ireland job, that he didn't understand the Irish psyche and that he probably should have attended more All-Ireland League games.

Warren Gatland was then parachuted in from the west of Ireland where he was coaching Connacht and on his arrival, Irish fortunes changed for the better.

A positive Five Nations followed, Ireland just losing out to Wales while there was no capitulation away to England. 'I never went in for all those major turning points. It's hard to make that straight call. A turning point is when you win. OK, that can sound kind of cold as well. When you look at it, we were not a great team for a long chunk of time and we tried bloody hard and we played as hard as we possibly could. But we weren't quite structured enough whatever the reasons were. Ultimately, there were things that started to resolve themselves as soon as we got a lot of the structure right, we got consistency in the team right, we got good performances out of it, we got monkeys off our back by beating teams, like France in Paris (2000) and then at home the following season, England (2001), Australia (2002) and South Africa (2004) – all these things are cumulative. And, because all of them were working and sorting out for us, we were then able to say yes, this is a turning point. You can't call them turning points at the time, but you can see them for what they were after the fact, and that doesn't necessarily mean you don't regress during that. You do know it's the start of something bigger and better.'

He savoured the victory in October 2001 at Lansdowne Road that deprived England of another Grand Slam. His try was a moment where Lansdowne saluted forward innovation in a move rehearsed on the training ground.

The sight of Wood barrelling over the line – and over Neil Back – is one of the great Lansdowne moments. 'It was one we had used a couple of years beforehand and, for some reason, we tried it once or twice that week. Well, once in training during the week, once that morning, once in the pre-match warm-up and we tried it in the game. It was good because it was simple: a throw to Mick Galwey, a simple pass to Anthony Foley and then a bit of unadulterated brilliance by Foley. You can't see it on the tape but I can tell you that it was. He passed a dead ball, which meant there was no weight on the ball, it was there in the air, so it wasn't going in any particular direction. It was such a perfect ball, I could have run any angle, I think there could have been a little subtle interference by Eric Miller at the back to stop them getting at me and then it was a little canter over the line. I had to score from there. I was going at full tilt because Foley's pass was perfect.'

He tried a drop goal before half-time — 'it was a bad decision, pure stupidity but luckily I got away with it' — and Ireland went into the break leading 11–6. An upset was on the cards. 'There was a turning point in that game. In the second half, I made a mistake, left a defensive hole and Luger ran through. We tried to chase back but he looked home and dry but [Peter] Stringer came across and ankle-tackled Dan Luger. It was incredible stuff.'

This was Ireland's third game in four weeks and, with twenty minutes left on the clock, England were raising their game as the Irish tired. 'Everyone ran themselves to a stand still. I remember badgering the ref to blow the damn whistle and, when he did, there was joy, but relief too.'

He'll never forget Jason Leonard's gesture at the end of the game. Team-mates and best buddies at Harlequins they had to scrum down opposite each other for eighty minutes. 'Immediately after the game, all the England players walked off the pitch except for Jason. He walked out onto the pitch to find out where I was to congratulate me and I remember saying in my speech that night that that was a mark of a sportsman. He must have been shattered at losing a Grand Slam but went out of his way to show that he was happy for me.'

Inside the dressing room, he led a rendition of 'From Clare to Here'. 'We were helped by what you might call an arrogant selection by England. They were picked on past form, not on present form and we felt we could intimidate a lot of their players. Halfway through the match, I recognised some of their lineout calls, and Malcolm O'Kelly told me they were the Lions calls that had been used on the tour [to Australia] that summer. We actually used their [English] lineout calls … they said afterwards that they weren't the Lions calls, but they were. That English team was eminently beatable and yet they nearly beat us. That was a huge thing to get over, that was one of those bogeys we had to get over and, subsequently, when you look at the English team, without the likes of Johnson and Leonard and others, you say to yourself, yes, we can beat them. But with Johnson at the helm, England was a much harder team to beat.'

He reacquainted himself with the All Blacks in November 2001. A Hickie try pushed Ireland 21–7 ahead and, for a long time, they kept New Zealand on the back foot. Eighteen minutes later, Reuben Thorne, Doug Howlett, Aaron Mauger and Jonah Lomu crossed for tries to make it 40–24. It was typical All Blacks, ruthless to the last. 'That was a game we should have won but lost for a variety of reasons. It was the angriest I'd ever been after a game. We were in a position to do it and we didn't, and if you're looking for a turning point that could have been one of the biggest.'

When Wood retired, a great leader was gone, but he contributed profoundly to Irish rugby's revolution years. 'With me going, with Claw [Peter Clohessy] going, Gaillimh [Mick Galwey] going, we were guys who went through an awful lot of the bad times – we had some good times, too, and it was a phenomenal part of my life. We now have a group of guys in there that almost expect to win. They don't have that sort of negativity in their background. I'd like to think we didn't have a huge amount of it either, but we're still tainted by the fact that we lost an awful lot of games when this present crew has won an awful lot of games. I take great pleasure in the fact that they win and I would like to think, that I had a lot to do with it in that a lot of things had to change.'

After Wood's retirement, Lansdowne seemed a less boisterous venue. He was capable of energising a whole stadium and electrifying 49,000 spectators with one barn-storming run into space or into a thicket of opposition shirts. Woodie was one of a kind.

He has returned to the old Lansdowne since his retirement as an expert BBC analyst and could be seen on a Six Nations day on the sideline below the West Stand curling the collar of his coat around his neck from the cold and the breeze. 'Without the crowd, the ground was a cold windswept great edifice long past its prime,' says Wood. 'It seemed to live for the big occasion; it came to life, struggling one last time to hold its place. It had an atmosphere and a noise level all of its own.'

Acknowledgements

When I began tracing Lansdowne Road's greatest matches and moments, its high points and low lights, it became a journey of sorts. Along the way a number of people have lightened the load, and their assistance and co-operation has been immense.

To all those whom I interviewed for the book, players and coaches past and present, and to all other interviewees who took time out from their busy schedules to talk to me, my heartfelt thanks for your time, openness and co-operation. Without your insights and candour we might never have had a record of your deeds and exploits from the world's oldest rugby ground.

A very special acknowledgement of my family, who've been there, steadfastly, since the book's genesis. Sadly, my dear mother, Maria, passed away one year after the publication of the first edition, but her support, advice and inspiration throughout my life – and in my writing especially – will never be forgotten.

To my father, John, my sister Yvonne, brother-in-law Mark

Southern (a massive Martin Johnson fan!) and brothers, Paul and Austin, and sister-in-law, Karen Walsh, your support has been unwavering since I cobbled together the first sentence for this book.

A special mention to my editor, Claire Rourke, who, from day one, has been hugely supportive of *Lansdowne Through the Years*. Her energy, dynamism, encouragement and understanding know no bounds. Also thanks to Ciara Doorley and Breda Purdue at Hachette Books Ireland for their assistance.

To Hugh Farrelly, a great wit and writer and supporter of this project, thank you, and to Tim Horgan whose encouragement was always appreciated.

Edmund Van Esbeck was the rugby voice I grew up with, and his knowledge, fairness and superb ability in reading a game made him the doyen of rugby writers. I am humbled Edmund agreed to write the foreword to this book.

To Liam O'Regan (RIP), the former editor of the *Southern Star*, who first published my local match reports when I was in my teens.

I would like to thank Tony Leen, Colm O'Connor, Declan Colley, Tom Ahern and Bob Lester and all at the *Irish Examiner* sports desk for their help and advice in the world of journalism.

And to those sports editors who helped me throughout my journalistic career, now I think is the chance to express my gratitude: John McHale (*Evening Echo*), Malachy Logan (*The Irish Times*), Geoff Thompson (*Irish Sun*) and Neil Robertson (*Irish Daily Mail*).

Also, can I just say to all my rugby writing colleagues – too many to mention – thank you for your help, advice, great company and for being there down through the years.

To Paddy Maloney, Paul McCarthy, Declan Ryan, Sue Crosbie (RIP) and Anne Kearney much gratitude for putting up with me late into the evening in the *Examiner* library, and to Joe Healy as well, thank you.

Special thanks also to Dr Larry Jordan, my principal at Christian Brothers College, Cork.

Special mention, too, to Karl Richardson of the IRFU for helping to organise some of the interviews.

To Steven O'Connor, who read parts of the manuscript and who offered sound opinion – a big thank you, and also to Sue Hitz and the use of her wonderful abode in Alden, Douglas, where part of this book was written. Cheers!

To good mates Gearóid O'Brien, Paul Sheehan, Niall Sweetnam, Seamus Murphy, Richard McMahon, Páidí Breathnach, Micke Jones and Seán Lyons – thank you.

Edward Newman
June 2010

Permission Acknowledgements

The author and publisher would like to thank the following for allowing the use of their copyrighted material in *Lansdowne Through the Years*.

Inpho Photography
Inpho section 1 page 1 (top); **Inpho/Billy Stickland** section 1 page 5 (top), page 8 (top), section 2 page 1 (top), page 2 (bottom), page 3 (top), page 5 (top), page 6 (bottom), page 8 (top and bottom); **Inpho/Patrick Bolger** section 1 page 1 (bottom), page 4 (bottom), page 5 (bottom), pages 6–7, section 2 page 2 (top); **Inpho/Andrew Paton** section 2 page 6 (top)

Getty Images
Mike Hewitt/Allsport section 2 page 4 (bottom); **David Cannon/Allsport** section 2 page 5 (bottom); **Richard**

Heathcote/Getty Images section 2 page 7

Empics/Press Association
Empics section 1 page 3 (top), section 2 page 3 (bottom)

Sportsfile
Pat Murphy/Sportsfile section 2 page 4 (top)

Bertie O'Hanlon section 1 page 3 (bottom)

From *Anam Cara* by John O'Donohue, published by Bantam Press. Reprinted by permission of The Random House Group Ltd.

Bibliography

Books

Inpho Sports Photographic Agency (ed. Billy Stickland), *Puting it on the Line*, Inpho Concepts, 2002.

McBride, Willie John & Bills, Peter, *Willie John – The Story of My Life*, Portrait, 2004.

O'Reilly, Peter, *The Full Bag of Chips – Ireland and the Triple Crown*, O'Brien, 2004.

Popplewell, Nick & Hayes, Liam, *Poppy: Time to Ruck and Roll*, Hero Books, 1995.

Scally, John, *Legends of Irish Rugby*, Mainstream Publising, 2005.

Van Esbeck, Edmund, *Irish Rugby – A History (1874–1999)*, Gill & Macmillan, 1999.

Newspapers

Irish Examiner, The Irish Times, Irish Independent